Web of Violence

By the same author:

Children in Danger

Web of Violence

A Study of Family Violence

Jean Renvoize

Routledge & Kegan Paul
London, Henley & Boston

First published in 1978
by Routledge & Kegan Paul Ltd
39 Store Street,
London WC1E 7DD,
Broadway House,
Newtown Road,
Henley-on-Thames,
Oxon RG9 1EN and
9 Park Street,
Boston, Mass. 02108, USA
Photoset in 11 on 12 Baskerville
by Kelly and Wright, Bradford-on-Avon, Wiltshire
and printed in Great Britain by
Lowe & Brydone Ltd

British Library Cataloguing in Publication Data

Renvoize, Jean

Web of violence.
1. Family—Great Britain 2. Violence—Great Britain
I. Title
301.42'7   HQ614   77-30408

ISBN 0 7100 8804 3

Contents

Acknowledgments

It would be impossible to mention individually all the people who have given me the benefit of their experience by letter, phone and interview, but without such widespread advice and help I would not have been able to embark on a book of this nature. I would like to express my deep sense of gratitude to them, especially to those who have recalled personal memories that were often still painful but which they felt may be illuminating to others who were now suffering what they had once suffered.

In particular I would like to thank Erin Pizzey, her colleagues and the wives at Chiswick Women's Aid refuge whose frankness and experience was invaluable to me: I would especially like to thank the girl I have called 'Janet' whose story is told in Chapter 1. Many members of the NSPCC have once more given me considerable help, in particular Christine Smakowska, the Librarian of the Battered Child Research Department, together with the rest of the department's staff and some of the mothers with whom they are working; and

Acknowledgments

Jean Moore, Senior Tutor at the NSPCC Head Office, and Fred Hedley of their legal department. I would also like to thank the National Women's Aid Federation for the assistance they gave me. Professor George Brown was kind enough to let me have details of the research into depression which he and his team at Bedford College have been conducting, while Dr Bentovin of the Hospital for Sick Children, Dr M. Green of the Royal Free Hospital, Dr G. Burston of Avon Health Authority, Bristol, Dr J. Cameron of London Hospital Medical School, Dr John Kennell of Case Western Reserve University, Ohio, and Dr Elphis Christopher of Haringey Social Services Department all gave me invaluable assistance and I am very grateful for their generous support. Dr J. Gayford of Warlingham Park Hospital, Surrey, not only supplied much of the evidence in the section on marital violence but was also kind enough to read through my manuscript and make some very helpful suggestions.

Finally, I would like to thank the authors and publishers concerned for permission to quote extracts from the following works: Dr J. Howells, 'Death and disorganization', *Royal Society of Health Journal*; Dr R. Gelles, *The Violent Home*, Sage Publications Ltd; various articles by Dr J. Gayford and Dr Selwyn Smith and colleagues, *British Medical Journal*; M. Borland, *Violence in the Family*, Manchester University Press, and Dr P. D. Scott, 'Battered wives', *British Journal of Psychiatry*.

Introduction

Violence has entered our lives to a degree that would have been unthinkable even a decade ago. Terrorist attacks, political kidnappings, bombs indiscriminately exploded among innocent civilians; all these horrors which once only happened to other people now are part of our own experience. There are periodic scares about mugging in the streets, and there is no doubt that adolescent crime has risen to a frightening extent. It could be that the growing acceptance of information about violence in the home (previously a subject about which no one wanted to know) is partly an attempt to shrink this worldwide expression of violence down to more familiar proportions. It seems easier to understand a drunken husband knocking his wife about than it is to understand one group of 'patriots' blowing up another group of 'patriots', each of whom bear similar names and share the same birthplace.

At bottom, politically-inspired or not, each act of violence is an individual act. Even in a mob where people will perform acts which they would never commit when alone, each separate member has had to cross the narrow bridge between being an individual with a mind of his own and becoming an irresponsible member of the mob. There are many people who are capable of stepping aside, whose personalities allow them to say, no, I will not do this. In the same way most adults when faced with increasing strain in family life do not relieve their feelings in violence. They do not batter their children, nor do they attack their spouses or their aged parents. But some people cannot restrain themselves in this way. Why not? What makes them different?

Short of genetic engineering we can do little about genetic inheritance. We can do a certain amount about environment, easing poverty, stress, overcrowding and other problems with which we are so familiar. But a growing child's environment is so much more complex than the rooms he lives in, the food he eats. The baby floating quietly in his mother's womb could not apparently have a more perfect environment, but what if his mother is a product of generations of people who have been deprived - emotionally or physically? What if she has married an unsupportive man, who perhaps beats her up while she is pregnant? Even before such an infant is born he is already many points down in comparison to other more fortunate babies.

I have come to see violence more and more in terms of a gigantic web in which countless generations of people are caught. A violent adolescent who has just kicked in someone's teeth is yet one more creature snared in the web, and probably it is already too late for him ever to free himself completely. Violence breeds violence. Not invariably, admittedly. One brother will escape, while his sister is trapped. Why? And has the brother really escaped or will the strains under which he grew up show in another way, such as over-determination to succeed, or a weak mildness, both of which can inflict their own brand of damage on his immediate family.

In this book I have looked at various types of family in distress. Who are these people who hurt each other? Why do they attack? How do they do it? When do they do it? I have gathered together many of the answers with which research is supplying us. Some questions have hardly begun to be answered, but others are slowly being clarified. I have not allowed myself to wander very far from facts. There are endless clues scattered around about which I would be delighted to speculate, but I must leave such pleasures for those more qualified than I. For example, Dr Daniel Stern of the New York State Psychiatric Institute has pointed out how highly aroused Western babies are in comparison to infants reared by more primitive societies such as those inhabiting the Kalahari Desert. There, a baby will be carried around everywhere by its mother and fed a little milk every half hour so that he never has cause to build up a high arousal level. He does not learn to cry from hunger because he never has a chance to become hungry - the moment he stirs his mother puts him to the breast. In the West a baby sleeping alone in its bedroom will probably have to work itself up to crying or even screaming point before its mother will realize it is awake. Middle-class parents in particular are likely to reinforce this high level of arousal by playing stimulating games with their children from the earliest age. Not unnaturally Dr Stern suggests that this system of early upbringing may be one of the reasons why we are 'such a keyed-up bunch of people'. But sometimes more problems are posed than solved by clues such as these. How on earth do today's liberated mothers who wish to do well by their children emulate the Kalahari Desert women without dangerously frustrating themselves, thereby risking the very relationship with their children which they are so anxious about? And isn't it also a fact that many deprived children, including battered babies, are retarded and apathetic because they are insufficiently stimulated?

The field of research is a fascinating and rewarding one, although it would be over-optimistic to expect any miraculous change as a result of research in the immediate future. Attitudes change very slowly. In *Children in Danger*, for example, one of my main themes was the lack of co-operation between the various professionals concerned with battered babies. Several years later, police submitting their evidence to the Select Committee on Violence in the Family (4 May 1976) made it clear that the split between those who consider that the police have no part to play in the treatment of battered babies and their families, and those who say that if a law is broken the transgressor must be prosecuted, still continues. For the rest, there has been on the whole a slow improvement, but economic conditions prohibit much experiment, so that new projects are rare and mostly on a small scale.

Finally, I hope no one will draw the conclusion that this book is an indictment of the nuclear family. Even kibbutzim have had to allow greater parent participation in their nurseries - humans cannot grow to their full potential if they are over-protected and reared like a greenhouseful of lettuces. We are an odd lot, we human beings, we seem to need a certain amount of rough treatment such as mild sibling jealousy if we are to develop fully. Even so, no one would pretend the nuclear family is a perfect system. But with what can we replace it? Marriage itself is under attack, and yet many of those who most object to it often in fact settle down with a single mate and behave exactly as though they were married. For it is difficult to live alone: most of us are happier with one other person who knows us intimately and with whom we can fully relax. But since this other person is usually of the opposite sex, children tend to result in spite of the availability of contraception, and yet more nuclear families are created, even if they are unofficial ones.

What we need is not necessarily to throw marriage out of the window, but to learn how to live with each other in tolerance and love, how to achieve the happiest possible relationship between parents and children from conception onwards, and above all, how to help those who are the worst victims of failed marriages. For unless they are helped, their personal tragedies will not end with their deaths but will continue to affect the lives of still unborn generations.

Janet's Story

Janet is a fine-boned girl with a quick, intelligent face. She is very responsive and laughs easily, but the laughter vanishes as quickly as it comes. She has been living in one or other of the women's aid shelters run by Erin Pizzey for eight months, ever since she left the boyfriend who used to knock her about. She has one child, a toddler named David after his father.

Bob, her current boyfriend, was brutalized from babyhood by his father. His mother ran away from her husband with her seven children a couple of years ago when she could stand no more of the continual beatings, and after a long stay at the Chiswick refuge has now been settled sucessfully in a house. The older boys, though, are very damaged: Bob himself returned to Chiswick to live in the Boys' House, an adjunct of the women's refuge. He found help there and the companionship of other adolescent boys much like himself, but he is not yet able to control his violence. At present he is waiting for his case to come up at the Old Bailey. One of the charges is that he beat up an innocent passer-by, fracturing his skull. Bob was hopelessly drunk at the time, and seemed to be under the impression that it was his father he was attacking.

Janet and Bob are now living together. They are hardly more than children - both are just eighteen. Bob has the lowering broodiness of a young Heathcliffe; Janet looks even more bird-like beside him. But she can give as good as she takes. The last time I went to see her she had been in hospital for three days after Bob beat her up, but not before she had thrown him down the stairs and kicked him black and blue. He has promised never to hit her again and he means it. She has promised to stop goading him, and she means it too. She has written scores of love poems to him in her neat round handwriting; sad, moving little poems. Knowing that he may go down for three years or more is putting an intolerable strain on both of them. Bob can't sit still - he jumps up abruptly from the bed they use as a sofa, then a couple of minutes later he flings himself down again, scowling ferociously at some inner thought. It is impossible to imagine him caged up in a cell. What sort of person will come out at the end of it?

The story that follows is Janet's life up to the present. Brought up on Merseyside, her story is no different from a thousand others. But the squeamish should be warned: the telescoping of such a life into a dozen or so pages intensifies its squalor, its horror. It seems impossible someone so young should have already suffered so much. Violent and unpredictable as she is, she is a girl everybody likes and wants to help. But where to begin? How do you start unravelling the tangled knots of such a damaged life?

Did you come from a violent family?

As far back as I know about. There's four generations of violence, right from me grandparents down to me own baby. I don't know back beyond me nan and grandad. He was just an alcoholic, used to beat nan up and beat the kids up too. In the end me nan kicked him out - I suppose he got weak and that - and she kicked me mum out too when she got pregnant with me. Me nan was a Catholic, see, and me mum'd had a baby before, when she was fifteen, and it was all very disgraceful for a Catholic. The baby got adopted, it was very hush-hush, but me nan wasn't going to stand for another one. So she kicked me mum out: she didn't want to know 'er. Me mum went to live with this man that was me father, and had me. She was only sixteen even then. They lived together for quite a while, then me dad - he was a sailor - brought his mate home from sea. After a bit me dad ran away back to sea - he didn't want to have nothing more to do with me mum - and his mate stayed on and looked after us. They got married when I was two or three, I think it was. He's an atheist from Manchester, so he didn't care, you see. Me real dad was Irish, but me mum come from Liverpool.

It was all right at first. Me mum used to hit me - just little things she used to hit me for - but when me dad came in (me stepdad Charlie - I always call him dad though) when he came in she'd be dead nice to me, 'cos he didn't like her hitting me. But when our Peter come along everything changed, everything completely changed. I was about seven when Peter was born, and from then on they didn't want to know me. They was drinking a lot by then and it got really bad. It was me brought the kids up; Peter, Robert, Mary and Jackie. I had to bring them up. Me mum's an alcoholic now, you see, so's me dad.

Did he start hitting you too, then?

Yeah. Real bad. Sometimes I'd hide behind a chair, you know, get in the corner of the room and pull the armchair up against me. He couldn't get at me body so he'd put his leg over the chair and sort of stand on me head and get me that way. He'd be drunk, you see. He was always batting me for anything, after the kids come along. They both went downhill, you see, they both became alcoholics and I had to bring the kids up. Someone had to.

Do you think it was having kids of his own that made him feel differently about you?

He started to bring up that I wasn't his child and that, and I'd

say, 'What d'you mean?' because I'd always thought of him as
my father, 'What d'you mean? what d'you mean?' I'd ask me
mum what he meant, but she'd say, 'Take no notice of him,
he's drunk.' This went on until I was about twelve, then one
day out of the blue, I found out. I'd run away from home and
they'd brought me back, and I was in the police car going to
court when me dad started going at me. 'You're glad now,' he
kept saying, 'this is what you've always wanted, to get away
from us, isn't it?' I said, 'What d'you mean?' He said, 'Oh piss
off, you know what I mean, you hate our guts.' 'I don't,' I said,
'I love you.' He said, 'Well, I'll tell you something, I don't love
you. So might be it's for the best.'

He got what he wanted. I was placed on a care order and
sent to Eton Lodge - it's an open approved school. I never lived
for any time at home after that. I didn't want to. It was too
awful. They were always fighting.

There was one time I remember especially. I was about
three and we'd moved back into me nan's house. She was really
good to me, me nan, I really loved 'er, but she's dead now. I
always remember hearing shouting and screamin', and I run
up to the bedroom and stood at the top of the landing, and I
screamed, 'Mum! Mum! Mum!' Me mum and me dad were
naked and he was biting her, biting big chunks out of her arm
and she bit his arm and he had a big piece of flesh hanging off.
After that I can't remember nothing, everything else was
black. Maybe I fainted, I don't know. That was the one real
scene of violence I seen. Apart from that I seen him punching
her in the mouth and that. She's lost all her teeth - he split her
mouth open and they were all knocked about inside her gums
and tha', and they had to take them out. Mostly he hit her in
the mouth, but he used to kick her in the back as well. He
made her lose two babies. He made her lose one when she was
nearly eight months pregnant and it was dead inside her for
two weeks before she had the courage, you know, to go to the
doctor's. She had septicaemia then and she was in hospital for
ages.

Had there been a particularly bad row that time?

No. He'd come in drunk, that's all. You see, sometimes she
says to him, 'Come on Charlie, we'll stay off drink, I don't want

to drink no more.' And he'll say, 'Yeah, yeah, yeah,' and then
he'll go off drinking just the same. So she says, 'Sod 'im, why
should I sit in, looking after the kids?' and she'd go off. Then
anything could happen when they come back in.

*So you went away at twelve. When did they let you go back
home?*

I didn't go back home. I came down to London when I was
fourteen and I worked for a year in Tesco's. Then I went
abroad. I went to France, Spain and Jersey. Then I got
deported.

Why?

Well, it's a bit complicated. See, me mate and me took some
money from where we worked. I took £350 and she took £700.
We didn't want to hang around and wait for them to pick us
up, so we went to Jersey, got a day passport for France, stayed
there a bit, smuggled through to Spain, come back to France
and then went back to Jersey. We worked as chambermaids
and that to earn extra money. It was all right getting false
cards in France but we couldn't get them in Jersey. It was in
Jersey they caught us. The CID had kept a trace on us, and we
were known to be missing, so when they caught up with us they
deported us back to England. They sent me to all sorts of
assessment centres but I kept running away from everywhere
they put me. I remember one time. They wanted to put me
into a Borstal because they couldn't control me. They took me
to this Borstal for me case conference and I just took one look
at it - it was all little cells, like a prison, and it was all dark
there, and there was a moat at the bottom and walls round it. I
wasn't going to have it, so I run away again back to London.

The police stopped me loads of times and asked me if I was
Janet — —, but I put on a cockney accent and told them to get
lost - politely, you know. They kept raiding the flat we'd got, so
we couldn't stay there properly, we had to break in ourself
when we wanted something.

I was still on the run from the police when I met David's
father, Dave. I met him at a party. I liked him and I went out
with him. Then his mother said I could stay with them so the
police wouldn't find me. He got me pregnant, though. He used

to beat me up and that. He raped me three times.

Why didn't you leave him?

It was better getting beatings off him than off me mum and dad. See, at first he was sort of protective towards me - he was really in love with me. I thought I loved him, but it was just infatuation with an older man - he was twenty-one or twenty-two then. I was only fifteen. He looked after me and visited me where I was hiding out until I went to stay with him and his family. He wanted to make love to me but I said no. He said, 'Are you still a virgin?' I said, 'Yes.' He said, 'OK then.' That was it. I used to be able to sleep in bed with him and he wouldn't touch me. You know, he'd kiss and cuddle me, but. . . . The first time he raped me he come into the bedroom drunk and I couldn't stop him. We was alone in the house 'cos his parents worked nights. Another time I was hiding in the lift shaft away from the police and he come up there, and he raped me again.

He didn't mind me being pregnant at first, but then he got jealous. I used to really take care of meself: I wouldn't do nothing, nothing strenuous. He pushed me down the stairs when I was eight months, because I thought more of the baby inside me than of him, you know?'

But you still didn't want to go back home?

I wasn't going to bring a baby up in that mess! The social services had got onto me, and they sort of made Dave me legal guardian - they thought I was better off with him and his mum than at me own home. Oh, he was always giving me slaps and that, but I thought nothing of it, I was used to it. We had a bed-sitter in his mum's house at first, then we got a three-up-and-three-down house. That's where I had David. But I got fed up after a bit, and then I did go back to me mum's.

It's funny, but I'd sort of got curious about me real dad. Me mum didn't say nothing, but one day she took me over to Liverpool to see this man. She didn't say why, just that she'd had a letter off him or something and we walked into the house - I always remember he had a check plastic tablecloth on the table, it stuck in my mind. He was fat, an'. . . . he was about thirty-six or something like that - it was me seventeenth birthday - and we just walked in. He said, 'I'm your father,' and, you know, the shock! I just couldn't believe it. I said to me mum, 'Is he *really*?' and she said, 'Yeah.' He said, 'Sit down and have a cup of tea,' and it was just like I was another neighbour, no emotion or anything like that. He just said, 'How're you doing?' I said to him, 'I got a baby and tha'' and he started getting . . . you could see he was a bit angry, and he went on to mum, 'You told me she was good, you told me all this. . . .' Because they used write, and I didn't know it, and he sent her money.

I liked him, though. He was funny, you know? He was Irish and that, and he was funny, a bit like Father Christmas. No, he didn't have a beard, it was just that he was all red-faced and fat and - oh, I don't know - I just couldn't believe it, I just started laughing. It was a silly lot of things he kept saying, and I kept laughing.

Did you see him again?

No. It's just not worth it. I can't see the point. Once is enough. I've seen him once and me curiosity's satisfied - there's nothing else to see. Me stepfather's more me real dad to me.

Did you stay back home long?

I did not. I'd hardly been there a couple of weeks when there was this scene. Jackie was trying to be sick. Jackie's the youngest. He had cancer in his stomach when he was a year old, and they cut it out but the scar's still there in the wall of his stomach, and his stomach muscles are very weak and he can't really hold his food. He has to eat it very slowly. It doesn't cause him no pain or nothing and it's not spreading, but he's sick easily. That night she'd let him get drunk - she drinks cheap plonk, you know? and thinks nothing of giving it to the kids - Jackie was two then. He was wanting to be sick and she was holding him sort of backwards so he couldn't be sick and lying him on his back and that. I come in - I'd been out on me own - and me baby was screaming upstairs, and I looked at them all and I thought, you know, oh God, what a mess. To leave one violent man, to come back to the same violent family.

There was a real uproar going on in the room. You see, Jackie wasn't by me dad, he was by another man. Mum'd been going out with this man for five years now - he's me dad's best mate. Yeah, dad knows all right. So there they all were. Her boyfriend was sitting there laughing at her because she was so drunk and tha', and me dad was getting real mad. I could see he was ready to. . . . I did the first thing I always do when it's like that, I get the kids out of the room, away from it all. But they're big now, and they wouldn't stay out. They were fighting me to get back in, they wanted to see what was going on. There was Peter, he was eleven, Robert nearly ten, Mary, she was about five. This was last year. Peter got so mad he punched me right on top of the eye and I had a big cut there. Me own brother Peter, he punched me right in the eye to get back to the room. They just stood there, and they watched her scream and I thought, oh God!

You couldn't see what was happening, everything was flying, you couldn't really see people, it was just everything - the big plate glass window had a bottle slung through it, someone cracked open a door with the poker, everything was gone through . . . she picked up this shovel, she broke the handle off - me father was shouting at her over sex - and she tried to shove it up her, she split herself and everything. Peter saw it, and the screams out of him - he went stiff, he was shaking and white, then he was sick . . . he was screaming all the time. Robert was the only calm one. I got him outside, and said to him, 'Robert, just go straight down to the phone and phone the police, give them the address and try and explain what's happened, but be calm about it.' I spoke very slowly to him, like this, and he understood all right. He said, 'All right Janet', and he just run. When the police came I was still trying to grab Jackie out of their arms so he could be sick, because his face was going blue. I kept putting me fingers down his throat and then he was sick, but he brought up some blood as well, so the police took him and me - and me baby as well - off to the hospital.

Back home it ended with the police kicking mum out, because the house is in me dad's name and he wouldn't have her there. She come to the hospital too and she had to have ten stitches. They kept her in and they put Jackie into care for twenty-eight days - he had malnutrition as well because she never fed him properly. But after twenty-eight days they let him go back home. Home! Yeah, dad took mum back again. He didn't have much choice, he's frightened of her now. She beats *him* up now when he's too drunk to stop her.

I went back to live with Dave soon after that, and we got a council flat. But it didn't work out. We got the flat in January and I left him in March.

Because he was beating you?

Partly. I've been in hospital four times. He broke me nose twice, fractured me jaw, pushed me under a car. I was running away from him and he said he was trying to grab me, but if he was I'd have fallen backwards, not forwards. But he didn't want me to leave him. He was very jealous of me.

Did you keep hoping he'd stop beating you in the end?

He'd make a marvellous husband, because I never wanted for anything. If I said I needed £50 for housekeeping, he'd get that £50 by hook or by crook for me. If I needed a new pair of shoes he'd get them within an hour of me asking for them. You know, I was really spoiled by him. He got me everything I ever asked for.

Did he have a regular job or did he pick up what he could get?

[She laughs.] Well, *you* said it! He really did what he could for me. He loves David, he really loves David now. He's come to terms with him now, but before he was really jealous of David getting more attention than he was. He broke David's arm when he was very small. I took him straight to hospital and I told them what had happened but they didn't do nothing about Dave. 'Insufficient evidence,' they said. Because I wasn't there when it happened. I was out on the front doorstep with a girlfriend. She wanted to call the police straight away, but I rushed him off to hospital instead. Oh yeah, the hospital called the police, and they listened to the story, but that's what they said, 'Insufficient evidence.' I said to Dave, 'How did the baby break his arm, then, doing a handstand?' 'No,' he said, 'I was trying to get his jumper off him and I yanked his arm and it must have broke.' The doctor said nothing, he never said nothing. The police went away. I went to the social services and told them but they never did nothing neither. The health visitor come once and saw Dave battering me and she run out and never come back again. It's true when David was first born I got a few visits until he was about two months old - after that, nothing. . . .

Well, as I said, David's dad got better to him, he come to terms with him, and he really loves him now. But I'd had enough. I left him in March and went to me mum's for a bit. I didn't really want to go there but I had nowhere else to go. But when I got to me mum's he come and snatched David away. It took the police four days to find him. I was frantic. I didn't know what he'd do with him. Then the police got him back, but the social services stepped in and I agreed to let them take David off me, just for three days, while I got a travel warrant to come down to London. 'Cos I knew I couldn't have David at me mum's. But after the three days, when I was all ready to come down here, they wouldn't let me have him; they said, 'No, you're not having him back, the twenty-eight days isn't up yet.' I said, 'I signed the papers for three days.' They said, 'Oh no, twenty-eight days.' They didn't trust me with David you see. I couldn't shift them so I came down to London and come to stay with Erin here at Chiswick and I told her all about it. She wrote to the social services and got David back for me, straight away.

You must have wanted him badly?

Yeah. I did. When I'm on me own with David I get on perfectly, I'm fantastic with him. I take him out every day, I always keep him clean and tha', and feed him, but I don't know, it doesn't go much beyond that. As far as take him out of his cot and kiss and cuddle him, I don't do much of that. But I do look after him. When I'm on my own, that is. When I'm living with someone I never seem to have the time, or can't be bothered. Mainly I just seem to want to sleep and sleep and sleep.

How does your boyfriend feel about David?

Bob loves him. He loves him more than I do. 'Cos I hit David, you see. I hit him when I'm angry with Bob. Like I said, I'm really good with him when I'm on my own, but when I'm with a man, it's different. . . . But I only hit him once, once at a time, I mean. I never keep battering him. I usually kick him, push me foot against his back, then he falls over and starts crying, and that's it. I'm sorry then. Immediately I'm sorry. I'm sorry as I'm doing it. I know what I'm going to do, but I just feel I have to do it.

Have you ever boxed his ears or hit him with a stick or anything?

[Shocked] No! Oh no! I'd never *ever* punch his face or anything like that, or hit his ears. I'd never punch him. I'll push him over or slap his face or his hands or his legs, but oh no! I couldn't, I just couldn't do it.

Because I know the pain. Not just the pain but the feeling of not being wanted. It's a horrible feeling. You feel sick inside you. You just want to die. You can't even cry. You know, the sad look he gives me, after I've hit him . . . it's really bad. It makes me feel. . . .

When I'm on my own with him, I don't even touch him, I get on marvellous with him. But I never ever felt - you know, the mother instinct you're supposed to have when a baby's born and you want to cuddle him. I just said to nurse, 'Take him away' [her voice is sad, restrained] 'just take him away.' Maybe it was something to do with Dave raping me, I don't know.

Bob's good with him, then?

When I hit David, Bob hits me. Yeah, Bob bashes me too. Or he would, if he got a chance. He was brought up to it, same as me. His dad was really violent - he used to beat him up a lot. He used him as a skivvy. His mum was good to him, maybe she gave him the occasional biff, but nothing much. She got bashed up herself, real bad, by Bob's dad. That's why she come to Chiswick, to get away from him. He really was violent, his dad.

But Bob's all right. I met him a couple of weeks after I come up to Chiswick. He was staying in the Boys' House. He's eighteen, same as me. We got on all right. Then I moved to the second stage community house, but I didn't like it there, not after the Chiswick house. At Chiswick the whole place is on the go the whole time, but at the second stage house I had just one little room and I was shut away from everyone all on my own. So I went to the squat and lived there for a while with Bob, and when we got kicked out of the squat we went back to Chiswick. I went round to the Boys' House practically every night, then Erin got us this flat.

He's selfish though. Like I'd only got damp jeans one night and he insisted on going out. I've got kidney trouble and I didn't want to put on damp jeans. I got seething mad, real mad with him. I picked up a corkscrew and went for him with it. He run out the door, and I chased him, then I come back to the kitchen and waited for him. Every time he come back I tried to get him, then I hid behind the door and when he opened it I stuck in his arm. It never went in far, only about half an inch. But if I'd got a sharp knife I'd have got him. I'd have killed him. I was hell-bent on killing him.

Are you just saying that, or did you really mean it at the time?

I really meant it. I'd have got him if I could. I'm not a violent person, I wouldn't say. But if I get mad, then I do let go, I suppose. I smashed a wall down twice and kicked in a door at Chiswick. I won't be stood on.

I had a fight at Holloway with ten girls. [She laughs.] I nearly lost me life. They was dying for a real cigarette and I had some. They got me on the floor and I got hold of one girl and I kept biting her nose and her face and her cheeks, and she kept shouting to them, 'Stop! Don't hit her! Don't hit her! She's killing me. *Aaaah!*' I was laughing! 'Cos when I fight, I laugh. I love it, a good fight. I really enjoy it. But if I really hate someone, I don't laugh then, I just talk to them. There was a girl who kissed Bob, got hold of him one night and kissed him. I just talked to her. I really put the fear into her, what I'd do. And I love it, because that's what happened to me, and now someone else is getting it, and if I can get someone in that state I'm really made up. I just got her by the hair and kept kicking her in the face. I must have kicked her about fifty times. She had two huge black eyes, big nose and all that.

You sound as though you really enjoyed doing it.

I did. I loved it. It made me feel really great.

What would you do if you met a quiet man, a peaceful man, a man who never tried to hit you?

He'd bore me to tears! I like a bit of drama. I love the argument, building up to a fight. [She smiles, thinking of it. Then her face changes.] But when the actual beating comes, I hate it. I wanna *die*. I feel like dying when someone beats me up. Bob says to me, 'Oh you love getting beat up, it turns you on.' I can't get through to him I hate it. I love the drama, not the fighting. I love the argument, and throwing things about an' that. But it's a dangerous game, I know that. I push Bob as far as I can, but then I see in him . . . I see the lust to kill in his eyes. Once he starts real fighting he doesn't stop. But I don't let him beat me. I get hold of his hair and say, 'Go on, just *one* punch off you, and I'll *kill* you' [she hisses the words] and he tries to lash out at me and I just keep hold of his hair and say, 'Go on' - quiet like - 'go on, hit me. Because you'll *die* before I do.' [The drama leaves her voice and she continues in an ordinary tone.] And he sort of calms down a bit. And I say, 'Bob, please stop it,' 'cos I get a bit frightened, you know? he looks so. . . .

Hasn't he ever landed a punch on you?

Oh yeah, but it's nothing. He's never really hurt me. If he did I'd kill him. Sometimes he tries to treat me . . . he can get practically any girl he wants, I don't know why, and he thinks I can be treated like common muck. Well, I can't. As far as I'm concerned I'm somebody, not just anybody on the street, I'm somebody and if I give him a good and easy life he should do the same for me. It's not just take, take, take, but give and take.

It's like sex, he wants it non-stop, and I can't cope with it, I'm just not that way inclined. I mean, I do enjoy it when I'm having sex, but it doesn't bother me, I don't crave for it. I didn't enjoy it at first at all, it wasn't until I was three or four months gone with David that I had sex at all willingly with David's father. I didn't really want it. Then I began, you know, to enjoy it, like a woman enjoys it. When David was born, afterwards I enjoyed it for a bit, then slowly, it just turned me sick. I was sick in Dave's face once when he was making love to me. No, I don't think he was a good lover - I wouldn't really know, I haven't had much experience with others. But he was no good compared to Bob. Just a quick bang bang, roll over and good night. Honestly, I'd sooner kiss and cuddle a man than make love to him.

When Bob goes on I tell him to go and get another woman, a bit on the side, it doesn't bother me. If it's only a sexual relationship it doesn't bother me. Yeah, I know I went for that other girl, when she kissed Bob, but it was only an excuse, she'd got it coming to her anyway. I wasn't really mad inside me, not the way I get sometimes. You see, I pretend to him that I'm jealous, so he'll think to himself she must be in love with me and all tha'. I do love him, I think a lot of him, but I'm not jealous.

But I won't be used! I don't see why I should get used all my life as a scapegoat, bringing kids up, getting battered. I was a scapegoat for David's father, and I'll do anything now for Bob, but he's so inconsiderate.

It can't be easy for him, brought up as he was.

But my father treated *me* like that too. His father wanted him to be a big man at three years old. My father wanted me to be a mother when I was eight. I'm sick of being used.

I feel I'm heading for a nervous breakdown. I just can't be bothered lately with anything. I took an overdose a couple of weeks ago and I was in hospital and this psychiatrist come to see me. He just got on me nerves. 'It's a cry for help,' and 'Can we help you?' and all that stuff, so I stood on the bed and ripped the sheet off. 'Yeah,' I said, 'I'm mental, can't you see! Go away, baby, go and play with your nurses!' and he said, 'Paaah! How disgusting! I'll be back to see to you later.' He said, 'You really are disturbed. You need some kind of help I can't give you.' Then this lady comes, she was very nice, but, you know, it just goes in one ear and out the other.

I don't know what help anyone can give me. The best time I ever had was the time Bob's mum had David for a month, because I knew he was safe. She's been rehoused, just her and the kids, and she's made a really nice home of it. I fretted for David for about three days, but I knew he was enjoying himself

because she's got kids and that. Sometimes it's all right.
Sometimes I just look at David and I think, Oh, doesn't he look
like his father. But lately he's been getting some of Bob's
characteristics; you know, his movements and that, and the
way he laughs, and it makes me feel better. I don't *hate* his
father, I still like him. I don't love him, but I feel sorry for
him. He wants to help me, he wants me back, he said he'd look
after me, there'd be no more beatings and that. Said he'd
learned his lesson. But I'd never go back.

Anyway, I think I'm pregnant. It'll be Bob's. Yes, I'm glad.
If I am having a baby I'll keep it. I'd just love a girl, I really
would. I was really very sorry David wasn't a girl, but now I'm
glad, because it's good to have a boy first. The eldest boy is
always protective towards his sisters and the younger ones.

What will you do if Bob goes down for a spell?

I don't know. I just don't wanna even think about it.

You won't go back home?

I went back a few weeks ago to visit them, and the situation's
just as bad as ever. The kids are locked in all night, all four of
them. Physically the older ones aren't too bad, because they
can reach into the cupboard and cook themselves something,
but Jackie can't. He's still only three, so he just goes hungry.
Me mum can't cook anyway. It's comical watching her trying
to cook a meal. She pours half the sherry into it, so we all get
drunk then!

Do you drink?

I *hate* it! I've been drunk about four times in all my life, that's
all. I only drink when I'm upset; you know, when I want to
forget things. If I go out with Bob, I only have Coke now.
When I do have drink, I go out of me mind, I can't even
remember the night before. I used to take a lot of drugs, but
I've gone off them as well. Me only vice now is smoking!

No, I wouldn't go back, not to that mess. She's no grandma
to take your baby home to.

How old is she now?

Me mum? She's thirty-four.

Battered Wives

Until the latter part of the nineteenth century women were bound by law to stay with their husbands however brutally they treated them. If they ran away their husbands had every right to drag them back again and, if need be, to lock them up to prevent their future escape. But in 1870 Frances Power Cobbe, a Victorian feminist and philanthropic worker, wrote a pamphlet called *Wife Torture*. This pamphlet crystallized a growing unhappiness with the law among many thinking men and women, and in 1878 Frances Cobbe had the pleasure of seeing the Matrimonial Causes Act passed, enabling magistrates to grant judicial separation with maintenance and custody of any children to wives whose husbands had seriously assaulted them.

The passing of this Act was of major importance in the fight to free women from their age-old subjugation to men, but a parliamentary act does not overnight change mental attitudes. Brutal treatment eventually destroys the ability to make firm

16

decisions and to act on them. Even now, a hundred years after the passing of the Act, many battered wives are as effectively trapped by their husbands as though Frances Cobbe and her fellow reformers had never existed.

Until Erin Pizzey almost single-handedly brought marital violence into the news again, the subject was buried. It was material for comedians and comic postcards with no application to the great majority of married couples. That violence should be spread throughout the classes and involve one's fellow citizens was as unthinkable as the idea that 'ordinary' parents should batter their own children had been in the early 1960s. But through the efforts of Mrs Pizzey and others wife-battering became once more a highly publicized subject, and in July 1975 the House of Commons published their *Report from the Select Committee on Violence in Marriage*. On the question of research the Committee (of which the indefatigable Willie Hamilton was chairman) wrote: 'The whole of our enquiry is being limited by the remarkable paucity of information about domestic violence. Only one or two studies are currently being conducted and very little money is being spent.' The Committee made urgent recommendations to the government and other bodies that further research should be carried out.

But research into such an intensely personal area of human relationships is difficult. Battering husbands dislike being interviewed: in any case they are usually out working when the interviewer calls. Richard Gelles (1972), when researching into physical aggression between husbands and wives found that even when husbands were at home they often insisted that the wife talk for the family. Or that if the husband could be persuaded to talk the wife would frequently interrupt, or eventually dominate the interview. Such interviews, when achieved, often led to altercations between the spouses, showing how close to the surface the marital discord was. In the end Gelles and his colleagues decided to interview only those spouses who would be the best informants: they ended with 66 wives and 14 husbands. Clearly such results must be biased, but no one has yet found a way of successfully overcoming this problem which is experienced by all researchers into family violence.

A further difficulty is that most people when they are being interviewed allow their answers to be influenced to some extent by their perception of what the interviewer is seeking. Few of us can totally avoid trying to impress when we meet a stranger, and battered/battering spouses are no exception. Some will tell actual lies. One person may wish to stress his or her peaceful nature and put all the blame for any violence onto his or her partner; another will exaggerate her toughness and sturdy independence; yet others will deny all violence because of their need to be thought of as members of respectable, law-abiding families.

Questionnaires carry the danger that, unless they are designed by experts and contain within themselves cross-checks of an elaborate kind, they can also give a false picture. Dr J. Gayford interviewed many wives both at Chiswick and elsewhere. (The words 'wife' and 'wives' are to be taken throughout this book as meaning legal wives, common-law wives, cohabitees, or a combination of all three.) He used personal meetings as well as a printed questionnaire, and had to reject the evidence of some whom he felt were lying, or who through lack of a desire to co-operate or difficulties of language gave misleading replies. Of the 100 women he finally selected he found none, on checking with other sources, whose evidence had to be invalidated (Gayford, 1975a). But even so his work - invaluable as it is - presents us with marriage purely from a woman's point of view. Direct research into the husband's life must be undertaken before we can get a fully balanced picture, although it is already quite clear that the image of an innocent little woman terrorized by her unloving husband needs updating. The picture of family life drawn in Chapter 1 is closer to the real home life of many battering families.

Janet's story demonstrates the different type of violence inherent in many problem families. The damage done to the young minds of the children is as traumatic, perhaps more so, than the damage done to their bodies. Janet and her siblings were not properly fed, their moral welfare was totally overlooked, they were exposed to alcoholism, often beaten for no reason, and were completely deprived of consistent loving reassurance. Violence and dishonesty is now an integral part of their lives; as Janet herself says, a good row turns her on, brings a bit of excitement into an otherwise drab life. But many people have still worse things happen to them: for one thing, none of the people in Janet's story were killed. Hundreds are, every year. The children were not molested sexually - many are, repeatedly.

The emotional damage suffered by children as a result of marital violence has hardly been researched at all; the facts and figures in the following section therefore relate mainly to the adult participants in marital battles, and are based on the small amount of evidence at present available.

As far as we know, a percentage of women are battered by the men they live with in every country in the world. What these percentages are future research may tell us: for the present we might speculate that in communities where male dominance is strong battering is likely to be more frequent. On the other hand it could be argued that violent confrontations are more likely to take place in homes where women are indepen-dent.

Dr J. Gayford's final sample of 100 women reflects the cosmopolitan character of Britain's larger cities. He was introduced to most of his subjects through the Chiswick Women's Aid house, but a quarter came to him through social workers, health visitors, etc. Unlike most refuges which shelter only local women, the Chiswick refuge receives women from all over Britain. One might therefore expect fewer immigrants to seek shelter there than if it took in purely London-based residents. In fact only 66 of the wives and 56 of the husbands were British (including Northern Irish) while 17 wives (21 husbands) came from the Republic of Ireland, and 9 wives (13 husbands) were West Indian. There was only one Asian wife in his sample, although some workers have found that a number of Asian wives, who come from a highly male-dominated society, are ill-treated by their husbands. The rest of the sample mostly came from Europe.

All researchers report that pregnancy is a particularly dangerous period. Jean Moore, senior tutor in charge of training at NSPCC headquarters, says: 'The peak time when violence is very often at its worst is when a couple cannot have intercourse, just before and after the birth of a child.' Pregnant women are often pushed down stairs or knocked over, sometimes losing their child as a result. Erin Pizzey has found that a high number of children coming to her refuge are physically handicapped in some way, and it seems likely that some of these have been injured in the womb.

Men kick, bite, and use fists and implements to inflict damage. Gayford reports that all the 100 women in his sample had been struck with a clenched fist, and 59 were also repeatedly kicked. Forty-four suffered lacerations, 17 of these being caused by instruments such as razors, knives or broken bottles. Nineteen women reported attempts to strangle them, and 2 attempts to suffocate them. Twenty-four had fractures of ribs, nose or teeth, and 4 had their shoulders or jaws dislocated. Nine were taken to hospital after being found unconscious. Two were left with defective vision, and 2 claimed their epilepsy was a result of head injuries. In 42 cases weapons of some kind were employed. Usually the first object that came to hand was used, but nearly a third of the husbands always used the same implement: in 8 cases it was a belt with a buckle. Richard Gelles (1972) reports that he frequently found that the assailant used the same method of punishment as had been used in his childhood, either directly on him or on his mother or other members of the family.

Sometimes blows are carefully placed so that they do not show. Jean Moore reports the case of a woman who now walks with a limp because her husband always kicked her on the ankle believing it would not show. Other men attack the skull or the ears, so that any bruising will be hidden under the hair, or they attack areas normally clothed. But most of the brutalities inflicted on the women at Chiswick are only too obvious when they first arrive, as Gayford's report shows. The following account is typical of many:

'He hit me with his fists, feet, and bottles, smashing me to the floor; then he started to kick, sometimes with repeated blows to the face and other parts of the body. He has kicked me in the ribs and broken them, he has tried to strangle me and taken me by the shoulders and banged my head against the floor. During my marriage of nearly four years I have received constant bruises all over my body, this has been more so during pregnancy. I have received black eyes, cut lips, and swollen nose. Most of my bruises have been to the scalp where they do not show. On one occasion I had bruises to the throat and abdomen and was unable to speak; on admission to hospital I was found to have multiple injuries and broken ribs.'

In addition to attacking their wives, men often attack household objects in their rage. Jean Moore told me of one husband who played bizarre games of noughts and crosses on the family three-piece suite, and of another who slashed his wife's clothes and threw them out into the garden. Some men smash windows, systematically working through the entire house, while others go berserk and demolish whatever pieces of furniture meet their eyes. If neighbours or relatives try to stop them they too will be attacked, so that soon the wives find themselves totally isolated from outside help.

How many women find themselves in this position is unknown. The Select Committee on Violence in Marriage sat for five months, attempting to gather as many hard facts as possible, including incidence. At the end the best they could do was to report that witnesses were probably correct when they talked of known cases being only the tip of an iceberg. The Welsh Office suggested that, extrapolating from a limited study made in Colchester, there might be 5,000 battered wives in Wales. The Citizens Advice Bureaux estimated they received 25,000 enquiries in 1973 with regard to battering, and felt that the numbers were growing. In a memorandum submitted to the Select Committee the Metropolitan Police report a study carried out over three months in 1974 at ten police stations in the Metropolitan Police District. This showed a total of 89 cases being reported to the police, suggesting a total of 6,336 reported cases a year over the entire Metropolitan district. They add a warning, however, that as many wives refuse to report assaults to any official body their numbers must be an underestimate of the true occurrence.

The figures for applications for injunctions against husbands molesting their wives and mandatory injunctions ordering the husbands to vacate the matrimonial home are increasing at a surprising rate in London, though not in other cities. Sir George Baker, President of the Family Division of the Supreme Court of Judicature, told the Select Committee that two years previously a judge sitting one day a week in the Royal Courts of Justice was able to cope with all the applications for injunctions as well as dealing with approximately 30 undefended divorce cases, whereas now, at the time of giving evidence (July 1975), a judge has to sit every day of the week to deal almost solely with injunctions. In the High Court in London vacation judges sitting for the holiday months of August and September dealt with 339 applications in 1972, 468 in 1973 and 502 in 1974. The major part of this increase, however, is probably due to publicity surrounding battering. Wives, social workers and solicitors are nowadays more likely to know about and take advantage of legal remedies (discussed in detail in a later section). But it is also possible that battering itself is on the increase.

In the USA G. Levinger (1966) studying families undergoing divorce reported that 37 per cent of American women cited violence as grounds for divorce. I was unable to obtain equivalent British figures, since 'cruelty' as used in divorce citations covers such a wide range of behaviour that no statistician was willing to isolate for me any particular figure which would be relevant to the kind of violence we are discussing. In Britain, two separate studies of women in Holloway prison (D'Orband, and Gibbens and Dell, quoted by P.D. Scott, 1974) both show that 17 per cent had been physically ill-treated by the men they had been living with.

To try to work out from the figures I have quoted an estimate of the number of wives in Britain who are battered would be a pointless exercise. Probably within three or four years we shall have gathered enough information to make some rough guess, but for the moment I can only say that we may safely assume there is a very high number indeed of women who are abused by their husbands, and that this number is almost certainly much higher than official statistics will ever be able to show as, until the violence becomes really severe, most women continue to hope that the situation will improve and do not report it.

Levinger, in his study of divorcing couples (1966), also looked at their social class. He found that physical abuse was an important factor in the decision to break up their marriage in 20 per cent of the middle-class couples and in 40 per cent of the working-class couples. Richard Gelles found that the less education the husband had received the greater was the likelihood that he would physically abuse his wife. But the opposite was the case with women. There was more violence in families where the wife had had some high school education at least, and he also found a fairly high level of conjugal violence among women college graduates. Gelles hypothesized that where a woman is more educated than her husband, the husband may feel frustrated that he is not providing his wife with the kind of life she might expect. A further explanation (put forward by other American workers and supported by Gelles) is that when the social status of a superior group (the breadwinners) is threatened by an inferior group (supported wives and children) physical violence is likely to erupt since such men have few other ways in which to prove their superiority. Gelles quotes the following case of an unemployed man who was less educated than his wife. The wife's father, who was a guest at his grandchild's birthday party, had to leave early to be at his work by three o'clock. The wife explains what happened:

'It was around two-thirty and we were cutting the cake. I had my son blow out the candles and make a wish and then help make the first cut. I had him give the first piece to my father because he had to go to work. My husband stormed out of the house . . . he came back loaded that night simply because my father had the first piece of birthday cake instead of him. . . . That was the first time he broke my wrist.'

Whether or not battering is more rife in the working class is at present being hotly disputed. P. D. Scott (1974) suggests that wife battering occurs 'alongside a constellation of other social inadequacies . . . the majority of cases are found in social classes 4 and 5.' Some writers suggest that in certain areas such as mining districts, where a man's physical strength is traditionally very important to him, it is normal for the women to receive a certain amount of roughing up. In a chapter on violence in community homes (Tutt (ed.), 1976) Millham, Bullock and Hosie, who spent considerable time researching in a poor mining community, writes that 'Attitudes to, and definitions of, violence are very much class determined', and report various incidents where wives and girlfriends appeared to take a certain amount of 'thumping' with positive pleasure. Typical of the comments boys made about their girls was, 'Oh, you just give her a good thump, and if she hits back you're made!' The authors conclude 'What seems in objective terms a violent action may mean something entirely different in another cultural context.'

Indeed it might. The authors apparently base their conclusions on what the males told them: they do not report having asked the women themselves what *they* felt about it. While it is possible that a certain amount of rough play might have excited these girls sexually, it is also likely they considered such treatment indicated a growing relationship between them and their boyfriends, and in a community where marriage is highly esteemed, such attentions could be welcomed for what they represented rather than for any pleasure they themselves gave. By the time a woman was married it would be a little late to change what by then had become an established pattern of behaviour. I can only say I have never met a single woman yet who enjoyed being hit. Janet, in the preceding chapter, summed up the feelings of many when she told how she liked the excitement of a row, but loathed actually being bashed.

Norman Tutt, in his introduction to the same book, comes to a different conclusion to P. D. Scott and to Millham, Bullock and Hosie. He agrees with other recent studies which suggest that battering is distributed evenly throughout the classes, while allowing that there may be pockets within various classes where a particular form of behaviour is normal which is not accepted as such in the remainder of that class. I think this last is most probably true. It may be of interest (though of no statistical value!) that of twelve women who attended a lecture on violence in the family at which I was present, three admitted during a later discussion that they themselves were battered, and all three turned out to be married to lawyers. Since none of the women knew each other previously and it was an open public lecture the coincidence was fairly remarkable!

Marsden and Owens (as reported by Margaret Gregory in Borland (ed.), 1976), interviewing in the general community, found that battered women came from all social classes 'except that labourers' wives were under-represented in proportion to the national average'. This last supports other research which suggests that where education is high enough to raise a few hopes but is too low to allow their fulfilment, stress and frustration is likely to be greater than among those whose expectations were always low from the beginning. Margaret Gregory also points out that middle-class women rarely enter the statistics because they are more likely to make their own arrangements, and are unlikely to flee to a refuge. But as anyone researching this subject who talks to middle-class women can verify, there are plenty of apparently smoothly-run congenial households where professional men's wives are terrified of their husbands' brutality, though they would almost die rather than let outsiders know about it. I personally am convinced that battering is spread throughout the classes, but where conditions are particularly stressful violence is likely to be greater. Money worries, homelessness, frustration at work, are obviously more likely among classes 4 and 5, but there is no lack of stress in classes 1, 2 and 3. As with baby battering it is unlikely, however, that we will ever know the true incidence of conjugal abuse among the middle and upper income groups.

We do know a little more about the age groups involved. It might be thought that most battering would be found amongst hot-blooded young husbands, but that does not seem to be the case. Of Gelles's sample, most conjugal violence took place among the husband's age group of 41 to 50 years (this group battered their wives more than twice as much as did the men in the 19-30 age group). An earlier American study (Snell, Rosenwald and Robey, 1964) found the average age of the wives was 37 years, which probably means the husbands were in general at least two or three years older. M. Faulk (1974), in a study of 23 men awaiting trial on charges of seriously assaulting their wives, found an age range of 20 to 70, with an average age of 39. A similarly wide range of ages is evident among the wives arriving at various women's refuges, with the National Women's Aid Federation reporting a high number of women in their late twenties and thirties. Gayford produces an age of 31 years amongst the women in his sample, and 34 for the men.

Thus the information so far available on age groups indicates that the marriages in which most battering takes place are well-established. Certainly many wives have been battered ever since they first formed a relationship with their men, but present knowledge suggests that in most cases abuse does not assume real seriousness (if it had existed at all before) until some years of marriage have passed. Perhaps approaching middle age and dissatisfaction with what has so far been achieved in life is an important cause of battering?

Another common assumption is that battering families are large families. From the very small amount of evidence available it seems possible that such an assumption may be false. Gayford gives a mean of 2.3 children born to the battered women in his sample, who themselves came from slightly larger families. The NSPCC in a study of 23 violent matrimonial cases (*Yo-Yo Children*, 1974) found that there was an average of 2.91 children per family. Since the average age of the children was 6.33 it does not appear that these are families where yearly births exacerbate any tensions already inherent in the marriage.

The same NSPCC report suggests that these families move house frequently, which makes it difficult for inspectors and social workers to keep contact with them. This has been a common finding also with families where children are battered, and I have seen the same phenomenon referred to with regard to other types of problem families. It would make an interesting piece of research if someone could explore just how common this trait is with all kinds of families who have in one way or another come under the official eye. Are these people restless because it is in their nature, or are they fleeing problems such as rent collectors, increasing neighbourly rejection, etc? Are they moving because they hope to find better housing, better luck? Does a change of residence help or make things worse for them?

There is one precipitant of battering about which a lot is known, and that is alcoholism. There is no doubt that alcoholism is very frequently connected with conjugal abuse, but we do not know whether this is because the kind of person who is liable to resort to violence out of weak self-control, poor self-esteem, natural irritability, etc., is the same kind of person who tends to seek support in alcohol, or whether it is that husbands who would not otherwise be violent take to drink because of frustrations at work or at home, as a result losing their normal inhibitions against aggression.

The Addiction Research Unit of the Institute of Psychiatry investigated the wives of 100 alcoholics, and found that nearly half had been beaten by their husbands. Seventy-six per cent of the men were quarrelsome; 49 per cent had broken furniture, windows, china, etc; the same proportion were very jealous and/or possessive, and 27 per cent had attempted seriously to injure or murder their wives. The Newcastle upon Tyne Citizens Advice Bureau in their evidence to the Select Committee on Violence reported that the most frequent cause of violence revealed in their case histories was the husbands' drinking habits, it being mentioned in 25 out of 73 cases. At the same enquiry the Tyneside Marriage Guidance Council gave evidence that

> Drinking is almost invariably associated with violent behaviour on the part of the husband. Newcastle Brown Ale seems to make husbands very aggressive and lowers their 'frustration tolerance level' so that what would, in other circumstances, invoke a harsh word, now invokes a blow.

Gayford found that 44 per cent of the husbands regularly came home drunk and beat their wives. Fifty-two per cent of all the men frequently got drunk and from time to time a further 22 per cent became inebriated. Gelles finds similar figures among his sample, drinking being associated with violence in 48 per cent of the cases. Gelles puts forward various evidence which suggests that alcohol and family violence are more closely related than alcohol and other types of violence. He also reports that aggressiveness was almost entirely a male reaction to too much drink: only one woman in his sample became violent when she drank. Nearly all the wives claimed that alcohol completely changed their husbands who, when they were sober, were responsible, pleasant men. Similar comments are often made by other battered wives: one told me her husband was 'ideal in every way a woman could want, except', she would add hastily, 'when he was drunk'. In fact, this particular husband neglected her, went out in the evening with men friends leaving her alone, and was clearly uninterested in her as a person. His virtues were that he gave her regular housekeeping money and saw that she was comfortably housed and fed, though the latter virtue was disappearing as drink began to ruin his career. This need to stress to outsiders that were it not for drink the home would be a model one appears so frequently it could almost be called a characteristic of battered wives. Gelles suggests that this may be because battering is clearly obnoxious to everyone, whereas alcoholism is nowadays considered an illness and may be thought of as being less reprehensible.

Many researchers and workers report that typically, when a man returns home drunk, he demands food and sex, in that order. The wife, angry that her husband has been wasting money on drink, may give them grudgingly or even refuse one or both. Her reluctance or resistance infuriates the husband, who then retaliates with physical violence.

There can be no doubt that alcoholism itself is increasing. Admissions to mental hospitals for alcoholism have risen from an average of 4.6 per cent in the five years preceding 1969 to an average of 10.5 per cent since then, and the latest rises are now up to 13 per cent a year. It is predicted that if this increase continues by 1985 alcoholism could account for nearly a quarter of all mental hospital patients as is already the case in Scotland. Obviously, whatever the precise nature of the connection between battering and drink is, alcohol plays a leading part in wife abuse, and with the continuing rise in alcoholism it is not unreasonable to fear that battering also will increase.

Although alcohol is by far the most important drug, other drugs are also implicated. Tranquillizers are prescribed far too frequently by many GPs who in spite of official warnings still hand them out as though they were no more harmful than the traditional coloured water masquerading as medicine, instead of investigating the real cause of the patient's distress. The effect of these drugs can be disastrous, particularly when they are combined with alcohol. There is some discussion of this subject in the chapters on baby battering, but I would like to mention here an example of atypical behaviour caused by the administration of drugs. Sydney Brandon, a psychiatrist, reports in his contribution to *Violence in the Family* (Borland (ed.), 1976) that the benzodiazepines such as diazepam (Valium) and possibly some other sedative drugs may occasionally produce explosive episodes in men who are not normally violent. He quotes the case of a twenty-two-year-old student taking Valium who went nearly mad with rage when he could not open the door of his room after fetching some milk. He dropped the bottle, pounded on the door, finally breaking it from its hinges. Seeing his girlfriend (she had been trying to open the door from the other side) he immediately attacked her and was only stopped by the intervention of neighbours. He had not been aggressive previously and on stopping the Valium he returned to normal behaviour.

Alcohol is also frequently associated with the gambling urge. Sydney Brandon finds that gambling is often brought up in discussions on family violence. Usually the man gambles on a sudden impulse - not many are compulsive gamblers. Brandon connects this impulsive type of gambling with the kind of person who finds it difficult to put off immediate gratification and to tolerate frustration. Obviously the disappointment of a gambling loss can easily lead to feelings of aggression, and who easier to attack without danger of a comeback than a frightened wife?

A quarter of the wives in Gayford's sample admitted that gambling was a problem in their home, while the Citizens Advice Bureaux report that financial worries, exacerbated by the husband's gambling, are often discussed by wives seeking their help. One may easily imagine a wife's impatience with a reeling husband who has not only drunk away much of the scarce housekeeping money but has lost further amounts by betting unsuccessfully on the horses. This picture may sound Victorian, but it is one that is still frequently reproduced in many modern homes, and could, if alcoholism continues to increase, become once more a problem almost on the nineteenth-century scale, the immensity of which resulted in our present-day licensing laws.

We have now looked at a number of statistics on some of the aspects of wife battering. Some of the samples are too small for anyone to claim universal validity for them, but until further research is carried out they make useful indicators. We have seen that marital violence is an international problem, examined the kind of assaults men make on their wives, and attempted to gain some idea of the size of the problem. We have seen that battering occurs in all income groups, though it is probably more frequent in classes 4 and 5, and discovered the rather surprising fact that most battering husbands are, according to present research, in their thirties or forties. The families concerned are usually small and they move frequently (though this last has yet to be confirmed by further research). Lastly, alcoholism, drugs and gambling are features that appear regularly in the lives of many of these families. But what of the characters of the people involved? What kind of people are the men who beat up their wives, and why do the women put up with it?

Sometimes people say to me, 'They must be mad, they must be mental', meaning both the men who attack and the women who submit. It is perhaps easier to envisage a violent man bashing up his wife than it is to understand why the woman does not run away the first time it happens to her. Let us dispose first of the 'mental' tag. P. D. Scott chaired a committee of the Royal College of Psychiatrists whose conclusions (Scott, 1974) were: 'As in crime and delinquency, the majority of wife battering will almost certainly prove to have no clear correlation with mental illness . . . yet all the varieties of mental illness may occasionally play a part.' In other words, once in a while a man may attack his family as a direct result of some severe mental disturbance or sickness, but in most cases of marital violence there is no evidence of what would be clinically defined by a psychiatrist as mental illness.

Dr Scott, who believes that the majority of battering is to be found in social classes 4 and 5, finds a striking similarity between battering and other types of social deviance. He considers that any classification of criminal or deviant behaviour will fit wife battering, and that you will find the same major groups in both. There will be the same hard core which is very difficult to help, and a large majority whose behaviour will easily be changed by skilled help. Another group are those who behave according to normal social mores for the great majority of the time but who will occasionally, in response to some powerful stimulus, 'go on a bender'.

To say that a man is socially deviant is a useful phrase for sociologists, and perhaps is no more than what the man in the street means when he calls someone 'mental' or 'off his nut'. Often it simply means that the person concerned is breaking the current conventions appropriate to his social background. We have already seen that in some parts of our society it appears to be fairly normal to 'give the old lady a few thumps on a Saturday night': a doctor in the Gorbals will not suffer the same shock as a doctor in Wimbledon if a woman knocks on his door with a bloody face and a few cracked ribs. But the great majority of our society is no longer prepared to consider women as men's property; they shun a man who breaks what they consider to be appropriate rules of conduct. They ask, if one man can control his undoubted superior physical strength and not use it to silence a recriminating wife or to settle a marital argument, why cannot another?

Everyone is agreed there is no one answer. Leaving aside the comparatively rare occasions when unbearable stress provokes an otherwise controlled and peaceful man to an outburst of physical violence, there seems no doubt that the majority of battering husbands suffer from a constellation of problems, some of which are psychological but none of which classify him as mentally ill.

Jean Moore feels that, as with battering parents, strong feelings of inadequacy and low self-esteem typified the spouses in the small sample she studied (described in the NSPCC (1974) booklet *Yo-Yo Children*). She writes, 'It seems to us that they experienced their marital partners as attempting to annihilate their very being and they hit out as one would with a wasp in one's hair.' The American researchers Snell, Rosenwald and Robey, looking at a very small middle-class sample, came to similar conclusions. They found that men who

31

beat their wives are typically passive, indecisive and inadequate sexually, while their partners are aggressive, even masculine. Other researchers have reported findings that bear out this picture, calling many of the wives domineering or bossy. The women themselves frequently comment that they are forced to take over all the running of their households to prevent the husbands from spending all the money on inessentials and to ensure that vital decisions get taken. Thus, in this role reversal, the wife becomes responsible for all that happens to the household and the people within it. When things go wrong the husband then blames the wife and considers himself justified in physically abusing her.

M. Faulk also confirms this picture, which is particularly interesting as 17 of the 23 men he studied had either murdered or attempted to murder their wives. Dr Faulk (who is a consultant forensic psychiatrist) categorized the men's relationships with their wives into five types. Nine of the men he placed into category 1 (dependent, passive men whose attempts to pacify their querulous dominating wives would break down, sometimes under direct provocation, resulting in a violent attack), and four in category 2 (the dependent but suspicious type who was very jealous of his wife, usually unjustly, but whose need for her was too great for him to abandon her - the tension caused by this jealousy would gradually build up and erupt in ever-increasing violence). A further husband fell into category 3 (violent and bullying) and five more into category 4 as dominating men with a strong need to prove themselves. The remaining five men who fitted into category 5 were husbands who had achieved a stable and affectionate relationship with their wives, but during a period of severe mental disturbance had assaulted their wives. The dependent, passive group was therefore the largest; in all, 13 out of the 23 accused men had dependent personalities, a surprising conclusion under the circumstances.

Low self-esteem and feelings of inadequacy are commonly accompanied by a sense of depression, both among men and women. Gayford found that 71 of the 100 wives in his sample were taking antidepressants or tranquillizers, and of 46 who were seen by psychiatrists, 21 were diagnosed as clinically depressed. In 9 of the 23 couples studied by the NSPCC one or other partner was being treated for a psychiatric condition, usually with drugs. Five of Faulk's sample suffered from depression severe enough to be labelled as a psychiatric disorder.

In some respects Faulk's figures are at odds with Scott's conclusions mentioned earlier, that there was no clear correlation of mental illness with wife battering. Of the men over 40 years of age in Faulk's sample 7 out of 8 had serious psychiatric illness. Seven of the 15 men under 40 years were psychiatrically disturbed. Only 9 out of 23 men in all had no psychiatric abnormality. However, we must bear in mind that these men were at the extreme end of the spectrum of battering, being on trial for serious assault including murder, so that one would not be surprised if a higher number of psychiatrically-disturbed cases than is normal were to be found among them.

In all the researchers' samples there are instances where both men and women have attempted to take their own lives. How seriously these suicide attempts may be taken cannot be judged, but no doubt there were many 'cries for help' among them. Gayford reports that 34 of the 100 women he interviewed had tried to poison themselves, 10 trying more than once. Seven attempted self-mutilation, 3 repeating the attempt, and 9 tried other methods. Twenty-one women admitted that the so-called suicide attempts were actually calls for attention, but 16 insisted they had meant to die. In Jean Moore's sample 9 of the spouses (of both sexes) had either threatened or actually attempted suicide. The various women's aid refuges report that from time to time the wives staying in their shelters attempt suicide - we may remember Janet's description of her own attempt and her scorn of the doctors who visited her afterwards. What struck me particularly while Janet was telling me about this incident was her matter-of-fact manner. She admitted she was not sure herself how seriously she had meant her suicide attempt - she thought she had intended to die but she couldn't really be sure about it. It seemed to me she meant it as an extreme form of communication, and communication implies a desire for a reply; it was a violent protest against the life that fate had doled out to her, plus a demand for help, although she already knew only too clearly that no one could really help her.

One must remember that many of these women have lived on the edge of tension for years; as Janet said, they are lost when the adrenalin falls. If you are used to being violently assaulted, perhaps it is not such a terrifying thing to violently assault yourself. There was a slight sense of bravado in Janet's telling, but more a sense of dreariness, an acceptance that - in the end - if you weren't saved in time, what did it matter? You might as well be dead, anyway.

One might add that Scott has written that he expects future research will show 'frank masochism or sadism in either marital partner is not a central feature of wife or baby battering'. Certainly I have not come across any workers in the field who have suggested otherwise. There is no doubt that large numbers of men enjoy fantasizing about sadism and/or masochism - one has only to look at any bookstall to see endless depiction of girls with their hands or ankles tied, while muscular men stand behind clutching rawhide whips; there are fewer covers depicting women with whips standing over manacled men, but there are some, and I doubt if much of their readership is female. But few of the men who quietly indulge in the titillating daydream of a beautiful girl kneeling submissively at their feet waiting to be whipped would dream of causing real pain to a real woman, and the motives of the few sadists who actually do carry out their fantasies are so remote from what we know about the usual wife-batterer there is no point in examining their obsessions here.

We have, then, a picture of two people - not classifiable as mentally ill but usually suffering some character defect such as low self-esteem or inadequacy - yoked together in violence, each advancing and retreating as the one or the other takes the initiative. For it would be quite wrong to assume that in all cases the man is the aggressor, the woman the innocent victim. Jean Moore has aptly described this situation as a power game between two people, which on occasion is fought out even to the death.

The jealousy that is so often manifested by battering husbands may be one aspect of this need for one partner to have complete power over the other. The jealousy is mostly of a sexual nature, and may reflect a doubt about his own potency on the part of the male. Women also suffer the agonies of jealousy - as with men, there need be no foundation for their constant complaints.

Gelles found that male jealousy was typically accompanied by a Gestapo kind of questioning which was continued until the wife, worn out, would admit to anything - false or true - in order to stop the interrogation, at which point the husband would beat her in revenge. Where it was the women who were expressing their suspicions they mostly regarded a beating from their finally exasperated husbands as confirmation that their husbands were being unfaithful, and were not then upset about the attacks as they might otherwise have been. But not all the women were submissive. Gelles discovered several wives who had attacked their husbands violently, one because she was jealous of her husband (who was in fact faithful), another because she objected to her husband's suspicions (founded in truth) that she was sleeping with a friend of his while he, the husband, was on night duty.

Gayford, discussing their husbands' jealousy with the women in his sample, writes that 66 per cent reported morbid jealousy on the part of their husbands. Nearly half the men had accused their wives of actual infidelity, and just under a third of flirting. Over a quarter checked their wives' movements and 4 per cent went so far as to claim they were not the fathers of their own children. Gayford had to rely on the women's own versions of what had happened, and 17 per cent did admit they had slept with other men. A few more may have done so in fact, but clearly in many cases the jealousy was delusory. Since half the men had had affairs during their marriage, Gayford suggests these husbands could be projecting their own behaviour on to their wives. Delusional jealousy is particularly dangerous since the man cannot be argued with, and it is in any case notoriously difficult to prove something has *not* happened. The tragedy of Othello and Desdemona is, of course, a classic example of this kind of jealousy.

In a report mentioned earlier on an investigation into the wives of 100 alcoholics, it might be remembered that half the husbands were classified as being very jealous. We also saw that Faulk reported that 4 of the 23 men in his sample were dependent and jealous, 3 of them suffering from delusional jealousy. This low figure suggests that beatings for jealousy are less likely to end in death or serious injury than for other reasons, but this study is seriously limited by its size, and all the findings will have to be repeated on a larger scale before they can be validated.

In an article in the *Guardian* (25 November 1976) I wrote about a man whose life had been totally changed when his best friend was blown up beside him while they were on army duty in Ireland. He went berserk, showered bullets everywhere, and broke his sergeant's jaw with the butt of his rifle. After some months in mental hospital he was released, but took to beating his wife. He seems now to be unable to let her out of his sight, and even when she is in the same room he keeps looking at her as though he needs to check she is still there. One day when I was with them she left the house to visit a friend. As she went out he could hardly contain himself. He kept going to the window to see if she was coming back, looked at his watch, suggested that perhaps he ought to telephone the woman friend she was visiting, although he knew quite well she had only gone out for a couple of hours and would certainly be back to get his lunch. When she was near him he often touched her, rough little pats that made her wince since she was still covered in bruises from the last time he beat her up. He made her show me her bruises, and as he pointed out the worst ones he appeared to be rather proud of them, much as a child will show with satisfaction a nasty cut that is no longer actually paining him. They are *his* bruises, *he* made them, and he is obviously possessive about them. I believe he feels obscurely that in this way he has made her flesh his flesh, and for a little while he rests secure. His wife says she cannot take any more from him, and his face freezes when she says this, but I don't know that she has the will to leave him.

The daily strain of living with such a man can be imagined. But living with a violent woman can be as painful, for women make up for what they lack in muscle power by using implements - paperweights, pots and pans, plates, a radio - whatever comes nearest to hand. Most women, though, are too frightened to retaliate when attacked by their husbands, as they fear it will increase the violence. Gayford found only eight women who claimed they regularly fought back, but it should be borne in mind that over three-quarters of the wives in his sample had actually left their husbands. Clearly, where battles end in feminine victory, a wife has no need to leave home. No one can have any idea how many battered men there are who cower in the privacy of their homes, but they do exist, and possibly in some numbers.

Gelles's results here were interesting. Even 20 per cent of the control wives in his study (normal members of the public with no recorded histories of marital violence) had struck their husbands, three of them hitting their husbands more than occasionally. In the high-violence families themselves over half the women had hit their husbands at least once and 20 per cent regularly joined their men in violent battle. He reports that in the most violent families 'both partners are offenders as well as victims'. In the less violent families mostly the husband attacks while the wife occasionally hits back or even starts the fight. Twice as many women as men used an implement such as a lead pipe, lamp or chair, and the only stabbing with a knife was done by a woman. Men mostly kicked, punched, slapped, hit or scratched. Women also attacked in this manner, but obviously their blows were less effective than their more muscular husbands'.

Gelles found that some women committed what he calls 'protective-reactive violence', named after the kind of bombing (such as that of Cambodia and Vietnam) which is intended to hit the enemy before he can hit you, and with luck incapacitate him. Some women were in fact able successfully to incapacitate their men by rushing to the attack when they considered themselves about to be threatened, while others had learned that they could floor a drunken husband without too much trouble. In these circumstances women may use an object such as a knife to give them added power, but all admit it is a very dangerous game, and that they often end up suffering the worse because of it. However, Gelles suggests there is some indication that women who do not risk fighting back may be more likely to be hit repeatedly, but adds that this evidence is not at all conclusive and no one really knows what a woman's best course is likely to be.

Behind all this violence we repeatedly see evidence that both partners need each other, for whatever complicated reason. In

February 1976 Mrs Alice — — was found guilty of two attacks on her husband, one with a poker and the other with an axe. The judge said he was satisfied that Mrs — — was suffering from a mental disorder and that she ought to go to a mental hospital. However, no suitable place could be found for her, so she was sent to prison, as all the evidence suggested she would repeat the attacks if she was returned home. But her husband wanted her back. Immediately, he lodged an appeal and six months later succeeded in having her released. His argument was that he and his wife had been drinking too much and as she was also taking tranquillizers 'she was not herself' when she hit him with the axe. When the Court of Appeal judge (having remarked to Mr — —, 'With a husband like you she will be better off at home than in prison') said to Mrs — —, 'Go away and do not bash your husband again', Mr — — wept, presumably for joy. Back at their home he told reporters that from the beginning he had wanted to forgive and forget and had not wished the case to go to court. Now he said happily, 'It's great to have her back again' and insisted he was not frightened of her, giving her 'a huge kiss' to show the truth of what he said.

Finally one might comment that the continued success of those many seaside postcards, showing little men cowering under raised rolling-pins wielded by vast-bottomed and -bosomed women, must prove something. Obviously, far more women than men are physically hurt in the marital war, but I suspect there are many men, through a variety of motives such as weakness, chivalry, incapacity through drink, etc., who take far more physical punishment than any of their neighbours would imagine. Since people buy these cards in their thousands when on holiday, and since comedians still regard the subject as good grounds for an easy joke, we may assume that in reality its occurrence is not all that rare. On a phone-in radio programme recently a man asked me how he could stop his wife from hitting him, which she did at the slightest excuse. He did not retaliate, he explained, because he had been brought up to believe that no decent man ever hit a woman. It struck me that the poor woman might have been longing for some positive reaction from him, for some slightly dangerous excitement in what otherwise was perhaps a dull marriage. But

I did not dare say so, in case some male listeners were to take my comment as an excuse for violence of a kind that was not at all what the man's wife might have been trying to provoke.

A high proportion of battering husbands have already had some brush with the law. Of Gayford's sample of 100 wives, over half the husbands had been to prison or borstal, 33 for violent offences. Other offences included theft, embezzlement, fraud, drugs, non-payment of fines, etc. Nine of the women's fathers had also been to prison or borstal, three for violent crime. Nearly half the Faulk's sample had had previous convictions. When this last group was broken down into those men who were over and those who were under 40 years of age it was found that the younger men were much more likely to have had a criminal past, two-thirds of them having committed offences, and a quarter some violent offence, whereas only a quarter of the men over 40 had committed an offence at all and only one a violent offence. Six of the 23 men had committed more than one offence.

For a variety of reasons which will be discussed later, battering husbands are rarely jailed even if they assault their wives in a manner which would certainly cause their arrest if the attacks were carried out against anyone else. Mostly the authorities do not move in with any effectiveness until a man has attacked his wife so brutally she either dies or is severely wounded. This slowness in taking action is extraordinary in view of the fact that many of these final assaults could have been avoided. P. D. Scott studied 40 prisoners held in Brixton on suspicion of having killed or attempted to kill their wives. Half of these men had either beaten their wives over a long period or had only battered more recently but with rapidly increasing severity. Why did not the wives take warning and flee? Why were they not given protection? Had this been done their lives would probably have been saved. Other studies show the same story: social workers, police and neighbours know a woman is being attacked, and yet the husband is allowed to continue his assaults until the final tragedy happens.

The remaining 20 men in the Brixton study had never before beaten their wives but had suddenly 'erupted in a single, final and fatal assault'. Even here one may suspect that the men must have been showing severe signs of stress before their terrible attacks, and no doubt many were on tranquillizers, today's panacea for all problems. One sympathizes with busy doctors who in any case know there are too few psychiatrists available to deal with every over-stressed patient, even if the doctors thought it likely such treatment would do much good. Nevertheless it seems to me we must develop some form of counselling or help in cases such as these, where a spouse may well be attacked through no fault of his or her own, but purely because a mental breakdown has caused a tragic change in the sick partner.

Most murders are committed against people known to their attackers. An article in *Newsweek* (1973) claimed that in Detroit (which the previous year had had the highest homicide rate of any large American city) four out of five homicides were committed by friends, relatives or neighbours of the victim. Gelles states that in 1969 the FBI reported that a quarter of all murders took place within the family and over half of these were spouse killings. In the London Metropolitan Police District alone there were 15 murders in 1972 where spouses or cohabitants were involved, 21 in 1973 and 23 in 1974. The Home Office figures for the whole country for 1973 show a total of 465 cases of homicide, 97 of which were committed by a spouse or cohabitee. Far more women than men are murdered by their spouses, but Scott quotes that out of 131 women in Holloway charged with murder or attempted murder over a period of three and a half years, 31 cases involved a husband or cohabitee. Many of these women had themselves been battered. We can see, then, that many cases of battering end tragically in death. Many more cause gross disablement, including brain damage, to the victims. Marital violence is emphatically not a subject for jokes about nagging wives or downtrodden husbands: quite apart from the ruined lives of the participants themselves, we must remember the effects on their children who are being brought up in an atmosphere of continual strain if not of downright terror.

Before we look at what happens to the children in a violent family it will be helpful to spend a little time on the subject of marriage itself. In past centuries people were more realistic about marriage than we are. They married to increase family fortunes, to heal a feud, to improve the strength of the stock, to gain a bed partner and a housekeeper or breadwinner and, of course, to ensure the continuance of the breed. Whatever the dreams of young girls about to be plunged into matrimony, if romantic love accompanied a marriage it was a bonus. No matter how well the reality was wrapped up, in law the man was the master, the woman the servant. Of course many women must have railed against male domination, and the discomforted man evading a nagging wife is a stock comic figure of history. But most women seem to have accepted the situation - they had little choice - and no one enquired too closely about what went on in the fastness of the private home. The women, their minds untaught and under-occupied, probably dreamed in their few idle moments of ideal lovers, and as education spread and romantic fiction proliferated, fantasies of joyous love culminating in blissful marriage unmarred by the slightest cloud became - instead of the wishful daydreams they really were - part of most adolescents' and many adults' expectation of life. The reality of marriage with its recurrent difficulties and need for perpetual adjustment must have brought not only disillusionment but also the shame of personal failure to vast numbers of people. Fortunately films have now moved away from the type of sugary nonsense which fades out in sunset's glow as the hero kisses the heroine and promises eternal love along with a gold ring, although there is a still buoyant market for the old-style 'woman's' fiction.

Dr P. D. Scott has written,

> To achieve a successful marital partnership is probably the most difficult of life's social requirements. . . . To be successful each marital partner must often defer to the other, especially if there are dependent children present. Failure to show this capacity to defer or to be unselfish inevitably leads to conflict, and conflict can easily build up to the point of violence. It is . . . realistic to assume that marital conflict is always a possibility in every marriage, and that it will occur when the difference in individual needs between partners exceeds their capacity to adapt.

There are two main points to be noted here. One is Dr Scott's acceptance that some conflict is virtually inevitable in every marriage. The second is his assumption that twentieth-century man (European man, at any rate) wants 'a successful marital *partnership*'. This is something that is absolutely new. On the surface of our minds most of us are aware that this is what we do want, but such a novel idea is not very well catered for in the depths of our consciousness. Most of the literature we read from early childhood on, most of the influences to which the growing child is exposed, most of our social mores, are still based on the concept that marriage is dominated by men, not that it is a partnership between two equals. For instance, until only two or three years ago a man received the bill for his wife's income tax, and still does so unless she goes out of her way to ask for separate assessment; some forms still request the signature of the 'head of the house', meaning the man; in a restaurant the man is given the wine to taste, and it is he who is presented with the bill. I am not attempting to fly a feminist flag, but to point out a very important fact not always appreciated in this context. We are trying to achieve in marriage nowadays something brand new, but our feet are still clogged with the detritus of thousands of years of habit and assumption. Men who give their wives an occasional thump are only doing what was the right of any man to do during most of the history of the world. This is not to say that most men did it - I doubt if many did - but it was their *right* to do so.

Today men have to face an increased pressure to succeed. In a world where all are supposed to be equal a man who fails has only himself to blame, while television not only preaches how desirable consumer products are, but also implies there is no one who cannot afford them. At the end of a day's hard work which has probably given him neither mental nor pecuniary satisfaction, the man goes home to a wife who, primed by the media, hopes and perhaps even expects that her husband will be considerate, helpful with the children, and an interesting partner capable of making meaningful conversation as well as innovative and satisfying love, however tired and fed up he is. Even if he were able to do all these things for his wife, how many men had this pattern set into them as a way of life by their fathers' behaviour, or their fathers' fathers' behaviour? We have to accept that it takes time, effort and a strong desire to succeed if we are to break age-old patterns, and it helps no one if we simply dismiss violent marriage as exceptional, sick marriages.

The last hundred years have seen extraordinary changes in our world, and anyone might have thought an ancient institution like marriage would have already crumbled away. Yet although the number of people marrying each other is now falling, marriage is still popular. There were 380,600 marriages in 1975 alone. It seems that, along with large numbers of other members of the animal kingdom, as a species we cannot ignore our inherited tendency to form permanent pair bonds, even if we no longer consider that the pairings must in all circumstances be lifelong.

While thinking in terms of ethology, one or two further comments may be made. Konrad Lorenz pointed out in his famous book *On Aggression* (1966) that strong personal bonds, including those of friendship as well as those with a sexual basis, only occur in highly aggressive animals, and that the more aggressive the species is, the firmer the bonds the animal is able to make. He also states that

As opposed to ordinary aggression, [hate] is directed towards one individual, just as love is, and probably hate presupposes the presence of love: one can really hate only where one has loved and, even if one denies it, still does.

One is supposed to be very careful when drawing conclusions about human nature from animal studies, but we cannot doubt that we are a highly aggressive species which can also love passionately. And yet we differ greatly from most animals in that we - who are probably the most aggressive species ever to inhabit this earth - have not developed a powerful inhibition against males attacking females of the same species. Certainly laws of chivalry have always insisted that men treat women gently and with consideration, but such laws have rarely been applied to wives. Why mankind has failed to develop this very important piece of social behaviour would make an interesting study.

The situation of modern woman is of course even further removed from the life pattern of the higher mammals than was the comparatively simple life of primitive woman. Women now leave the family dwelling to go out to work in situations and with people unknown to the husband in ever-increasing numbers. The latest census figures show that 860,000 more women were going out to work in 1971 than were 10 years previously. Forty per

43

cent of women with children worked outside their home as compared with 27 per cent in 1961, and the percentage of married couples who were both working rose from 32 to 47. A woman who is earning money and taking responsibility may feel she has more right to expect pleasure from a marriage than a woman who stays at home after her busiest time with young children has passed. She may even want to take up the traditional man's attitude - I bring home the money, where are my slippers and my food? Needless to say her husband is unlikely to welcome this change with open arms: he will probably want the extra money *and* his slippers and food too. I do not know how often this kind of situation is responsible for wife battering: I have seen no research figures on it, but it is one obvious possible cause of conflict.

A further factor that has some bearing on the incidence of conjugal violence in our present society is that the proportion of girls marrying very young is increasing steadily, particularly among unskilled manual workers' brides. In 1970 we know that 33 per cent of all brides under 20 were pregnant. Pre-marital pregnancy, early marriage and low social class are three factors clearly associated with the breakdown of marriages, and their combination is an unfair loading against the possibility of a successful marriage. Margaret Gregory (in Borland (ed.), 1976), collating various information, suggests that, like the parents of battered babies, battering couples marry at least three years earlier than average. Many of these marriages take place to legitimize a baby, which in itself may have been conceived out of a desire to achieve through lovemaking an affectionate relationship otherwise missing in both parents' own families. Eighty-five per cent of Gayford's sample had had sexual intercourse without contraceptives, and 60 per cent were pregnant before they married or cohabited. But enforced marriage is not the best strengthener of affection, and the original relationship between the two new parents may in any case have been based on illusion, the fruit of need rather than of perception.

I think it highly likely that marriage of this kind, unconsidered marriages undertaken mainly as a result of a search for an affection hitherto lacking, will prove to be as common in wife-battering families as it is believed they are in child-battering families. As we have seen, good marriages are not easy to achieve, and probably the best way to ensure one is to have come from a happy family oneself. The poor home life so typical of many battering men has not shown them how to achieve the very thing they most long for - exactly the opposite - and disappointment will almost certainly embitter them, so that sooner or later they repeat the pattern in which they were reared.

Frequently the wife herself has also seen a fair amount of abuse in her own family. If she has been brought up in a household where there is usually a high level of tension she tends to choose a similar type of man to her father, although she may imagine she is choosing someone quite the opposite. When she quarrels with or nags her mate she often accepts a blow without complaining, considering she 'asked for it'. As we saw with Janet, she may enjoy the excitement of a row, even though she dreads actual physical retaliation.

It might be tempting to shrug one's shoulders and say, 'Oh well, if they're going to play that game, they must take what they get.' But one must look further. What have many of these girls got in their lives in the way of excitement? Quite likely they married young, are stuck at home during the earliest childbearing years, have become mothers before they have had a chance to discover their own identity, too frequently getting little enjoyment even out of sex because working-class prudery and ignorance of techniques of lovemaking still persist. Out there, outside the home, is the big wide world, but they cannot enter it. When finally they do their jobs are probably dull, mind-limiting, and if at home they can goad their man into a verbal battle at least a few sparks will fly, adrenalin will start flowing and with it a sense of well-being which makes what follows almost worthwhile. One has only to look at Janet's sad little story to see the hopelessness of such lives. As she and Bob clutch at each other for support they are like a pair of leaves floating swiftly down a river towards a waterfall. The most you can hope for is that somehow they will survive the maelstrom and not sink before their time.

A question frequently asked is, why do these partners choose each other in the first place? Some of the answers have already been suggested. People with unhappy backgrounds try to find happiness, but do not know how to set about achieving it. Girls, in order to escape a miserable home, will often fling themselves into the arms of the first man who wants them and, not bothering with contraception, soon become pregnant. If well-intentioned advisers persuade them to abort the baby or to have it adopted, as often as not they become pregnant again almost immediately, for they want a child, they want a family. Unfortunately it does not follow that they will love the child they actually have - on the contrary, they are likely to be disappointed in it, and will find themselves tied down and exasperated by motherhood - but they continue to love the *idea* of family, and will continue their attempt to found one. The kind of boy who acts tough may have a charisma for a girl of this kind; here, she thinks, is someone who will protect her and her future family from the world. If he is jealous of her she feels flattered: at last someone really cares about her.

One would think that if the man's jealousy or toughness takes the form of aggression towards the girl she would be warned off, but this is by no means necessarily the case. A quarter of the women in Gayford's sample were battered by their men before they married or set up home with them. Intimacy was usually achieved early in the relationship: as we have already seen, 85 per cent slept with their future husbands and 60 per cent were pregnant by the time they came to live together. How universal these figures may be is unknown: most of the women in Gayford's group were from the less privileged end of society, and statistics are not available for middle- and upper-class girls in similar situations, but I imagine unhappiness prods better-off girls into searching for affection through sex in exactly the same way as their less well-off sisters.

Gayford felt that for many of the women there was little choice in what type of man they married anyway. The society in which most of them were brought up took a certain amount of violence for granted; often the local pub was a central focus and the men they met there and elsewhere mostly had similar backgrounds to their own. Perhaps the future battering husbands also had a need to establish a home, and instinctively picked on similarly-motivated girls: it is difficult otherwise to explain such carelessness about contraception. Certainly 37 of the husbands had already been through at least one marriage each or a period of cohabitation with another woman, and the failures of the first relationships, often through their own violence, do not seem to have damped their hopes for the success of the new ones.

Surprisingly, Gayford writes that 47 per cent of the women in his sample stated they came from happy homes, many feeling that all their erring partners needed to reform their lives was a 'good stable marriage'. I must admit to finding this figure of 47 per cent suspiciously high. For most girls, choosing a partner is a highly complicated procedure. Although the myth has it that today's girls will sleep with more or less anyone, researchers into the sexual experiences of the younger generation have shown they are as selective as ever, and that promiscuity is rare. Going out with a boy is one thing, sleeping with him - especially without contraceptives - is another. I cannot believe that such a high proportion of well-balanced girls from happy families would allow themselves to become deeply involved with boys or men of a disturbed, aggressive kind. Time after time when I have been interviewing battering mothers or battered wives they have told me their own childhood was happy, yet almost always facts would eventually emerge which indicated a very different story. Lack of insight, a desire to bury unhappy memories, pride - there are many reasons for this reticence, and I would guess that had Gayford been able to interview the women in greater depth, facts about their past might well have emerged which would suggest a different interpretation. One must remember that severely battered women have been damaged emotionally as well as physically. It is unrealistic to expect them to view their situation with impartiality: inevitably they lay most, if not all, of the blame on to the men who have hurt them. After some years of a miserable, painful marriage it is understandable if in retrospect their childhood seems virtually ideal to them, whatever its reality. They do not want to share the blame for the marital break-up; it was their husbands' fault, and any suggestion their own past might have some relevance is bound to be met with denials.

But once there had been a time when even these warring couples thought they loved each other. Researchers usually find that where a marriage is still viable the partners retain a strong need for each other's company. They will fight each other almost into the ground, until finally one partner leaves for a short time, maybe going off with another woman or back to mother's, but nearly always he or she returns, ready for another round of the battle. Whatever it is that binds them together - similarities in character, in background; qualities the other lacks and admires; shared needs; or even just familiarity - it is a powerful force that is not easily broken. As we will see later when we look at the experiences of women's refuges, it is not enough to say that women stay with battering husbands for economic reasons: in very many cases there are other factors at work as well.

One thing that some feminists are extremely reluctant to accept is that many women do provoke violence, even though, as has already been pointed out, they hate it when they get it. On the same radio programme mentioned earlier a girl phoned in and commented that she and her mates at work, talking one day, had found that they all liked to tease their boyfriends 'until we got them really mad'. Some wanted to see how far they could go without retaliation, others just enjoyed the teasing. Thinking about provocation in those terms one smiles, recognizing a pattern probably typical of adolescent girls exploring their first relationships with the other sex. Both partners will be making these and similar explorations, seeking to find how much power they have over the other, what makes a member of the other sex happy, angry, excited. But grown women who still engage in the provocation game must have learned from experience what its end will be, yet many cannot resist continuing to play it. Jean Moore found that some of the women in the NSPCC sample who were married to jealous men would provoke them by flirting at staff dances, going out without their husbands to dances and returning late, or setting up situations with their mothers (who often egged them on) which implied infidelity, even though the wives were in fact perfectly faithful.

Others, by withholding sex, would provoke scenes of violence for which the following day the husbands, on their knees, would beg forgiveness. Promises not to ask for sex again would be extracted from the repentant husbands, but inevitably the promises would be broken and the whole scene replayed. In these cases the women seemed to take some pleasure in the power they held over their husbands; all of them must have known that what they were asking was impossible, and that sooner or later their husbands' desires would force them once more to demand sex.

Many wives have spoken to me of this pattern of violence followed by repentance, when husbands would plead for forgiveness with tears in their eyes the morning after a brutal attack. Often the men would deny any memory of the assault, refusing to believe they could possibly have caused the bruises or cuts their wives exhibited. Since the husbands were often drunk when they made these assaults, drink would be blamed and forsworn, until the next time. Interestingly, although many of the wives had ceased to hope the beatings would really stop, most believed their husbands genuinely meant what they said at the time.

The drama of repentance and reconciliation is reported so frequently that one wonders exactly what part it plays in the battering syndrome, what it means to both partners. Mrs Moore, for instance, quotes a woman whose house was full of china knick-knacks, for which she had a passion, each of which had been given to her by her husband as an apology after a beating-up. To suggest she had deliberately inspired beatings in order to add to her collection would be ludicrous, and yet she displayed the objects with pride, had not flung them from her in disgust as one might have expected. It is tempting when writing about social problems to over-simplify, to see things in terms of black and white. But the complexity of the relationship between two cohabiting people makes such simplification dangerous - they may appear to hate each other, but to separate them may be to destroy them. People can be so devious they don't even know themselves what they are really up to.

The conclusion that a certain amount of violence is provoked cannot be avoided. How frequently violence is caused by such provocation, and how frequently a totally innocent woman is battered through no fault of hers other than an original misjudgment in the choice of marriage partner, no one knows. Without interviewing in depth both partners of hundreds of violent marriages it would be impossible to draw any valid conclusions, and it has already been seen how difficult it is to arrange any interviews at all with husbands.

Much provocation is obviously unintentional on the part of the wife. Pregnancy itself provokes many men; most researchers agree this is the most dangerous time for women. Far from deliberately inviting attack, the mothers' greatest anxiety will be to protect their unborn children, but this concern for someone other than their husbands can be enough to inflame the jealousy of these insecure men, especially if sexual intercourse is restricted or denied them altogether. In addition, if the pregnancy was the reason for the marriage, the man is likely to have mixed feelings about the forthcoming child or, if there are already other children, he may well be reluctant to have the responsibility of yet another mouth to feed. The attacks may reflect this ambivalence without there being any direct intention on his part to induce a miscarriage, though this is the not infrequent result. Pregnant women are kicked in their bellies, thrust downstairs or beaten up time after time, and one can only wonder what effect these traumas must have on the children who survive these attacks when they are eventually born.

Sometimes violence begins when children have annoyed their father. The mother, interceding, receives the blows intended for them. At other times it may be merely a bad mood on the part of the husband that sparks off an attack, or, as we saw earlier, a gambling loss, particularly when combined with too much drink. Gelles found a significant increase in marital violence around Christmas and the New Year, a time particularly associated with family harmony in myth, but which in fact often causes stress in the most normal of families. As in families where children are battered, many warring couples have little contact with other people, hardly know their neighbours and have no friends to turn to in times of trouble. Their isolation must be intensified at this festive time of the year, when all around them they see evidence of other people's enjoyment in contrast to their own unhappiness. Gayford, in a personal communication, reports that he has made similar findings, and has also noted an increase in attacks on other public holidays.

As we have seen then, in spite of, or perhaps because of, the difficulties these couples face - both as individuals and as a bonded pair - they remain together far longer than anyone, looking in at their marriage like a stranger through a window, would suppose possible. Usually the partnership continues until the death of one of the pair, a death that in most cases is from normal causes, but which from time to time is a result of an act of violence by one upon the other. Whether, as a result of the increasing availability of refuge and forthcoming changes in the law, battered women will leave their men in increasingly greater numbers remains to be seen. The men may be jealous, weak-charactered, bullying, drunken, unsatisfactory in many ways, the women may be demanding, nagging, taunting, ego-destroying, but however many of these faults each may have, the other provides a familiar foothold in a shaky, uncertain world. To break away from a marriage, however insecure and unhappy it might be, to risk complete loneliness, is a step few men or women have the strength to take. Remnants of love, the tie of familiarity, hold them back. But there is one trigger that acts more effectively than any thought of self-preservation ever can, and that trigger is mother love. When children become involved in the violence, when the man lifts his hand or his foot and hits out at them too, many women at last find the courage to say 'enough', and go and pack their bags.

Children of Violence

A woman who sees her children being attacked by her husband may be stirred at last into leaving him, although until then she has been prepared to put up with his violence when it was only she who was being beaten. What she may not yet understand is that the emotional damage already done to her children simply by living in a violent home may be potentially more harmful to them than the physical blows now being inflicted.

No child likes to hear his parents quarrel. Imagine the pain a child must feel, then, when he sees his father yanking his mother's hair out, or hitting her face repeatedly with his fist while the blood runs. I remember one battering mother who told me how she used to watch her father knock her mother down, prop her up against a wall, hit her until she fell down again and continue until she passed out. (This, incidentally, was one of the women who, when I first met her, told me she had had a happy childhood, by which it turned out she meant she had a close relationship with her mother of whom she was still very fond.) In that particular family the mother remained with her husband, who never touched the children, until the last of her children had grown up and left home, whereupon she immediately walked out on him. Her daughter, whom I met several times, seemed a well-balanced woman, intelligent and with considerable self-insight. I always found it difficult to believe she had nearly killed her own baby daughter by cracking its skull on a window-sill.

In 1973 the NSPCC, disturbed at the effect of violent marriages on children, set up a study group to research into the problem under Jean Moore. From the many families on their books they chose for their pilot study 23 families, comprising 45 parents and 67 children, where violent matrimonial conflict was an outstanding feature. Their findings were published the following year in the pamphlet already referred to, *Yo-Yo Children*, and as a result of this study Essex County Council donated £19,000 to the NSPCC for a unit to be set up in Essex in co-operation with local social workers. Called an action research unit, its primary function is to discover more about marital violence, particularly with regard to the effects on children, while actively helping a limited number of clients. The unit is now functional, but it has not been in existence long enough to evaluate its experiences.

The original pilot study, although on a small scale, provided much useful information. It was discovered, for example, that there was an extraordinary amount of movement among these families. One of their inspectors remarked, 'Some of these kids don't know whether they'll wake up in the morning in the same bed in which they went to sleep the night before.' The NSPCC described one particular case which had been referred to them because a family of three children were left alone for a weekend in the charge of a young boy. They discovered that in seven months these children, all under five, were moved at least twelve times. First the mother left home with the children, no one knew where, but they all returned the following day. The whole family then went to stay with the maternal grandmother, until they were eventually rehoused. But the quarrels continued, and now it was the father who left home for ten days. The mother also left the new house and went back home to her mother's, taking the children with her.

She returned for a brief period to her new home, but soon went back to her mother's again, the children accompanying her each time. But she could not settle, and after a bit she brought the children back once more to her husband, but this time she only remained for a few days, when she disappeared with two of the children, leaving the third with its father. Some days later the mother suddenly appeared at her own mother's house, her two children still with her. Later the third child joined them. The father, not prepared to lose his family, came to the grandmother's house and removed all the children, taking them back home with him. The grandmother snatched back one child, whereupon the father put the remaining two children into care.

The importance of the maternal grandmother in this story was typical of many families. It was found that in 11 of the 23 families the mother's mother played a very active role, not only in giving shelter and financial help, but also sometimes in stirring up trouble. The daughters were often very influenced by their mothers, behaving as though they were still children and handing over responsibility. Jean Moore told me of one case where the grandmother would encourage her daughter to dress up and go out with her in the evenings, both women deliberately giving their furious husbands the impression they were going to dances to meet men. The resultant quarrels between the four, often ending in violence, were of such a complicated nature they alone would have provided a student psychologist with enough material for an entire thesis. It is significant there were only four cases in the pilot study in which the father's relatives were involved.

It also became obvious from the pilot study that the parents used their children as pawns in their marital battles. One child might be left behind when a partner departed as though to indicate that the parting was only temporary, or a favourite child would be removed to ensure the remaining spouse would attempt to get the departed ones back again. Treated as hostages, as pawns for blackmailing, dragged about from house to house, witnessing scenes of violence and horror, it is no wonder most of these children showed signs of disturbance. At school they were often introverted, nervous kids shutting themselves away, or they let out their strain in unruly behaviour. But often they were too tired to go to school, having been kept awake half the night by rows or the dread of a returning drunken father. Frequently the parents were too occupied with their own miseries to bother about their children's schooling, and since in any case the families moved so often the children were often unable even to get to their schools. Obviously relationships with other pupils and their teachers suffered, as did their school work, none of which helped to bolster their already damaged egos. The neglect of the children included lack of proper surveillance. One three-year-old child, for instance, was allowed to wander up and down the street outside its house, and was eventually run over and killed.

Occasionally the children were caught in the cross-fire of blows between the parents - in nine cases they were either hurt physically or threatened with violence. Faulk's research on 23 men accused of seriously assaulting their wives showed that one or more children in at least half the families had been physically involved. Some were hit by their father while trying to protect their mother or when going to fetch help, while others were punished by one or other of their parents with more severity than can be considered normal. P. D. Scott, studying a group of men held on the charge of murdering or attempting to murder their wives, found that out of 17 men who had children at risk, 5 admitted they had abused their children. Gayford found that over half the men in his study were said to have attacked their children, and 37 per cent of the women admitted they were hitting their children 'quite violently'. The NSPCC's Battered Child Research Team report (*At Risk,* 1975) showed that 36 per cent of the fathers in the families in their study had on occasion been violent towards their wives as well as to their children. A third of these drank heavily, and their abuse was frequent and consistently more violent than that of the rest of the husbands.

Clearly then, there is a considerable overlap between child abuse and the battered wife syndrome. As we have just seen, it is not only that sometimes battering husbands also attack their children, but that the wives themselves sometimes pass their sufferings on to their children by punishing them too severely. This 'pecking order' can and sometimes does degenerate to the point where the frustrated mother's swipes can turn into dangerous battering. An awareness of this new danger to the children can be one of the main reasons for a wife's belated decision to leave her battering husband, though she is unlikely to admit it unless directly questioned. It may be imagined how desolated such a progression must make a child feel, and it is no wonder the women's aid refuges are now discovering that one of their worst problems is how to deal with these highly disturbed children, particularly adolescent boys.

In response to an article, a reader wrote to me about her own marriage from which she had fled two years previously. She herself is recovering from the experience - 'I am now just beginning to see myself clearly and am enjoying peace' - but she is very aware she and her children have all been 'emotionally scarred'. In particular she is concerned for her elder son, who is now eleven years old. She writes:

It took fully ten years to convince me utterly and conclusively that my husband's violence was permanent and that he wasn't going to be able to change. He is in fact like two people, and I read up about schizophrenia but he doesn't fit into that description. Many people who knew both of us were amazed at what I did - run off leaving everything the boys and I have ever owned, leaving my husband, my teaching job, home, personal belongings. Many judged me, not knowing all the facts, and when I got through my divorce I vowed I wouldn't attempt to justify that action any more.

On the direction of the welfare officer, who knew how violent and uncontrollable my husband could get, court bailiffs were brought in near the end of the divorce case to enable me to leave home. The welfare officer also reported in the witness box that he very rarely recommends that children don't see a parent, as the children are often used as pawns. But in our case he took the position I suggested, that my husband have a 'no access' judgment against him, and that was granted.

My sons were nine and seven years when we left home two years ago. They have had all those years in a tense situation and witnessed violence and received violence. My eldest boy came to terms with the separation from his father easily, as his father favoured noticeably my younger son, and although both got heavy treatment with the belt, the youngest one got away with less beating. So at first it was the younger one who was in a conflict. He had been, even when we lived at home - one minute his father was cuddling and playing with him, the next moment he orders him to strip to his underwear and beat him with a belt - for what? - not straightening his trouser belt satisfactorily. Now the younger one is better, he still has fights at school, but is normally able to cope. But the older one reacts very badly if I tell him off, or slap him. In fact, although I don't let him realize this, he strikes fear into me when he turns on me and seems as if he would punch me just as his father did. I don't want to dramatize this, as it happens very rarely, but I know it is a direct result of behaviour learned from his father.

There is far more potential damage to the children than the risk they themselves may be battered or their school work may suffer. Jean Moore and her colleagues found a variety of pitiful reactions in the children they were studying. A four-year-old boy's facial eczema always worsened when his parents' quarrels were particularly violent; another young boy kept a bizarre notebook of the dates social workers and police visited his house, feeling obscurely these records might have some protective influence on his family; a third would hold his breath during rows, bringing on what at first were taken to be epileptic fits; a fourth spent much time attempting to mediate between his warring parents. Women's refuges report that bedwetting among even ten- and eleven-year-olds is common. The girls are usually frightened, withdrawn children who may occasionally explode in emotional outbursts. Nearly all the boys are either withdrawn or straightforwardly aggressive.

Obviously the upbringing these children have received has caused many of their difficulties, but probably many have in addition inherited genetically some predisposition to neuroticism or emotional instability. E. P. Rice *et al.* (1971), investigating a group of mentally sick hospital patients, found that nearly half their children manifested neurotic traits and behavioural difficulties. Again, many of these disturbances

57

were no doubt the result of the physical mistreatment a large number of these children had received, but it is also likely that many may have been genetically ill-equipped to deal successfully with such a troublesome upbringing.

H. Swanson in her chapter 'The Biological Value of Aggression' (in Tutt (ed.), 1976) has pointed out that when mice bred from an aggressive strain are removed from their mothers and suckled by non-aggressive foster-mothers, they will show less aggression than their litter mates who were reared by the natural mothers or by foster-mothers from the same aggressive strain. Of perhaps even greater interest is the finding that if immature mice are housed next to cages containing mice which fight regularly, the young mice themselves are more likely to fight whenever they have the opportunity. Both these examples demonstrate the importance of environment, but equally the fact that there can exist 'aggressive strains' of mice from which to choose the samples for experiment shows that a predisposition to aggressiveness can indeed be passed on genetically. Clearly, both heredity and environment are vital influences in all animals' make-up, including that of the human animal, but since genetic engineering is not feasible for us, we must do what we can with environment.

Jean Moore's study group (NSPCC, 1974) straightforwardly writes

> The social worker may be faced with the decision that if the marriage can only work when surrounded by violence and the children are being damaged by this violence, the children may have to be removed and placed in a stable environment.

The problem is, *what* stable environment? Any relatives may themselves be disturbed - the grandparents have between them produced this errant family and may not be the best people to rear children, and any uncles and aunts also may have been affected by the same family environment.

But placing children in institutions also has its dangers. Millham, Bullock and Hosie, writing on community homes in the DHSS book *Violence* (Tutt (ed.), 1976), comment on the identity problems that boys in institutions face, especially with regard to sex. Middle-class boys in boarding schools, they say, have the advantage of long traditions of working out their developing sexual role - 'they can dance, paint, design clothes, act and even wear drag at the school concert without arousing much stricture' - whereas the working-class boys' code of conduct forbids any tentative display of the feminine side of their nature so that their tensions will probably be alleviated instead by over-aggressive behaviour, which is also intended to hide any possible self-doubts about their own masculinity. 'Violent, aggressive behaviour is', the authors say, 'an unmistakable badge of courage' in a milieu where 'a small physical handicap such as a stammer, squint or even retarded sexual development can engender considerable anxieties and consequent aggressive outbursts'.

Where children are placed individually in foster homes this type of problem may be overcome, but it is not easy to find people willing to foster overbearing, disturbed adolescents. Many of the children solve the problem of whether or not they should be removed from their own homes by breaking the law, thereby putting themselves into some form of community home. Millham, Bullock and Hosie found that boys who exhibited violence in their approved schools were more likely than others to have come from families some of whose members, the father in particular, were violent; they were also more likely to be less intelligent than the other boys, and to have spent long periods in residential care. Often they will have been separated frequently from their fathers during their early formative years. (This last situation appears to affect girls less than it does boys.) A further finding was that this periodic absence of the father tends to make boys less aggressive while they are young, but as they grow into adolescence their aggressiveness increases. Repeatedly the researchers found an ambivalence in the attitude of the fathers to their sons' upbringing, sometimes rewarding aggression, sometimes punishing it. Meanwhile the fathers themselves habitually used aggressive behaviour, which was seen by the growing boys as a model for their own future conduct. The researchers noted a clear correlation between difficult behaviour in boys at an early age and later violence during adolescence.

59

Unfortunately even if - in an attempt to lessen the likelihood of their own later violence - we remove children from a violent atmosphere, we cannot entirely eradicate the memory of past incidents. There is experimental physiological evidence which together with psychological and psychiatric findings suggests that no experience is completely lost. Experiences may become deeply buried out of the reach of the conscious mind, but it is now thought that every single experience we have ever had is physically retained by the brain. We do not yet know how far a scene of violence witnessed, say, by an infant of eighteen months and totally lost to his conscious memory may affect his later behaviour, but it seems unlikely on the face of it that there will be no effect whatsoever. It could be that once a child, however young, has witnessed violence it will be impossible to eradicate the increased possibility he or she will use violence in later life. Certainly if the child continues to be brought up in a violent situation and is taught by methods involving violent punishment we must expect that that child will in adulthood turn naturally to the use of violence both as a method of gaining what he or she wants, and also as a method of controlling marital partners and raising children.

Dr Gayford was asked when giving evidence to the Select Committee on Violence in Marriage whether it was possible that children could be tested early in life for 'early recognition of a low frustration tolerance'. His reply (slightly edited) was:

We do not need a special test for this. All one needs is to observe these children and one can see a pattern developing. By the time they are about seven they are having tantrums, they are losing their temper, attacking adults, even in play, quite viciously. They have been brought up in an environment of violence and they have seen their father battering their mother. By the time they are 14 the male children can really let rip with violence and if something does upset them they have learned that violence does pay. . . . They not only attack their parents but they also attack their teachers at school. One must realise that if there is a background of family violence the children are at risk, and unless something is done for these children they will become the battering husbands of the next generation.

Gayford was basing this last statement not only on his own study of 100 battered wives, which showed that 51 of the husbands and 23 of the women had been exposed to family violence in their childhood, but also on other research which has come to the same conclusion. Gelles quotes a number of American studies which have all found that adult males convicted of violence have very often been exposed to violence in their childhood. He refers to Guttmacher's evidence (1960) showing that a group of murderers under study had commonly experienced a high level of violence when they were growing up and that they had identified themselves with their aggressors, learning by example that aggression was a solution to frustration. Gelles also quotes Tanay (1969) who found that 67 per cent of the homicidal offenders he was studying had undergone a violent upbringing, and another study in which it was found that murderers had not only been treated more severely than their siblings when they were young, but that they had been treated more severely than had other types of prisoners. As a result of these and other studies, including their own, Gelles and his colleagues came to the anticipated conclusion that people who as children had witnessed violence between their parents would themselves have violent marriages much more frequently than people who had had peaceful childhoods.

But adults who had themselves suffered violence as children varied in their marriages. Those who had been frequently abused when young were more likely to attack their spouses than people who had never been beaten as children. However, those who had been attacked *infrequently* were less likely than either of the previous two groups to attack their spouses, including those who themselves had never suffered childhood abuse. The reasons for this last finding are not yet clear.

What is clear is that violence undoubtedly breeds violence. Prof. D. Walters wrote in his book *Physical and Sexual Abuse of Children* (1975) that in 1972, acting as consultant to a state department of corrections, he had worked with a group of 20 men sentenced to be executed. 'Most of them had been severely punished and beaten in childhood. Not one related that "the rod was spared." To anyone working in corrections it is abundantly clear that violence does indeed beget violence.' Examples are endless. This very week while working on this section I read in my paper about a man who had just been gaoled for life for raping his twelve-year-old daughter and for indecently assaulting his thirteen-year-old son (*Guardian*, 18 November 1976). He had faced 27 charges of alleged sexual offences and violence to his own children and six children of a neighbouring family. One of the children remarked, 'I didn't know what it was like in any other family. I am just starting to realize this was all unusual.' The man, who beat the children 'with a degree of violence which went far beyond what anyone in the 19th or 20th century would consider proper parental control or punishment', forced the children to submit to joining in a sexual wrestling match, the loser of which had to do whatever anyone else wanted for the rest of the day. This 'game' he called 'Slave for the Day'. We do not have to wait to see how the children of this father will develop. At the time of writing, out of his four older children one son is already awaiting trial on a murder charge, another is in a children's psychiatric hospital and his two daughters are in council care. Violence does indeed beget violence.

The Law

Whereas it took a long time for the government to stir itself into action over baby battering, it responded more quickly when wife battering became headline news. On 26 February 1975 the first meeting of the newly-appointed Select Committee on Violence in Marriage was held, when, naturally enough, the first witness to be examined was Mrs Erin Pizzey of Chiswick Women's Aid. The sessions continued until the following July with evidence, written and oral, from ministers, High Court judges, psychiatrists, police, doctors, social workers, various groups and many individuals. In the Report summarizing their findings the Committee wrote:

> A general impression must be recorded at the outset. We have been disappointed and alarmed by the ignorance and apparent apathy of some Government Departments and individual Ministers towards the extent of marital violence. Hardly any worthwhile research into either causes or remedies has been financed by the Government.

They go on to report that responsibility is diversified between seven different government departments: the Departments of Health and Social Security, of Education and Science, and of the Environment; the Home Office, the Lord Chancellor's Office; the Scottish Office and the Welsh Office. 'Only in a very few of these Departments does the problem of marital violence receive anything other than a very low priority either in terms of manpower or financial resources.' They ended by urgently recommending that the Committee should be re-established in the next session so that more information, particularly with regard to battered children, may be received. This recommendation has now been acted on.

In view of the economic crisis under which we are at present suffering and the stringent cuts recently made in public expenditure it is obviously fruitless to cry that large sums of money must be spent on helping violent families, much as one would like to do so. Small amounts of government cash have been allocated towards limited research (which will be detailed later) but about the only change we can hope for in the near future will be a change of heart rather than a noticeable extension of facilities. Much can be done without a penny being spent. Changes in the law will greatly help wives, as will a change of attitude by the police. And if social workers would face up to facts, and stop insisting that families must be kept together at all costs, that would be another significant advance.

Meanwhile, the government is shuffling forward as usual with all the vivacity of an elderly arthritic elephant. The Department of Health and Social Security, probably the department most directly concerned with marital violence, submitted a memorandum to the Select Committee in which they write:

Generally the Department's role requires it to take a lead in exploring, with health service, local government, professional and other bodies and groups, any problems that appear to call for a new or more effective response from the agencies for whose work they have responsibility. This process leads to the formation of policy, and action such as the issue of guidance, the allocation of resources to particular developments, the commissioning of research, or grants to voluntary organisations may follow. Policy must however be realistic, and take full account of the availability of resources and all other claims on them: questions of priorities must be settled before action can start. It is the Department's intention, as more facts become available and in the light of the Select Committee's work, to prepare guidance designed to help social service departments, health authorities and others in their response to the problems of battered wives.

The penultimate sentence is obviously the vital one, if vitality can be associated at all with that paragraph. 'Policy must be realistic', 'availability of resources', 'questions of priorities' - how well we all know those phrases.

The DHSS continue this passage by discussing liaison with other departments. Briefly they remind us that the Home Office is responsible for the police, for the aftercare and probation service and for enforcing the law. The Department of the Environment is responsible for housing and accommodation for the homeless (more of this later when discussing the plight of fleeing women); the Lord Chancellor for civil law; the Department of Education and Science for children's education; and the Welsh and the Scottish Offices for their own special variations on English law and custom. With so many departments involved it is easy for us to see how individual attempts at action can flounder in a bog of memos, committees and meetings. It will require the devoted work of many campaigners before noticeable results, as opposed to endless discussions, are achieved.

Let us look a little more closely at some of the officials whose work brings them into close contact with those errant members of the public who will insist on bashing up their nearest and dearest.

Because there are always policemen on duty twenty-four hours a day, seven days a week, it is the police who are often the first officials to come into contact with a bout of marital violence. Their role has been the cause of considerable discussion recently because it is generally considered that they treat wives and cohabitees quite differently from ordinary members of the public. Violence which would call for the instant arrest of the attacker in a street brawl is often overlooked if committed by a spouse, the injured wife probably being advised to give her husband a kiss and make it up.

The police explanation for their partial approach is that over the years their experience has been that wives usually refuse to appear in court to testify against their husbands, which is highly embarrassing to the police officer who has brought the charge, as well as being a waste of everyone's valuable time and money. Nevertheless, it is their duty to keep the peace, and to shrug their shoulders and say 'wives are unreliable, they always back out so there's no point in trying to take action' is to neglect that duty. *Of course* a woman who is being terrorized by her husband is going to back out of giving evidence against him in court. In addition, it may not only be fear of her husband's reprisal that stops her, but also a desire to keep her marriage alive - whether for love, convenience or financial reasons is immaterial.

A woman who is being battered either needs protection from her husband while waiting for her case to come up so that she may be free from his bullying, or, if she wants to remain with her husband, she needs some form of threat held over her man's head to restrain him from attacking her whenever he feels like it. Since the police know too well the problems involved in securing a conviction in the former case, and feel the latter case is outside their concern, it being a civil matter, their usual reaction is to dismiss marital violence as unimportant unless the injury is so severe it cannot be ignored.

I want to look at this whole problem in some detail as, to a woman under attack, nothing is more important than that someone should effectively protect her from her attacker. Whether they like it or not, this role of protector falls naturally on to the shoulders of the police. In too many cases this help is not given, and it is vital that public concern should stir the various police forces into changing their attitudes to maltreated wives. Reforms are being made in the law, and it could well be that the public at large now imagines that battered wives' problems are over. But there is still a great deal to be done, particularly with regard to the response of the policeman on the beat to an appeal for his help. Called in by a neighbour or a terrified child, he is often the only official person the wife sees. He is her sole source of advice and protection. She is likely to be too confused, too demoralized, to seek help elsewhere.

Before elaborating on the reluctance of the police to interfere in marital disputes it may be necessary to digress a little to look at how the law works and how it influences police opinion. At the time of writing, considerable changes are being made in the laws relating to marriage, and as others are still under discussion it is pointless my explaining in great detail either the law as it stands at this precise moment or what the reformers hope to achieve. The two most relevant areas of concern to us here are the laws relating to injunctions (civil law) and to convictions for bodily assault (criminal law). Briefly, up to now the system has been that when the police have been called in after a marital row, only if the policeman on the spot considers the wife's injuries really serious will he either charge the husband and arrange for a summons to be taken out against him or, more likely, recommend the wife herself to apply for such a summons. Since she rarely knows how to do this, and is in any case usually far too bewildered and browbeaten to undertake such a complicated course, this advice is normally useless. Even if a charge for common assault (the most usual charge) succeeds, the husband will either be let off with a warning or be given a small fine or a few weeks in jail. He will then be free to return to his wife and work out his bottled-up anger on her. It is true that some men are shaken by their first court appearance and their behaviour improves, but for a great number of men it is merely an additional irritant and their wives' suffering is proportionately increased. And, of course, for at least four or five weeks while they wait for the case to come up, the wife has been entirely at her husband's mercy. It is not a course of action a woman is likely to undertake a second time.

Few policemen take the trouble to advise a woman that she may apply to a county court or divorce court for an injunction prohibiting her husband from attacking her. If she does somehow obtain this information she has in the past found that it has been necessary to apply for a divorce or separation from her husband before an injunction can be granted, and this is an action most of these women are reluctant to take. Even if she persists and succeeds in having an injunction granted the wife is still not really safe, for injunctions have to be served personally on the husband, and this in itself can take months. Until the man has personally received the injunction he is as free as he was before to bash up his wife without incurring any special penalty. Even after the injunction has been successfully served the husband can still attack his wife with some impunity as (at the time of writing) only a court bailiff has the power to arrest him - the police have not had the power to do so. Husbands frequently evade local bailiffs simply by moving to another area outside their jurisdiction, occasionally returning to molest or threaten their wives in comparative security.

However, a new Act has recently been passed (thanks to the determination of Jo Richardson whose Bill it was) which came into force on 1 June 1977. Under this new Act a judge may order a copy of the injunction to be served at the local police station, and if the husband breaks the injunction the police will now have the power to arrest him. They will be entitled to hold him for twenty-four hours, during which time they must contact a judge who will be able to deal with the matter as he thinks fit. This is an important advance, and at last gives teeth to the granting of an injunction, but how effective the new system will be depends on the willingness of the police to implement the new Act. We shall see in a few moments what the attitude of the police was to this reform before it became law.

A second important reform is that the Act has done away with the necessity for applying for a separation or divorce at the same time as asking for an injunction, which means that many women who have been put off by this will now feel free to go ahead and apply for an injunction. Jo Richardson also wanted the power to grant injunctions to be given to magistrates' courts - at present this may only be done by the more formal and often physically distant county courts - but it was pointed out to her that the Law Commission intended to recommend many far-reaching changes regarding matrimonial jurisdiction. In October 1976 the Law Commission Report was published. One of its recommendations was that future legislation should enable magistrates to make 'personal protection orders' prohibiting husbands from using violent behaviour against their wives and children, and 'exclusion orders' which would forbid husbands entrance to the matrimonial home (although in fact magistrates already have the power to bind over any parties whose behaviour is likely to promote a breach of the peace). These orders will be easier for wives to obtain and they should be a valuable instrument in protecting women. In the following November the Home Secretary stated that he hoped to implement the Commission's proposals as soon as parliamentary time permitted, and no doubt this reform will also soon become law.

Unfortunately for women in Scotland, these reforms do not apply to them. Their laws differ in many ways: for a common assault prosecution, for example, *two* witnesses are necessary, and as two are almost never available in a marital fight, a Scottish wife rarely has recourse to the courts at all. In addition she cannot have an injunction granted while she is still living with her husband, which means she is forced to leave him if she wants legal protection. With the forthcoming changes in English law the position of the wife in Scotland will appear even more unfortunate than it does at present.

We have looked at the law regarding injunctions and have seen that the police have now been drawn into an area they previously considered beyond their province. The second area concerning them - the decisions as to what kind of assault has been committed - remains unclarified by any reform. I doubt if many ordinary members of the public are aware of the personal power each policeman holds. It is up to the individual policeman on the beat to decide what kind of assault has occurred, whether it is common assault or the more serious aggravated assault, actual bodily harm or grievous bodily harm. Since the breaking of the skin or the blacking of an eye is unequivocally a *serious* assault (see Alex Lyon, Minister of State, Home Office, in his evidence to the Select Committee 11 June 1975 - p. 433 of the Minutes - who states 'A black eye is actual bodily harm') it is a little difficult to understand why the complaints of so many women are regularly brushed aside by the policemen to whom they have appealed for help. With injuries ranging from black eyes to broken ribs, smashed teeth and cracked jaws, time after time wives who have fled to women's aid refuges for shelter have reported that the police have merely told them to 'be a good girl and kiss and make up' as though they were toddlers who had been smacked by a baby brother. Top-ranking police tend to deny at official enquiries that such a thing can happen, but as the Report from the Select Committee on Violence in Marriage testifies, the evidence is quite clear. Obviously it is now essential that precise instructions are issued to every policeman in the force, particularly those at the lower level who are the ones who actually come into personal contact with the victims of this type of violence.

Why are the police so reluctant to intervene? As I have already said, the first reason given is nearly always that the wife withdraws her evidence the morning after the event. Either she will deny the assault ever happened, or she will say it is over and done with and she wants to forget about it. Bedfordshire police, the first to drop the customary low-profile policy towards domestic violence, found that, in spite of active interest and sympathy on their part, out of 288 cases of violence in the home only 77 men were taken to court. This was because in 184 cases the wives or cohabitees decided they did not want the men prosecuted, and out of the remaining 104 cases, 18 victims refused at the last moment to give evidence in court.

For a charge of common assault to be successful the wife must be a witness. If the policeman has proof of physical damage, such as a doctor's report, he can subpoena the wife against her will, but he cannot force her to talk if she chooses not to, in which event he is most unlikely to win his case. The terror of the wife, who may well have been threatened 'with the beating of her life' if she speaks against her husband, may be evident to everyone in court, but a conviction cannot be obtained without firm evidence. The husband will then be freed and the wife left without any protection.

Chief Superintendent Mildred Dow has stated that in some areas, notably in cities, police will sometimes lock up a man while waiting for the case to come to court when they are convinced he has seriously assaulted his wife, but in rural areas he is more often left free. Obviously, with the husband in custody, the wife is more likely to testify. Even so, if the wife is unwilling, most policemen dislike making her testify, even though she may be a compellable witness if there is proof of the assault, on the grounds that they do not wish to be partly responsible for the probable wrecking of a marriage. They also point out that as an adult citizen of a free country her wishes ought to be respected.

Policemen are very aware that arresting someone has a powerful effect on that person, even if he or she is freed a few hours later. The individual policeman is very conscious of the seriousness of arrest, so that he has to consider not only the extent of the wife's injury but also whether or not in his opinion the man ought to be arrested. Michael Chatterton, a sociologist studying the police, found that in less serious cases of injury they would only arrest if they personally felt the offender deserved it, becoming, in effect, quasi-magistrates (in Borland (ed.) (1976). They would talk to both assailant and victim, sum up the characters of each, and consider if the victim had got what he or she deserved, and if the attacker was provoked into his or her action.

Whether or not, therefore, a woman is given protection depends to a considerable extent on whether the particular policeman who happens to be around at the time of the assault is sympathetic or hard, a man with a happy marriage or one with a nagging wife he can hardly bear. Mr Bohan, of the Police Department, Home Office, confirmed this independence of the individual policeman in his evidence to the Select Committee. The chairman had asked him whether the Home Office had any power to ensure that, in cases of serious assault, all police forces would agree to instruct their men to arrest an assailant on the spot rather than to issue a summons which would allow him freedom to 'influence' his wife. Mr Bohan replied, 'It is very much a matter of the constable's discretion under the law with which even chief constables themselves would be very reluctant to interfere except by the most general directions.'

Clearly none of us want police powers to be so wide that any policeman can throw a citizen into jail on the slightest complaint of someone with a grudge. Indeed, this fear of a police state is used by the police themselves as an argument against over-enthusiasm on the part of their men. In the end, the public gets the police force it wants. But we know that the police do not make sufficient use of the criminal law to protect wives when they have suffered assaults of a seriousness that would have led to charges of grievous or actual bodily harm had they been occasioned in any other circumstances. Policemen who argue that there is no need to change the law as it is already adequate are quite right - it *is* already adequate; what needs changing is the police application of the law. We can guess at various reasons why the police attitude is as it is: (a) they still feel basically that a woman is a man's property and his home is his castle; (b) they find the whole thing acutely embarrassing and escape from the situation as soon as possible by assuring everyone concerned, themselves included, that by next morning it will all be over and forgotten; (c) they know that if it comes to the question of needing the woman to testify she will be a reluctant witness and her marital position will almost certainly be worsened instead of improved; or even (d) the policeman concerned is over-stressed, his area is under-manned and he feels the force has more serious things to deal with than a row between husband and wife.

This last argument is a strong one. A recent survey carried out in a city centre division of one of our larger cities showed that as much as 22 per cent of all the weekend emergency calls for police action were concerned with domestic disturbances. The police feel they already have enough to do, and in particular do not want to undertake the enforcing of injunctions. Their attitude is made clear in the following extract from a memorandum submitted by the Metropolitan Police to the Select Committee:

The Civil and the Criminal Law have always been separated for good reasons, and it would be wrong both constitutionally and practically to extend the Criminal Law to enable Police to exercise powers to enforce orders made within the Civil Jurisdiction of the Courts. The Police Force is already over extended with the enforcement of the Criminal Law generally and preserving the Queen's Peace with all that entails. To add the wide sphere of injunctions issued under a Matrimonial Jurisdiction to their diverse responsibilities would place an intolerable strain on manpower resources and be to the detriment of safeguarding other members of the public.

This extension to their responsibilities, as we have seen, has now been made. If the Metropolitan Police feel that the enforcing of injunctions will place them under an intolerable strain we may assume they will be even less ready than at present to take aggressive husbands into custody or to advise wives to obtain injunctions against them. In the same memorandum it was argued:

> There is no need whatsoever for any change in the police role. . . . That some husbands do assault their wives, even quite seriously, and are not punished for it, is not the fault of the police, but is caused by the 'human element reaction' in the attitude of many such wives.

Mr Lyon, Minister of State, Home Office, confirmed that the law was already adequate with regard to police intervention:

> Where it is a matter of common assault without any injury, I think there probably is something in the suggestion, judging by the evidence you have heard and also by the attitude of the police when they saw you, that they do not intervene because they think it is a civil matter and because they do not think there is much danger to the wife. . . . If the atmosphere is changing, as undoubtedly it is . . . and it is felt that this is an area in which the police ought to intervene more regularly, the power exists for the police to intervene if they wish to do so.

He then goes on to suggest that the Committee present a report proposing that the police should intervene more often, ending, 'If [the Committee] did we would bring it to the attention of chief officers.' The Committee have taken him up on his word, and it will be interesting to see what comes of it.

Certainly there is great reluctance at the Home Office and among the police in general to alter the law as it stands. When the Committee argued during this same hearing with the Minister that 'the law shows a degree of complacency with its particular machinery which seems to be in direct conflict with the evidence of the unfortunates who have been battered', and that if the law were adequate there would be no need for the Committee at all as 'there would not be so many battered women facing quite intolerable conditions while we are actually sitting here', the Minister's reply was, 'That is an assumption and I do not necessarily accept it.' A little later a member of the Committee commented, 'Mr Lyon, are you saying there is no solution to this problem?' Mr Lyons: 'I am not sure there is anything this Committee or the Government can do about it. There is a solution; the solution is husbands ought to treat their wives better.' Committee: 'That is not a solution, it is a pious hope.' Mr Lyon: 'It is the only solution, with respect, in personal relations. There is only one real solution, that is that human beings should treat each other better.'

Thankfully, the Committee, in their Report, reject the idea that nothing can be done. They suggest that special instructions be given to all new recruits and regular written guidance issued by the Chief Constables. Where there is evidence of any injury they want the assailant arrested immediately and protection given to the wife. Police intervention, they say, would reduce the problem of violence in this country and 'contribute to the prevention of a number of homicides'. They reject the shortage of manpower as being a sufficient excuse for police tardiness in dealing with marital assaults.

A major problem the Home Office must face in changing police attitudes, however, is their own lack of direct authority. Each Chief Officer of police may decide on his own prosecution policy, and apart from a few special cases the Home Office has no right to intervene in his decisions. All the Home Office may do is to send out circulars suggesting what it would like to see done, but it cannot insist, for each of the various forces guard their independence jealously.

To illustrate briefly what we have been talking about I would like to quote Mrs M. Miller, a member of the Select Committee, who spoke of a constituent of hers. In the previous week her constituent's husband had been brought home from hospital by ambulance. The driver assisted the man to his front door, which was no sooner opened by his wife than the husband struck her to the ground. The driver called for the police who, after a question or two, said, 'It's a domestic matter, there is nothing we can do about it.'

Finally, I can do no better to exemplify the attitude of a great number of policemen than to quote once more from the Metropolitan Police memorandum to the Select Committee. Having presented their evidence, they sum up the essence of what they have been saying in their Conclusion:

27 While it is accepted that a major cause of crime is 'the efficiency or otherwise of the police' it is not accepted that this factor applies in the case of 'battered wives'. The main contributory cause of this syndrome is the aggression factor and the psychological reasons for this are beyond the scope of police to prevent.

28 Similarly, it is submitted that the equal status of women in society today precludes any preferential treatment for them: otherwise the law could fall into disrepute.

29 The role of the police has always been, and must remain, that of complete impartiality when performing their duty of enforcing the law and preserving the Queen's Peace.

Whoever drafted paragraph 28 must have taken a great deal of surreptitious satisfaction from it. The prejudice it reveals is too pathetic to comment on, other than to say that to talk about equality is sheer cruelty in view of the evidence we have been considering. But what if a woman *were* physically equal to her mate, or even heavier and stronger? What if a twelve-stone woman battered in the ribs of an eight-stone man, blacked his eyes, knocked out his teeth and chucked him out of the house in the middle of the night with only his pyjamas on? Would the policeman then be so assiduous in preserving his impartiality along with Her Most Gracious Majesty's Peace, and advise the man to kiss his wife like a good chap and make it up? I very much doubt it.

Refuge

Because there is never a time when they are not on duty it is probable that the police come into contact with more marital violence than any other official body, as once the actual violence is over the matter is closed for most wives until the next bout. Fear, confusion, pride - all combine to prevent a woman from seeking further outside aid. But occasionally other officials are drawn into the web of violence. Most, however quickly fight free again.

If a woman's injury is bad enough she will see her doctor, but she is unlikely to tell him the real cause of it. He may guess, he may know perfectly well from long experience exactly what caused the bruises, the cuts, but it is a rare doctor who probes the woman's reluctance with a determination to help her marital problems. The woman will probably admit to depression, sleeplessness, 'nerves', and the usual treatment is some form of tranquillizer and a bottle of sleeping pills. Of Dr Gayford's sample, most of whom had been battered severely enough to cause them to leave home, 71 per cent had been prescribed antidepressants or tranquillizers, and nearly half had been referred for psychiatric help. Half of these referred women were told they were depressed and were treated with either physical or chemical agents.

Even if the injury is so severe that hospital treatment is necessary the woman is still unlikely to confide in the casualty department staff. If she does admit the true cause emergency staff rarely do more than stitch up her cuts, set her broken bones, and send her home. Babies who had obviously been battered used to be given the same kind of treatment - and in some hospitals still are - but publicity and a growing understanding of the problem is gradually changing this pattern of official negligence. But battered wives are still left to their own devices unless they are prepared to make a fuss.

This state of affairs must be remedied. There ought to be a fool-proof system in every hospital which is automatically followed by any member of the casualty staff, from the youngest nurse to the consultant, who suspects he or she is dealing with a woman who has been battered by the man she is living with. At the very least, contact should be made with local social workers or health visitors who can visit the woman and offer her help. All general practitioners and hospital doctors have a responsibility for the health of their patients which ought not to cease the moment a pill is prescribed or a bandage applied. Packing a woman off to a psychiatrist is not sufficient answer either; the social services department must be informed, since they are unlikely to hear of the case in any other way. Many GPs also have regular contact with local health visitors who are in an excellent position to offer aid; if this kind of co-operation were to be extended all over the country many of our social problems would be well on the way to solution.

Unfortunately, contact with the social services department does not at present necessarily bring a battered wife any relief. Most social workers still seem to be under the sway of their old ethos that the family must be kept together if humanly possible. For this reason many battered children have been left with their parents when it would have been wiser to separate them within a year or two of their birth, and while social workers are now beginning to understand that a bad parent may not, after all, be better for a child's development than a good fostermother, few seem to be prepared to apply the same reasoning to a marriage. Margaret Gregory, a psychologist, has written that marital violence is not mentioned in the literature of social work, and that few social workers have had much guidance or training in how to deal with it. This, together with poor facilities for emergency housing, accounts in her opinion for their failure to provide effective aid to battered wives.

Certainly nearly all such wives who have had contact with social workers report they have been urged to 'try again', usually for the sake of the children, even when they have already suffered many years of increasing brutality. It is this belief in the sanctity of marriage that in the past has blinded so many people to the existence of so much suffering, and it is no coincidence that the rise in the public concern for wife battering has occurred at the same time as the easing of the divorce laws and the demand for real equality of treatment by the women's rights movement. It is amazingly easy to allow ourselves to ignore other people's misery if we feel our viewpoint is morally justified. But few of us now feel that divorce itself is immoral; it is a sad, often tragic act, one no one would willingly undertake, but for most of us purely religious qualms about it are a thing of the past. Yet there still remains a sense that no one may come between man and wife. This feeling, reinforced by their training that the loving presence of two parents is vital for the successful development of a child's psyche, seems to be particularly strong in social workers.

They are in a very difficult position. There is no doubt that children need consistent 'mothering' (though not necessarily by their natural mothers or even by a female), and full development is difficult without regular contact with caring adults of both sexes. Also social workers, more than most of us, learn early on that human relations are nothing like as simple or as easily managed as much writing would have us suppose. They know only too well that the putting on of a wedding ring does not ensure a couple will live happily ever after. When, therefore a wife complains to them about her husband it is a story they have heard in one form or another thousands of times before. They have to harden themselves to a certain extent to the woes they face daily, and if they feel that for the good of the whole family the mother must put up with a certain amount of rough treatment from her husband they will not hesitate to tell her so. After all, unless their imagination betrays them and informs them how agonizing a deliberate assault by a once-trusted partner must actually be, what their eyes show them is merely a fading bruise, a cut, a piece of Elastoplast, and have they themselves not at some time also suffered occasional bruises, cuts, or even worse? In the long run, they tell the wives, all will be well, so stay; stay for the sake of the children, of your husband whom you must have loved once and whom you will soon love again.

But this insistence is beginning to change. The fact that now there is somewhere to send the women to has helped. The National Women's Aid Federation report that the majority of the women who flee to their refuges have been sent by their social workers. Erin Pizzey has a different picture, but then she receives desperate women from all over the country who come to her because Chiswick is the only refuge they have heard about. Many social workers are now realizing that what battered women need above all else is a respite, a time to withdraw and sort out their minds in peace. Many of them eventually leave the refuges and return to their husbands. Whether this will continue to be the pattern when facilities improve is as yet uncertain, but aiding a woman to leave her home for a short time may in fact be the best way to preserve a marriage. The shock of the parting is often enough to make a man realize how much he needs his wife, and while it may not completely cure him, it does at least give the wife more confidence in her own ability to think for herself and to order her life a little more to her own liking.

Erin Pizzey's book, *Scream Quietly or the Neighbours Will Hear* (1974), describes in detail the setting up of the first refuge in Chiswick in 1971; it is a book full of horrifying descriptions by the women themselves of their sufferings at the hands of their husbands and lovers. In the wake of this first refuge there followed many others, and there are now many refuges spread throughout the entire country. The exact number is unknown since not all of them are affiliated to the

National Women's Aid Federation. The NWAF claim there are 73 affiliated refuges in existence, but not all of those listed are still functional, and Erin Pizzey doubts if there are in fact more than about 50 refuges which are currently accepting women. Unfortunately the very success of the women's aid movement has recently inspired the government to declare that further monetary help for projects concerning battered wives is unnecessary. After deliberating on the many recommendations made by the Select Committee on Violence in Marriage, in December 1976 the government published a report which made it clear they consider the combination of public economic restraint together with the enthusiasm of concerned voluntary bodies sufficient excuse for them to take no further action. The Select Committee's urgent recommendation that twenty-four-hour crisis centres should be set up in every large town and enough refuges provided for one family in every 10,000 (in itself a conservative estimate of the number who might need such shelter) has been rejected. The need for crisis centres is accepted, but the government hope that voluntary bodies will organize and staff these.

This report has bitterly disappointed those who have been working so hard for government participation. We all know there is little enough money to spare, but do we use what little there is as efficiently as we might? A growing number of people feel, for instance, that far too much social service time is spent behind desks in large offices instead of actually working alongside clients. Crisis centres dealing directly with people in need could well be one of two or three main focal points around which social work should be organized. Voluntary workers can bring an immediacy, a freshness to such work, but they need the guidance of trained professionals in the fraught situations which must be the daily experience of successful crisis centres, not left to fend for themselves as best they may while the government breathes a sigh of relief at getting one more problem off its chest.

At present battered wives get little help in finding out what escape routes are open to them because they are very loath to take their problems outside the family, feeling that once the social services have been contacted they might never be rid of them. At a crisis centre, on the other hand, it would not even be necessary to reveal one's name and address if one did not want to. Workers at such a centre could give women in need unbiased advice as to the options available to them. These boil down to: temporary shelter in whatever housing or hostels the authorities have made available for local homeless families; moving into a relative or friend's house; putting the children into the care of the local authority while the mother fends for herself; or, lastly, flight to a refuge. The first is very unsatisfactory, particularly as there is nothing to stop a man from entering his wife's accommodation, attacking her or the children and forcing them to return home. These men are unpredictably violent and often smash up furniture, doors, other people's property in their rage, so that a battered wife will probably find herself shunned by others sharing the housing. Relatives and friends, however fond, may equally be terrorized by a husband determined to get his way, and after a violent incident or two the wife is likely to find herself with no alternative but to give in and return to her own home. She can always ask the local authority to look after her children for her while she goes off on her own, but few women are prepared to do this, feeling separation from the children would be even worse than continuing to live with their husbands.

Until the opening of refuges for battered wives, there was no real alternative to these measures. Sometimes a woman in desperation would run away, with or without her children, and helplessly roam the streets, but in the end there would be nowhere for her to go except back home. Now, thanks to the devoted work of many sympathizers, any needy woman in Britain can find her way to one refuge or another where she will find, at the very least, a roof over her head and people like herself who know from experience what it is to be battered.

An unknown number of wives leave their husbands soon after marriage when the men's violence becomes evident. We hear little of these women since they mostly resume their single life without needing any help from outsiders. But for women with children the decision to leave home is a desperate one. It is not usually taken until the children are visibly seen to suffer, either directly from violence meted out by the father or from the distressing emotional background, or even from an increasing irritability sometimes leading to over-severe

81

punishment on the part of the mother. It means leaving behind a familiar home, well-loved furniture and personal effects which may have been bought with the woman's own earnings, removing the children from their schools, parting from friends and neighbours, and abandoning a marriage in which the wife had once placed all her hopes.

Money problems, already a recurrent worry in families where drinking and gambling frequently co-exist with violence, are worsened when a woman leaves home. If she and her family stay with friends or relatives she will be unable to pay for their food; if she needs to make long journeys she will not be able to afford expensive fares for the children and herself without borrowing. If she applies for Social Security she will have to convince the officials of the legitimacy of her claim, while at the same time persuading them not to reveal her new address to her husband. Even then, unless she agrees to start divorce or separation proceedings she may lose her claim.

For the refuges themselves money is also a perennial problem. The DHSS does give a grant to the National Women's Aid Federation, but it does not go very far. Many refuges are helped by their local authorities, but others have to rely on fund-raising events and charity. The Chiswick refuge is not a member of the NWAF, and the grant which the DHSS made to Chiswick in 1974 is now being phased out on the grounds that DHSS grants are given on a national rather than a local basis, and that since there is now a nation-wide organization concerned with battered wives (the NWAF) the Chiswick refuge no longer qualifies for a grant. Erin Pizzey wrote in her book that as women come to the Chiswick refuge from all over the country it is unfair that the borough of Hounslow should have to bear the whole country's burden. Hounslow have since solved this problem by also withdrawing their support; since October 1975 Chiswick refuge has no longer received an urban aid grant, nor any other financial aid from Hounslow.

So much - from the very foundation of a refuge itself to the provision of third-stage housing - depends on the quality of the relationship developed between a group organizing a refuge and the local authorities and social service departments. In some cases social workers have themselves been original members of a group setting up a refuge, but their training usually makes them dislike the idea of clients 'going it alone', and they mostly feel there ought to be a resident warden in charge of the refuge. Some have also objected to the strongly feminist beliefs of a few of the members, male social service directors especially being alienated by such an approach. Such differences of opinion have led to many social workers and other like-minded persons disassociating themselves from the NWAF groups. But a number of groups have succeeded in forming a good working relationship with their local authorities with the result that urban grants have been secured for them, enabling the refuge to employ play leaders and occasionally full-time staff (*not* called 'wardens'). A friendly local authority can frequently make available temporary accommodation or turn over to the group houses unsuitable for other uses instead of leaving them to rot, as too many authorities still do. Occasionally financial help comes from other sources. Bovis, for example, paid for the large house in Chiswick High Road which has become internationally known simply as 'Chiswick'. Other large companies have given money to other refuges, many of whom would otherwise have been unable to start up at all.

But, as the Report from the Select Committee on Violence in Marriage pointed out, local authorities have a duty (under s.21 (1) (b) of the National Assistance Act 1948, confirmed by the Secretary of State in February 1974) to provide temporary accommodation for people in urgent and unforeseeable need. It is clear that this duty is not being carried out by many local authorities and the Report suggests that all local authorities should be made aware of their duty. It also adds that the temporary bed and breakfast accommodation often given to women and their children is both expensive and unsuitable, and the money would be far better spent in setting up specialized refuges.

A further aid to battered wives once they have settled into a refuge is that the helpers there, who have been quick to learn their way through endless red tape and obscure rulebooks, can usually ensure they receive Supplementary Benefit, rent allowances and clothing grants. But for the helpers to be able effectively to assist the women they must first find a suitable house to set up as a refuge, and it is at this primary level that many good intentions are scuppered by the unwillingness or downright obstruction of local authorities.

Hounslow's main reason for withdrawing financial aid from Chiswick is that they consider its 'open-door' policy wrong on several counts, namely (a) the fire risk involved when as many as 100 people or more are sleeping in a house licensed for 36, (b) the health dangers (insufficient baths, lavatories, etc. for over 100 people) and (c) the extra burden placed on Hounslow's schools, social services, housing departments, etc. who have to cope with refugees from all over Britain. Erin Pizzey admits the validity of these arguments, but argues back that since women are still flooding to Chiswick there is obviously a continuing need for an open refuge and that she personally is totally incapable of turning any battered wife away. She has written in explanation of her own motivation that she herself had a violent father:

> the most tragic thing that happened to me as a child was being unable to defend my own mother . . . it is impossible to forgive yourself for something like that. Now it does not matter to me what the problems are or what reasons people give me for closing the door of the refuge. The open door is for my mother; that is why it will never close.

Civil servants must shake their heads over such an emotional statement and remark that that is no way in which to run a refuge. Nor is it only civil servants and local authorities who differ from Erin Pizzey; the NWAF itself is against many of her policies. It is certainly ironic that the woman responsible for the very existence of the present concern for battered wives and who was one of the pioneers of women's aid should not belong to the government-aided Women's Aid Federation.

The reasons for the split are both personal and political. I think it is doubtful if these can ever be reconciled. Erin Pizzey is a large, vital, emotional woman with great warmth, love and energy. I myself have rarely seen her other than in the role of archetypal mother hen, sitting cross-legged in her ballooning kaftan on a giant cushion on the floor, imperturbably giving out advice, listening, organizing, chiding, laughing, the calm

centre of a roomful of bustling women and men. But she can,
if she wants, bawl as loudly as any of the inhabitants, and they
know and respect this. She does not demand that you succumb
to her personality - indeed, she is perpetually trying to build up
independence of action in her mothers - but there is no doubt
that she is queen bee and everything centres around her. Those
who work with her, both men and women, are tough,
energetic people with minds of their own, but they seem happy
enough to work within Erin's overwhelming aura. She is a
natural leader, and she has achieved a great deal in an
incredibly short time, thanks mainly to the forces of her
personality. But inevitably she has infuriated many en route. I
can well understand how the mere sight of her sitting there
guru-like in the centre of a mob of women must be almost a
physical affront to certain types of people. She breaks every
rule: for example, she quite properly deducted income tax and
national insurance from her staff's salaries, but then she went
and spent the money on food and other necessities for the
refuge and now cannot pay the Inland Revenue its dues. She is
no modest retiring saint: she annoyed many by making a
publicity trip on the Continent with a vanload of women
although the coffers were virtually empty. She has only one
criterion, and that is that if a woman is being battered and
needs help she should be given it, no matter at what cost or
inconvenience to herself or to anyone else.

The National Women's Aid Federation is quite a different
kind of set-up. Few would deny that at the top it is politically
inspired. One of the organizers has said that a refuge can be a
place of 'extremely exciting politicization' of women. They
appear to believe that curing social inequalities will
automatically cure violence. They are of course particularly
concerned with the inequalities between men and women.

I am always depressed by the violence with which the more
militant feminists regard men. One sometimes has the feeling
that for some of these if every man were mysteriously to die
overnight the result would be purely beneficent. To replace
male domination by female domination is obviously as
pointless and as dangerous as replacing one dictator by
another, but it is difficult if not impossible to preach common
sense to revolutionaries. Anger, guilt, fear, hatred: these

emotions are often the unacknowledged spur that goad on the leaders of new movements, and the plight of battered women stirs strong emotions of one kind or another in most people who have come face to face with it. I do not therefore mean it in any derogatory sense when I say that it has seemed to me that for some of the women in the NWAF the desire to free women from the bondage of men is stronger than the simple desire to help women who are suffering, and that this difference is the real basis of the split between Erin Pizzey and the NWAF.

The NWAF is altogether a much tidier set-up than the refuge at Chiswick, more likely to be approved by officialdom. They have rules and they keep to them. They are strictly democratic, disliking with revolutionary ardour the concept of a single charismatic leader. As with all women's movement groups they feel women have been led long enough, and that in order for women to be fully liberated they must by 'consciousness-raising' learn to work as a cohesive whole, while remaining independent individually, without the permanent leadership of any one person. At meetings, for instance, chairwomen are usually elected, but for one session only, principally to avoid any risk of the majority sinking back slave-like into apathy while someone else organizes them.

When I interviewed members of the NWAF (I may not say 'leaders') at their administrative head office in Camden I found this insistence on equality made progress difficult. At first there were only a couple of women present in the office and they were unwilling to speak to me at all until two more had turned up to provide a 'representative' group. Indeed, for some time it was I who was being grilled, interrogated quite openly as to my attitudes on various subjects, and it was quite clear that anyone with a strongly differing viewpoint would receive little sympathy from them. I was not allowed to use my tape recorder (this was the only time this has ever happened to me, no matter whom I had been interviewing) nor was I even allowed to make notes of what they were saying other than to write down one or two basic facts agreed by all the members present. They gave me one pamphlet and sold me another, assuring me that all the *facts* I wanted to know were inside these booklets (as they were). They explained that the reason for their refusal was that the NWAF was a collective, and no single individual could represent the views of the whole. What was in the printed pamphlets had been subjected to committee and approved, and was therefore the true voice of the Federation.

I came away chilled, though impressed by the efficiency of their organization. The contrast between the earnest, frosty little group I had just met, and the animal warmth of the packed Chiswick living room could hardly have been greater. How far this atmosphere is reflected in the various NWAF refuges, however, depends on local conditions, for the refuges are run by all kinds of different people. Attitudes to men vary greatly, for instance, depending to a large extent on how any particular group originated. The official NWAF attitude is not anti-male: their report, *Battered Women Need Refuges* (1976), states that although men are not allowed to live in the refuge they can play a useful part as play leaders and helping with house repairs, etc., thereby helping resident women and children to regain confidence in males, a similar attitude to that at Chiswick.

The NWAF itself came into existence as late as 1975 as the result of a Women's Aid National Conference held in 1974 in a church hall much used by Chiswick. It was at this point that political differences between Erin Pizzey (who typically had taken along a large group of women from her refuge) and the other delegates became clear. Erin's emphasis on the desirability of treating the whole family, *husbands included*, was contrary to the opinion of most of the other delegates (who saw the organization as an expression of the women's movement). The Chiswick battered wives made their feelings about the other delegates and their opinions of men quite clear - with little concern for decorum apparently - and the result was that the whole Chiswick group walked out, cutting itself off permanently from what was to become the following year the National Women's Aid Federation.

By now many women throughout the country had already become conscious for the first time of the problems of wife battering and they had set about organizing refuges themselves. Some women's action and women's liberation groups turned themselves into women's aid groups; other groups of women already meeting regularly for one purpose or another found out how to set up a refuge, as did church groups, social workers, magistrates and a few individuals who had been impressed by Chiswick's example. For many of these women politics played no part in their life; others were staunch members of one party or another. Many were happily married and their interest was purely altruistic. Their coming together in a Federation has helped them to organize themselves more efficiently, but although the way each invididual group is run depends on many factors, such as the amount of aid they receive from their local authorities and the personalities of the originators of the group, there are certain rules which most follow. They do not, for example, approve of resident wardens. This is because they feel women must learn to look after themselves and not go from one situation of dependence straight into another.

Self-help is perhaps the most important tenet of the Federation. They consider that battered women in particular lack self-confidence and that taking responsibility for the day-to-day running of the refuge helps restore their confidence. In most refuges voluntary women's aid helpers call in every day to give help and advice, but it is the women themselves who run the houses. On the face of it this sounds a sensible decision, but in practice it is not as simple as that. The first time I visited Chiswick they were busy settling in a woman who had arrived during the night from Ireland with ten children. When I mentioned the principle of self-help to Erin Pizzey she pointed to the mother and said, 'Look at her! What she needs is a month's solid sleep while someone else bathes, feeds and gets those kids off to school for her. She's had to look after herself and those kids all her married life - what she needs now is a bit of kindness and love, not a lesson in independence. That comes later, when she's recovered a bit.'

Interestingly enough, there seemed less genuine equality between helpers and battered wives at a NWAF refuge I visited than there is at Chiswick. By 'equality' I mean the total lack of a sense of 'us' and 'them'. There was equality between the helpers all right, but because they were so keen to build up the women's self-confidence and independence their contact with them was much more remote than at Chiswick, where it was often difficult to know who was helper and who was client. At the NWAF refuge which I visited helpers were mostly in their office, to which the mothers only came when they wanted something. Each woman cooked her own food, had her own cupboards. I saw none of the women talking to each other as they worked or cooked; isolated, each got on with her own life, looking as sad and lonely as though they were still shut up in their own private house or flat. Contact with the helpers was mainly for advice in claiming Social Security, coping with pursuing husbands and so on. A weekly group meeting was held, but again it was mainly to sort out problems and complaints. There was no attempt at group therapy, either formal or informal. The women helpers coming to the refuge were undoubtedly kind and sympathetic, giving up much of their time to this voluntary project, but they knew surprisingly little about the women living in their refuge other than external facts.

At Chiswick everyone knows everyone else's most intimate details and group therapy is one long continuous process, sometimes not even stopping in the middle of the night when bad dreams or an occasional suicide attempt arouse neighbouring sleepers. Some may shudder at such intimacy, but Erin's firm belief is that for years these women have been isolated from others by their shame and that now their greatest need is to talk, to listen, to laugh and to be supported by the presence of others with the same traumatic background. When I left Chiswick the first time I had the feeling I had been to a party, my main impression being one of smiles and laughter mixed with intense seriousness. It has been an extraordinarily invigorating experience, a feeling repeated each time I have been there since. Without this continuous stimulus of personal exchange the women become depressed and are liable, out of boredom, to return prematurely to their husbands. In addition, at Chiswick there is a constant flow of professional visitors both from Britain and from abroad - social workers, doctors, lawyers, journalists, TV and film camera units - whose presence keeps up everyone's adrenalin level so that consciousness is heightened and a sense of liveliness, even crisis, is maintained. As the women gradually become accustomed to living apart from their husbands and their personal desperation decreases they begin to help others, until their self-confidence has increased to the point where they are ready to leave the hectic atmosphere of Chiswick and live more quietly in second-stage housing.

Psychiatrists might be appalled at the crude amateur analysis going on all the time, but it seems to work well enough. Criticism usually evokes a smile of acceptance, and if occasionally anger or tears result, hugs and warm pattings follow. This temporary reversion to childhood, with kindness following criticism after a 'naughty' act, seems to suit most of the women there - very few leave. Those who do so are nearly always women who have come to Chiswick after leaving their husbands for the first time.

At the time of writing there are 94 women's aid groups affiliated to the NWAF with 73 refuges between them, although, as mentioned earlier, it is uncertain that all 73 are fully functional. We may assume that some of these are more like Chiswick in atmosphere than the refuge I visited. But most refuges have only a few women in them, partly because of limited accommodation, and partly because of their closed-door policy. Once the official quota for any particular house is filled, a woman in need who arrives unexpectedly will probably be sheltered overnight, but the next day she will be moved on to another refuge with more room or to temporary local authority accommodation. At Chiswick no one is turned away and families are only moved on when they are ready to move. Yet in spite of the numbers, the house is kept scrupulously clean. The neat rows of bunks covered with floral duvets, though packed close together, remind one of a school dormitory, and many a sailor or serving soldier would regard the accommodation as plush. Some nights, it is true, there are so many residents mothers have to take children into their bunks, the kids sleep two to a bed, and spare mattresses fill gangways, but there are worse things in life than that.

Living closely with other women who have severe problems including disturbed children can never be easy; privacy is impossible most of the time. Which type of refuge will be most appropriate for any individual depends on many factors. In practice, however, I think that after the first shock of the immersion, most women would find the warmth of the

Chiswick method preferable. With only a small group of four or five women one would still feel the need to preserve social pretences to a certain extent, keeping a stiff upper lip and so on, whereas a few weeks of relaxed floating in a pool full of potential lifesavers, even if they do at times splash and shout when one would rather be quiet, might in the long run be more therapeutic.

This period of relaxation is only possible if the mother is temporarily freed from the task of looking after her children. Whenever possible refuges arrange playgroups for the younger children or try to get them into a nearby nursery school. The over-fives can be placed fairly easily into local primary schools if it appears the mother will be staying in the area for any length of time, although it can take months to find a secondary school which will accept older children. But in most refuges babies and the younger toddlers have to be looked after by their own mothers, no matter how weary they are. Obviously it is far better if other women can chip in and care for the youngsters until the newly-arrived mother has recovered her strength.

It must be borne in mind that these are no ordinary children. It is almost impossible for a child whose mother has been badly battered by her husband to be mentally unscarred. Many have seen their mothers repeatedly knocked to the ground, kicked, beaten and subjected to verbal abuse and obscenities. Perhaps they have tried to protect their mothers, or perhaps they hid themselves in terror. Small boys no older than three or four may show violence to other children or even adults, copying their father's manner. Adolescent boys, bewildered by the change in their life which has thrust them unprepared into an almost totally female community, can be frighteningly violent outside as well as inside the refuge, and are often picked up by the police for assault or other criminal activities. The girls tend to be sullen and unco-operative, many of them experiencing sex at a very early age as they seek the affection they never knew at home. Many of the kids wet their beds and soil their clothes. They have nightmares during the night and tantrums during the day. Toys get broken, doors battered in, windows smashed and walls kicked until the plaster falls off.

The emotional needs of these children are immense. They need patience and loving to a degree beyond the capabilities of ordinary playgroups or schools, for their suffering is not merely caused by having seen their mothers being hit or having been hit themselves. Sometimes their fathers love them deeply but alternate warm affection with outright bullying. Their mothers may be confused and distressed to the point where they are incapable of affection of any kind, ignoring their children's physical needs and leaving them to fend for themselves, or they may alternate over-possessive love with coldness or even downright brutality. As a result the children's feelings swing between love and hate, hope and despair. Some days they will admire a parent and emulate him or her, other days they reject and despise them. If they are boys the assault upon their emotions tends to force them to one extreme or the other; they grow up to be either too subdued or over-violent. The girls may have an impaired capacity for mothering, and their own babies, too often conceived at fifteen or sixteen years of age or even earlier, may be neglected little mites, white-faced and underweight. No one who has seen children in a refuge and given half a thought to their past and their probable future can fail to have been moved by them.

I have said before that this pattern must be broken, but I cannot repeat it too often: these children must be rehabilitated and watched over if we are to prevent the growth of yet another generation of violent marriages and battered children. We have seen how many battered wives find it difficult to live without the sense of peril, of excitement to which they have become accustomed. For some this has been their way of life from the day of their birth, and they have never known any other existence. It is no wonder they chose men with backgrounds like their own, even though they had sworn all their childhoods to find a man as different from their father as any man could be. We choose our spouses for reasons deeper than we are aware of, and once we have chosen we are stuck with our choice unless we are capable of making the great effort of backing out. The children standing silent at their mothers' side when they first arrive at a refuge soon reveal by their behaviour what damage has been done to them. Unless they are very lucky, within a few short years they in their turn will be enduring the same agony their parents have suffered, and are probably suffering still.

Second-stage accommodation becomes necessary once women have recovered from the first trauma of leaving their husbands. Their main need now is peace and time to discover their true feelings towards their men, to evaluate the chances of a successful reunion, and to decide whether or not they could make a more successful life for themselves and their children on their own. This is the stage at which they must once more fend for themselves and resume the responsibilities of day-to-day living.

Dr Gayford (most of whose sample, we may remember, were women living in the Chiswick refuge) found that four-fifths of the women in his sample had already left and returned to their husbands before finally coming to Chiswick, over a third of them having done so on more than four occasions. Half had usually gone to stay with relatives, most of the others went to friends or found rooms in hostels or hotels, 11 per cent had gone to hospital and been given in-patient treatment, while a further 9 per cent had just drifted about with no roof over their heads.

In over half of Gayford's sample the children had become involved in the violence, and many women gave this as the reason for their leaving home. But in spite of this danger, most had returned to their husbands at least once before the final flight to Chiswick. Seventeen per cent explained they had succumbed to their husbands' threats and violence, while a further 27 per cent had given in to their husbands' pleas and promises of reform. Fourteen per cent had gone back because they had nowhere else to go, and 13 per cent returned because their children were still with their fathers. Out of all those who had returned, only 8 per cent had gone back because they felt sorry for their husbands or because love prompted them.

Once the women had arrived at Chiswick, however, they mostly stayed. This pattern still remains unchanged. Currently it is reckoned that of the women coming to Chiswick who have left their husbands for the first time ever, roughly 60 per cent return to the marital home, but two-thirds of these arrive back at Chiswick within a short time. But of those who have left their husbands before, about 80 per cent stay at Chiswick until they are ready to move on to second-stage housing. It should be borne in mind that many women have to travel a considerable distance to come to Chiswick, and no doubt most of these are very conscious they are making a final desperate bid to change their lives. Others probably stay because the knowledge that second-stage accommodation is available encourages them to break out of the habit of living from day to day, enabling them to envisage for the first time a hopeful future. But perhaps the main reason that most of the women no longer feel the need to return to entirely unsuitable violent husbands is that at Chiswick refuge they find the atmosphere every bit as dramatic as the one they have left behind, but with the difference that the excitement ends not in the horror of assault, but in supportive friendship.

An acknowledged problem that has to be faced during rehabilitation is that wives who have finally separated from their husbands tend to remarry a similar kind of man. Obviously the need for excitement is partly the reason in many cases, but it is also unfortunately true that there are not many stable men available who are prepared to marry a divorced woman with little or no money of her own and with two or three disturbed children to take care of. It is only men who themselves have been left and who are desperately looking for a new partner who are likely to take such a woman on, with inevitable results. Many women continue to repeat this pattern of taking up with a man, having a child or two by him, leaving him because of his violence, setting up with a new partner who eventually proves every bit as violent, perhaps having yet another child, then once more moving on. Janet's story in Chapter 1 is typical of this pattern, although it is hoped in this case that Janet and Bob will be helped to settle into a new style of life. Very often press stories about babies who have been severely battered or killed by their mothers' cohabitees show a similar background, the battered child usually being the offspring of a previous partner.

It is easy enough to dismiss women such as these and say they obviously like being battered, but this is to ignore the fact that most of them are young - some are still only sixteen or seventeen although they are already mothers - and they still have lively sexual desires like anyone else. They want affection and they want sex, and they will take up very quickly with a man who appears to offer them both. Because of this danger it is essential they are given support and understanding for quite a time while they sort themselves out. During this period they need sexual freedom to make and break relationships without going to the extreme of actually setting up house with their new partners. They have to discover for themselves where they are going wrong, and learn to distinguish between one type of man and another. While this is happening support from friends who are perhaps also undergoing the same type of experimentation is invaluable, but they also need tactful supervision to ensure they are taking contraceptive precautions. A pregnancy at this stage can be disastrous, encouraging the woman to choose once again a man who is quite wrong for her.

Applied intelligence and will-power has little to do with this gradual change in a woman's focus; the damage is very deep-rooted, and the settling into an entirely new pattern of relationships can only be achieved over a long period of time. Battered women may tell themselves that all they want is a quiet loving man who will protect them, but, unless they have an opportunity to learn to understand themselves and to slowly build up self-respect and confidence in themselves, this is not the kind of man they will in fact be attracted to. It also has to be accepted that for some women the unconscious motives which direct them to choose dangerous men are too powerful to be overcome without professional help; unfortunately, given the present scarcity of effective psychiatric help, for these women the prognosis is poor.

Second-stage housing, then, is clearly essential if violent marriages are to be reduced in number. There are some local authorities who understand this and who make available annual allocations of council housing or of short-term property destined for eventual destruction. Other authorities insist there is no difference between the plight of a battered woman who has left her home and ordinary homelessness. Indeed, many housing officials insist that as a woman's departure from her marital home is voluntary she is not really homeless at all, since she can return at any time to her husband, an option not open to others on their already over-filled housing lists.

But once a woman with children has obtained a separation order or a divorce the local authorities will usually agree to transfer a council tenancy which has been in the husband's name to the woman. In the case of privately-rented accommodation the same transfer can be arranged if it is a protected or statutory tenancy. Frequently, though, the wife is made responsible for forcing her husband to move out, which she clearly is incapable of doing. Even if the law does this for her she may well find her furniture has been sold or wrecked and the accommodation badly damaged.

Without a legal separation few councils will agree to change the tenancy, even if the woman has several children and they are all homeless because of the husband's behaviour. Gayford found that 86 per cent of the husbands of the women he interviewed were still living in the marital home. Surely it is much more sensible when a marriage has broken up because of the husband's violence for the husband to be allocated single man's accommodation and for the woman to be allowed to return with her children to her own home?

But even this is not always the solution. Naturally enough the man will object to being turned out of his home, and he is likely to turn up at any hour of the day or night to threaten or terrorize his wife and the children. Sometimes he wants the marriage to start up again, at other times he simply wants vengeance. Many women know that the only way they can sleep in peace is to remove themselves far from the district in which they were previously living and set up home elsewhere. Where local authority tenancies are held the obvious move is for tenancy rights to be transferred to whatever area the woman has moved to, but although many people, including the NWAF and the Select Committee on Violence in Marriage, have pressed for automatic co-operation of this kind between all local authorities, such co-operation still does not exist. Since it is rarely a question of a neat swap being arranged between two authorities a national pool of housing will have to be formed, and if some areas should receive an unfair number of requests for tenancies, special provisions will have to be made to assist them.

Until all local authorities are prepared to work together in this way, the burden must continue to fall unfairly on the few authorities who will accept battered wives onto their housing lists. The fear of this responsibility is of course one of the main reasons why many authorities will not assist in the setting-up of refuges in their area, as if a woman has become resident it is more difficult for them to refuse her their help.

Once a battered wife has successfully recovered from her experiences and is capable of standing on her own feet again she wants to settle down into third-stage or permanent housing. If she has not remarried then the best solution might be for her to live with one or more women in the same position as herself, but this is usually very difficult to arrange. It is almost impossible to obtain a local authority tenancy or a mortgage in the names of two unattached women. Many of the council flats intended for a married couple and their family would be ideal for two mothers and children to settle into. Together they could avoid some of the stresses inherent in single-parent families, and would be able to give each other adult friendship and support. In many cases one of the mothers would be able to go out to work while the other kept house, thus relieving the local authorities of a financial burden, but it is very difficult to make officialdom see the sense of this kind of arrangement. Certainly many women would be very happy in this kind of accommodation, or in council houses where several women could live with their children, one or more of them working during the day outside the home.

Women living alone who have been battered feel continuous fear: each time the doorbell rings they suspect their husband or ex-husband has found them, and this, together with the loneliness any single mother of young children must face, often drives them into yet another unsuitable marriage. Mortgage companies are notoriously unwilling to allow women to take out mortgages to buy houses: they are even more so under circumstances such as these. But there is no reason why council mortgages should not be granted - after all, if a woman cannot work she has to be supported by the local council. How much more sensible if she is aided to support herself.

For obvious reasons it is women rather than men who receive the bulk of attention whenever marital violence is discussed.

97

We saw earlier that a few men also are attacked by their spouses, and a great number undoubtedly suffer emotional battering. Very little work has been done specifically on the male half of violent marriages, but perhaps the most important advance of all would be to find out how to deal with and if possible cure men who are potential or actual wife batterers.

We have seen how badly most of them seem to need a woman around. If their wives leave them they follow them no matter where they go, hammering on doors in the middle of the night, breaking in at windows, abducting children from schools as hostages - there is nothing they won't do to get their wives back. They weep and promise reform, and their tears are genuine. But their promises are rarely kept because they are incapable of keeping them. If their wives finally succeed in escaping from them they find another woman and eventually treat her the same way. Yet few of the wives I have spoken to seemed to feel really vindictive about their husbands - so often they protested how admirable their husbands were in all ways but one, that if it hadn't been for drink, or gambling. . . . Dr Gayford asked his sample of 100 women just this question and found a similar response. Only ten wanted their husbands to suffer or die. A third merely wanted them out of their lives so that they could build a new future, while a further third felt their men were disturbed and needed help. Ten considered them so violent that it was imperative they received long-term custodial care.

These were the reactions of women in a refuge like Chiswick, where they are encouraged to think about causes and their own natures rather than to throw all the blame onto the male sex. Seeing what is happening to the male children in the refuge also helps this growing understanding. The reader might remember the mother mentioned earlier whose letter to me described how her own son was already showing signs of her husband's temper and how it deeply distressed her. At Chiswick this problem of violent adolescent boys became so pressing it was finally decided to set up a special Boys' House. What is happening there deserves a study to itself, but briefly, Erin Pizzey took over a tattered old house due for demolition close by the M4. The boys, whose self-image had not been improved by having to seek shelter with their mothers in a refuge full of women and kids, appreciated having a house to themselves. The agreement was that they would pay rent (they were all receiving Social Security, rent allowances, etc.) to Erin and her colleagues, who would save it to spend on the house as they thought necessary. The boys were given equipment and some help to make the house habitable, and were then left to get on with it, although a close eye was kept on them. It worked reasonably well at first, but gradually enthusiasm died. The day came when the boys refused to pay their rent; bit by bit the house was broken up and the furniture smashed and burnt until there was not an undamaged bed, chair or carpet left.

Erin and her colleagues decided the boys needed to learn a lesson. They sat tight, refusing to give any more help, saying firmly that the boys had had their chance; now they must either get down to work to repair the damage and save up their allowances to replace the smashed furniture or put up with the discomfort they had brought upon themselves. Winter was approaching and biting winds began to blow through the broken windows. Gradually the boys' stubbornness broke down. First one boy repaired his room, then others began to follow. Now they are paying their rent again and it looks as though Erin's firmness has paid off.

One important result of the experiment has been that the boys have been taking out their internal angers on the house itself rather than on outsiders, as some of them were doing before. They all have too much spare time, unfortunately, as none of them work at regular jobs. With Social Security money in their pockets they drink, play cards, bet, take out girls or just laze around. Their records are too bad for most people to even consider employing them, and they are not yet ready to accept responsibility, but one or two boys have begun to earn extra money by working in the main refuge or helping redecorate some of the second-stage housing, and it is hoped that gradually they will all settle down as their outlook begins to mature.

They are fortunate in that they all know whenever they want friendship and understanding Erin and her colleagues are always ready to give it. Some have preferred to stay on in the

Boys' House after their mothers have left the Chiswick refuge, enjoying the support of living with other lads of their own kind. No one knows how they will turn out eventually: it is too early yet for any permanent results to be estimated. How they would have turned out if they had been left without being helped is only too obvious: their behaviour, their police records all pointed to a definite path, a path leading straight back to the kind of life they came from, only this time it would have been they who were perpetrating the violence.

When one knows the background of these boys one may be almost too ready to discover signs of violence in them - a morose silence that otherwise would have been seen simply as a normal adolescent mood is interpreted as brooding male-volence. Violent men may betray no outward signs of their disturbance at all to those who are not specifically looking for them. There are numerous battered wives married to highly respected doctors, lawyers, teachers, stockbrokers and other professional men, whose behaviour to others is impeccable. Mutual friends will often refuse to believe the wife if she should break down and describe her married life, assuming she is ill and suffering from hallucinations, or, at the least, grossly exaggerating.

At a refuge I was visiting I saw a pathetic little incident which left me feeling sorrier for the husband, whom I had seen, than for the wife, whom I had not. It appeared that the husband had agreed to bring his baby to the refuge for his wife to collect, as when she ran away from him she had left her children behind. The helper at the refuge had phoned the mother, who was then staying elsewhere, advising her not to come to the refuge herself as her husband would probably be hanging about hoping to contact her. Eventually the husband arrived - a meek little Indian who appeared far too timid to swat a fly, let alone beat a wife - empty-handed. 'You've cheated!' said the helper angrily, 'You only made this appointment in order to see your wife, you never meant to bring the baby at all!" The young man, obviously completely out of his element in this extraordinary country where strange women could speak to men like that, looked confused and stuttered that he could not bring the baby as it was ill. He turned for confirmation of this to another Indian who had come with him. But their combined protests were ignored and the door was firmly slammed in their faces as though they were a pair of itinerant beggars. Looking very dejected they walked slowly away down the refuge steps.

A couple of hours later, just after I had left the house and was getting into my car, I saw the man return. He was holding a small boy of three or four years by the hand, and was accompanied this time by three Indians. Not knowing what they intended to do, I waited in case there was violence and help was needed. Once again the same two men mounted the refuge steps, together with the child. The other two men waited out of sight behind a hedge. I could not hear the conversation properly, but I gathered that the boy had been brought along to confirm the illness of his baby sister. The helper, half hidden behind the chained door, retorted loudly that it was all an excuse, the man had never had the slightest intention of parting with his baby, and all he had ever meant to do was to get hold of his wife and force her to go back with him. Again I could not hear properly what the husband was saying, but obviously he was pleading with her. In mid-sentence the door was slammed once more in his face. He waited a while not knowing what to do next, still holding the little boy by the hand, then he came slowly back down the steps. For a minute or two he talked with his friends, then they all got into a large car and drove off, the child sitting silent looking out of the window.

No matter what he had done to his wife, what possible help was it to anyone for him to be treated like that? If he failed to get her back, would such treatment help improve his behaviour to the next woman he took up with? What effect would the witnessing of his loss of face have on the relationship between him and his little boy? On the child himself?

At Chiswick, husbands are talked to, reasoned with whenever possible. Erin Pizzey reports how she has often sat sharing a packet of cigarettes *outside* the chained door of the refuge while men wept and pleaded with her to let them in. She could not allow that, but at least she listened and treated them like human beings. A further advantage of this kindness is that a little sympathy can help a man to control his anguish, unlike one husband who drove his car straight into the front wall of a refuge where his wife was living, half demolishing it.

It soon became obvious to Erin Pizzey that the husbands themselves needed help as much as their wives did. Eventually, in the summer of 1976, she was able to persuade the GLC to lease her a house in Islington, not far from the rehabilitated elegance of Canonbury Square. It was no rich man's mansion but a small dilapidated terrace house with neighbours none too happy when they heard about the new project. It was not easy to find the right person to run the hostel. There was no money; everybody had to doss down on the bare floor on second-hand mattresses, but gradually the place was being repaired and redecorated. None of the men there cared much about appearances anyway. I use the past tense because a few weeks ago the Men's House was forced to close owing to lack of funds. Erin Pizzey hopes to open it again as soon as possible, but her present financial position is so insecure that unless some wealthy benefactor comes along it may be many months, even years, before that can happen.

The basic aim was to provide a community where battering men could live while they attempted to change their life-styles. Help in sorting out Social Security claims and other such problems was given, but, as at Chiswick, the main source of therapy was the general talk and discussion between the men themselves and with the helpers. Twice a week evening group therapy sessions were held to which men who were living elsewhere were invited. Women were encouraged to attend these sessions - not necessarily battered wives, but women with problems of their own who were prepared to discuss themselves and to listen to others in open give and take.

When I first went to the Men's House a tall, bulky ex-soldier called Henry was living there. Henry, whose jealousy I have already discussed in Chapter 2, had been a very peaceable chap, not at all given to violence until the day his best friend was blown up beside him in Ireland. His friend, a corporal, had been ordered to investigate a house which it was suspected had been mined. Henry blamed his friend's death on the sergeant, who, he felt, was more experienced and should have gone in himself. As the explosion died away Henry went berserk, showering bullets around him. Then he attacked the sergeant with the butt of his gun, breaking his jaw.

Treatment at a military mental hospital followed, which only confirmed Henry's growing detestation of authority. As he put it, it was just 'a load of bloody officers in uniform doing their morning rounds dishing out pills and tranquillizers to keep everyone quiet' - there was no attempt at regular psychiatric treatment. Afterwards, demobilized, he found himself unable to hold down a job, and he took to bashing up his beautiful quiet-eyed Greek wife, whom he had never touched in that way before. As they were homeless the local authorities allocated them temporary housing in a dreary street crammed full of unhappy people like themselves. A neighbour turned out to be an expert at forging Social Security Giro cheques, and soon Henry was helping to pass them. Henry is no big-time criminal, and was quickly caught. Now he has convinced himself that the Social Security people are out to punish him, and when he has any dealings with them you can see him struggling to control his violence.

I went one day with him and his wife to see their social worker. Because he had to wait twenty minutes or so Henry became enraged, stalking round the room, trying the doors, complaining 'she's making us wait on purpose, just to get back at me'. The overworked social worker, a slight girl with long fair hair, was sympathetic but I don't think she knew quite what to do with this enormous man with the restless hands who never looked her straight in the eye. His wife Evi spoke little English, so he spoke for her, digging her in the thigh or poking her in the back to emphasize whatever he was saying about her as though she were an inanimate object.

Meanwhile their little boy George knelt on the floor scrawling on some papers. On the cover of one of the booklets he had been given to play with was a picture of a man and a woman - flat and featureless like two gingerbread people except that one was wearing a skirt - whose two linked hands were held above their heads to form an arch under which sheltered three children. George scribbled furiously over the woman's eyes, blacking them out. Then he did the same to the children. The man's eyes he touched with a single stroke of his crayon, then he pushed the booklet away as though frightened at his temerity. I picked up the booklet and asked him, one by one, who the two adults were. 'Mummy and Daddy,' he replied. When I asked him what they were doing he stayed silent for a moment, then he suddenly gave an odd smile and banged one fist against the other, making at the same time a loud hitting noise with his mouth. The appalling irony was that this picture was meant to illustrate two fosterparents guarding a group of children under the safe shelter of their united love, but George had interpreted their touching of hands in the only way he knew.

Henry is a pathetic man. He is not all that bright, but he is certainly not stupid. As a boy he was spoilt by his father, he says, and his bulk protected him from trouble in the Glasgow streets in which he grew up. As a result he expected things to go his way without bothering too much about other people's feelings, but he had never wanted to hit people before. Now, he explained to me, if he gets irritated he just lashes out. 'Like when Evi tries to tell me something and I don't understand her English. "Why don't you speak English better?" I say to her - bang! wallop! - "I can't understand you" - bang! wallop! wham!' He smiles as he says 'bang!' and 'wallop!' and is quite unperturbed by the fact that Evi is sitting right beside him. He pulls up her skirt to show me the yellowing bruises where he had hit her a few nights previously, and he seems rather proud of them. He obviously feels she totally belongs to him, and that her bruises are his mark, binding the two of them together into one flesh. He insists that Evi will never leave him, but she shakes her head at that and says in her own stumbling way she has had enough. Little George has started to be affected, and the previous week he had gone for Henry with a hammer in an attempt to protect his mother. He is only three and a half.

There are other men who have been to the Men's House I could describe, men with very different backgrounds to Henry, whose fathers beat them, whose mothers lived a life of terror and poverty, whose entire lives are tales of disaster and tragedy. It must be accepted by all of us who make any claim to a social conscience that, even if a man's brutality appears to have alienated himself from any right to sympathy, he is nevertheless a human being who did not choose his birth or his upbringing, but who had it thrust upon him. If he is not helped in time, if his pattern of life is not changed, he will go on committing violent crimes, go on finding and injuring a succession of women, and go on spawning children who will grow up deprived, unstable and possibly only too horribly like himself.

There are a few men who are too damaged to be helped at all. Others, though badly disturbed, might respond to the right sort of treatment if it were available. Obviously one should not allow violent men to continue making and breaking relationships with a variety of women, subjecting each of them to pain and sometimes maiming them. There is no doubt that if these men had treated a number of citizens other than their wives or cohabitees in this manner they would certainly have been locked up for lengthy periods. But incarcerating a man in jail only solves the security aspect of the problem; it does nothing for the man himself.

It has been suggested that violent men of this type should be put into regional security units, the provision of which - most probably in the grounds of hospitals for the mentally ill or mentally handicapped - has been under discussion for some years now. The need for facilities for patients needing treatment in secure conditions was first discussed in 1961. In an interim report in 1974 the Butler Committee (set up in 1972 to speed up matters) urgently recommended that special units should be set up in each region. As yet these long-desired units have hardly passed the planning stage. In a speech in September 1976 David Ennals, current Secretary of State for Social Services, regretted that people were already referring to these proposed units as 'mini-Broadmoors', and emphasized that it was the intention of the authorities not to accommodate dangerous psychopaths in them but the kind of disruptive patient who causes chaos in ordinary mental hospitals, mentally disordered offenders and those with personality problems. As Mr Ennals so rightly said, 'The time has come for action. I am determined that these treatment facilities will be provided.'

With the right staff these units could well be one of the answers to the problem of what to do with violent husbands. One can envisage a time when men found guilty of wife battering will be automatically sent to such places for treatment, instead of being jailed for a few weeks or merely given yet another warning. Ten years ago one could have ended with this note of enthusiasm, but in today's climate I must admit to a fear that it will be some years before enough units are built for such treatment to be nationally available, and that even when they are built it is unlikely the staff-patient ratio will be as generous as it ought to be; nor is it probable that the quality of the staff will be as high as it would need to be if any permanent effect is to be achieved. A limited staff of male nurses who are in essence wardens aiming at keeping the 'patients' quiet, relying on tranquillizers and sleeping pills to assist them and reporting to a psychiatrist who sees each patient individually for only half an hour once a week, is the picture that is only too likely to emerge in spite of the good intentions of all those concerned with the project.

Without money we cannot expect sufficient staff of the right calibre to be attracted to such a difficult and exhausting job as rehabilitating these men, while half-an-hour-once-a-week psychiatric help does little in my experience other than familiarize patients with technical terms, leaving them with a greater understanding of why they are as they are, but with no increased ability to deal with their problems. It is probably better than nothing, but it is nothing like enough. Some units, I am sure, will do much better than this, but I fear that others will be built reluctantly and treated as unimportant annexes to the main hospital or dumping grounds for disruptive patients.

One way out of the difficulty of insufficient funds is for the patients to treat themselves as far as possible. Group therapy is now a respectable form of treatment, and if mental nursing staff can be thoroughly trained in how to run therapy groups much progress could be made. Groups badly run can be very destructive so the group leaders would have to be chosen and taught with care. With a sympathetic psychiatrist attending some of the group therapy sessions, as well as seeing each man individually for the normal weekly half hour, quicker progress could be made and everybody's understanding greatly improved. If all the nursing staff could be trained in group therapy methods the entire waking day could be constructive, instead of a succession of dreary hours that somehow have to be got through. It is too much to hope that all mental staff will turn out to be talented at this kind of work, but there is no reason why the great majority should not benefit considerably from the training and their work made more interesting for them as a result. As for the patients, there are few stronger morale-builders than feeling that one has really helped and been necessary to another person, and if a man's attitude to himself is changed he has taken the first steps to changing his attitude to society also.

What of the future? It is clear we cannot expect large sums of money to be poured into research. The DHSS has given limited grants to several universities: Keele is well launched into a three-year study directed by the head of the Department of Sociology, Professor Ronald Frankenberg; at Bristol they are investigating the effectiveness of the various agencies which come into contact with battered wives, while the University of Kent at Canterbury is looking at the role of refuges. The Home Office in consultation with the DHSS have set up a Marriage Guidance Working Party which, among other issues, is considering family violence, and there may be other working parties I have not heard about. But the truth is that few government departments are sufficiently interested to lay out money for research into what they mostly regard as a not very pressing matter.

It looks as though we must continue to rely on voluntary bodies and enthusiastic amateurs for the main stimulus to progress in this field. At the beginning of Chapter 3 I described the new NSPCC unit sponsored by Essex County Council. This aims to explore the reasons for marital violence and its effect on children while, in co-operation with local social workers, at the same time providing a caring service for a limited number of clients. It is hoped that in spite of recent economic restrictions other councils will copy Essex's initiative and enable further units to be established. This kind of research need not cost too much as the clients have to be treated in any case, and the burden of this, which would otherwise have fallen solely on the local authorities, would now be shared by the NSPCC workers. Without grants to aid them the NSPCC, being a voluntary body relying on public contributions to keep going, cannot afford to set up further units. This would be a great pity because a research action group of this kind, dealing with marriages which are still viable, can provide information unobtainable by research conducted after the patient has died, as it were.

As we have seen, shortage of money has also prevented the government from setting up crisis centres in spite of urgent recommendations by the Select Committee on Violence in Marriage. As the Committee wrote in their Report, if 'one or two crisis centres [were] set up as action research projects . . . to determine their effectiveness and value . . . research and service money [could] be most effectively used simultaneously, and a very specific question examined.' I have already stressed the need for a number of crisis centres to be opened, and I hope that voluntary workers will be inspired to take on this work, as the government has now made it clear that they will not do so. I feel sure that many local councils would co-operate to the best of their ability, especially as such centres would be open to all who needed them, whatever type of crisis was being faced. To attempt to restrict them to any specific problem would be a mistake, and would almost certainly restrict the amount of aid local authorities would be prepared to give.

One great advantage of such centres would be that advance warnings of severe crises could be picked up and acted on. A number of battered wives know quite well that one day their husbands' increasing violence is likely to end in their being severely injured or even killed. Nevertheless few take action, mostly because they are frightened either that their husbands will abuse them even more severely if they do so, or that their husbands will be arrested and taken away from them. If a centre were to become a well-known and trusted local amenity such wives might be encouraged to talk in private to the helpers in the confidence that no action would be taken without their agreement to it. M. Faulk pointed out in his article in *Medicine, Science and the Law* (1974) that out of the 23 cases in which men were charged with seriously assaulting their wives or cohabitees (including 8 cases of murder and 9 of attempted murder), 70 per cent of the women had had early warning signs of their husbands' violence and yet no precautions against further violence had been taken.

Even without the provision of crisis centres on a national scale so that any woman anywhere can obtain unbiased advice, the knowledge that there are now numerous refuges available for them to flee to means that in future more and more women will find the courage to leave their husbands before the assaults become too violent. There are too few refuges to cope with the need that would arise if all the women in this country who are battered should suddenly decide to rise *en masse* and leave their husbands. Such an eventuality is unlikely, but unquestionably the demand will become greater as women become less inclined to passively accept ill-treatment at the hands of their husbands. We need more refuges, more research into how refuges should best be run, and above all, we need more second- and third-stage housing, especially for the kind of woman who has been badly mentally scarred by her experiences and who would be far happier living close to or with other women who have suffered in the same way as herself.

The Select Committee urged that children should be taught about marriage and likely conflicts at school. They also suggested that children be instructed on the law as it concerns family life, and how to use the social services and other helping agencies. At first, remembering one's own schooldays, this might sound a rather dubious exercise, but today's fifth formers are far more sophisticated in such matters. They are already taught about sex, VD and contraception, but this is as limited a help in setting up a permanent relationship with someone as it would be to teach a trainee cook only how to eat, how to treat stomach ulcers, and the dietary requirements of the human body. Adolescents know already that married people quarrel; apart from personal observations they have almost certainly seen dozens of television plays, serials and comedies about marital conflict. They are lucky children if they have never witnessed any discord in their own parents' marriage. Discussions of the stresses and inevitable personal problems that arise in any marriage, explanation of how a child's own upbringing will affect his/her later attitude to women/men, warm assurance of the rewards that a mature, close relationship can bring - serious and enlightened discussions of subjects such as these would surely fascinate most young adolescents and help them not only later in their lives, but straight away in their early explorations with members of the opposite sex.

It is easy to be split-minded about children, on the one hand seeing all schoolchildren as innocents who ought not to have their illusions sullied by reality, while at the same time knowing that a growing number of them at an increasingly early age are turning into young thugs and criminals. For vast numbers of children school is a place that relates in no way to the reality of their lives. It is something to be got over as soon as possible because the real world is outside. Any attempt to close this gap can only have beneficial results. The kind of disturbed children we have been reading about earlier all go to schools of one kind or another, and are to be found among those schoolchildren whom the Select Committee suggested should be taught about marriage and its problems. They know plenty about violence already, and any illumination that can be brought into their lives by making them understand that their own personal problems are not unique will help to lessen their inner turmoil to some extent.

We are hearing increasingly about the growing problem of juvenile delinquents. Many are very young indeed: in 1975 29 per cent of offenders arrested for indictable offences in the Metropolitan Police District were aged between 10 and 16. Half of all the people arrested were under 21: 51 per cent of 103,252 arrests. The 1969 Children and Young Persons Act has been severely criticized by many magistrates, police and social workers who think it merely encourages youngsters to feel they can break any law and get away with it. The police have no desire to throw as many youngsters as possible into jail: the Police Juvenile Bureaux, for example, do excellent work in helping prevent many youngsters from settling into a life of crime, and the police contribution in this field is often overlooked. Nevertheless everyone knows that the present methods are not working and that new ways must be found of treating juvenile offenders.

Various suggestions are regularly put forward, but the most interesting to me are those which aim at changing the children's attitudes. We saw how at the Chiswick Boys' House the boys have too much spare time, Supplementary Benefit having taken away the necessity to work. Sullen and bored, they eventually broke up their own home. The Inner London Probation and Aftercare Service decided to try out a new method with a similar group of slightly older lads. They had many ex-offenders on probation in their care between the ages of 18 and 22, none of whom had managed to keep a job for more than three months during the previous year. Some had not worked for two years or more, and all of them were out of the habit of doing steady work. The ILPS took the attitude (based on the success of a New York scheme) that if you make a man work so that he doesn't have time to get into trouble and if you pay him well so that he becomes accustomed to real money in his pocket, with any luck he will eventually turn into a law-abiding citizen. They set up what they call the Bulldog Manpower Service, which organizes a variety of jobs like clearing up derelict land, dockland reclamation work and renovating old houses. The boys are paid well for their labour, but if they are late for work or break off early their wages are cut. Until they have become used to the routine, friendly probation workers keep an eye on them, even calling at their rooms to get them out of bed if necessary. At first the boys tend to moan, but when at the end of the first week they receive a worthwhile wage instead of the usual £15 or so Supplementary Benefit, their attitude usually changes. They are encouraged to feel responsible for the work they do and to take a pride in its success. The congenial company and the varied jobs given them keep them interested and busy so that they do not have time to be bored or 'clock-watch'.

The aim behind the scheme is that at the end of six months the lads should be capable of setting out on their own and working for an employer of their own choice. The secretary of Bulldog Manpower feels that although the scheme has been given a large grant from the Home Office it is virtually paying for itself by the saving of unemployment money and Supplementary Benefits, together with a probable saving on future prison and probation services, plus the taxation on earnings which the young men have to pay back to the government (one of the less pleasant aspects of their rehabilitation as far as the ex-offenders themselves are concerned).

This excellent scheme has proved its success, and now the ILPS hope to extend it. Projects of this type are the way of the future; of course some offenders are too violent, too disturbed for such a plan to be practicable, but for large numbers of people - women as well as men, old as well as young - rehabilitation is possible, and so much preferable to yet another useless spell in prison or remand home.

In September 1976 Whitehall proposed that a new-style national advisory council, probably consisting of magistrates, educationists, social workers and policemen *working alongside* a team of ministers, should be set up to examine the incidence and nature of juvenile crime. It is hoped that such a committee would result in better co-operation between various departments, while at the same time giving ministers close contact with people working outside Whitehall itself. At the time of writing nothing positive has yet emerged from this proposal, but it is a move in the right direction.

Although this particular scheme relates only to juveniles it would hardly be able to avoid tackling the subject of disturbed home backgrounds, including marital violence. Real understanding between all the caring agencies together with willing governmental assistance is going to be necessary if all aspects of violence in the home - from the small child terrified as it watches its mother beaten up to the ageing grandparent sent sprawling on the floor - are to be explored and alleviated. At present the drain on our national resources as a direct result of family aggression is immense: there can be few projects that will return such a large reward in monetary as well as emotional terms.

Granny Bashing

When I was a laddie
I lived with my granny
And many a hiding ma granny gi'ed me.
Now I am a man
And I live with my granny
And do to ma granny
What she did to me.

(Traditional rhyme quoted in
a letter to the *Guardian*)

Granny bashing cannot be treated in the same way as other
subjects in this book, partly because there is so little research
on which to comment, and partly because it appears to bear
little resemblance to the more usual types of violence. Most
doctors will have come across old people living with relations
who are suffering from neglect, but few find obvious cases of
straightforward abuse. Although there are of course some
families in which everyone including the cat is regularly

kicked, it seems likely that in most families where granny bashing takes place there has not been any previous violence. Even 'violence' may be too strong a word for an action that might amount to no more than a shove or an exasperated shaking, and yet the results of such an act can be catastrophic to an elderly person with little resilience.

It is only very recently that anyone has been prepared to consider the subject at all. Along with death, old age remains something we prefer not to think too much about.

Most of us attempt to ignore the fact that with any luck we too shall reach old age. While the aged were a comparatively small proportion of the population, society at large could afford this attitude. But those days are over. We are living in an ageing society. The birthrate continues to fall, while more and more of us are surviving until our eighties or even nineties. Eight million out of a population of 47 million are above retiring age (60 years for women, 65 for men). Life expectancy has changed tremendously in the last hundred years. A century ago a boy at birth could expect to live to 41 years, and a girl to 45. Today's newborn boy has a life expectancy of 69 years and a girl 75 years. During the ten years 1965-75 there has been an increase of 19 per cent in the population of people aged 65 and over, and as more of these than previously will survive into their 80s and 90s we can expect a staggering increase of about 21 per cent of people aged 75 and over during the years 1975-85. This increase will of course eventually halt as the optimum age for man's survival is reached, but the greatest increase for the over-75s and -85s has yet to come. Between 1971 and 1991 it is estimated there will be an increase in all of about 40 per cent of people aged 85 and over, and by 2011 this will have enlarged to an increase of around 62 per cent.

Dr Geoffrey Burston, Geriatrician at Avon Health Authority, Bristol, who has been concerned for some time with the problem of elderly people who are suffering non-accidental injuries, has pointed out, 'The elderly are increasing at an alarming rate - we are producing one new old person in this country about every five minutes - and there's no doubt this increase is causing problems on a large scale.' Just how great the incidence of abuse to old people is no one knows, but since some doctors and nurses are now beginning to look for signs of abuse, they are finding them. The principal of a nursing service centred in Southampton, for instance, reported that seven cases of ill-treatment to elderly persons had been reported to her within five weeks. But it is quite impossible at the moment to make even the vaguest estimate as to how many old people suffer physical abuse in one form or another.

There has been even less research into this side of family violence than into the other aspects discussed in this book. In June 1976 David Owen, then Secretary of State for Social Services, promised that the DHSS intended 'to give a higher priority in future years to research to the elderly than hitherto', while gerontologists such as Dr Alex Comfort add considerably to our understanding of ageing, but the subject of abuse of the elderly is roughly at the stage baby battering was at when Dr Kempe first coined the phrase 'child battering' in 1961. There is even the same difficulty in persuading people that it happens at all. Dr Burston found that when he made enquiries among medical colleagues many admitted it had not even crossed their minds to look for signs of non-accidental injury among their aged patients.

Notoriously old people bruise easily. Merely gripping an arm or wrist too tightly when escorting them over a road can cause bruising, and loose slippers or low lighting can easily result in a tumble. It is difficult for a doctor to decide whether or not the type of bruising he is dealing with is accidental, but Dr James Cameron, the pathologist, says that if you know what you are looking for you can usually tell. Grip marks on both arms probably imply a shaking; unexplained bruises on the back or the chest - the result of a rough push - in addition to the bruising incurred by the fall itself, may indicate what really happened. If it is claimed that the patient bruises particularly easily a haematological examination can show whether or not this is so. If suspicions are aroused old injuries may be revealed by ultra-violet light which will show up any previous bruises as a darkened area. These only become noticeable three months after the injury occurred, but they remain for at least a year.

Dr Cameron remarks that it is as important to be suspicious when dealing with accidents to old people as it is with children, but of course there is an important difference in that an elderly patient may be able to explain the 'accident'. However, many patients are in a state of confusion when they enter hospital and their ramblings are likely to be ignored in favour of the explanation given by the accompanying relative. Often this is on the lines of 'she went to the loo in the middle of the night and fell down the stairs'. The fall, in which the head was probably banged, plus the shock, is quite enough to drive an elderly person into temporary incoherence. In addition, old people are often encouraged to take too many drugs, both by their doctors and by their family. They take increasing numbers of sleeping tablets to get them through the night, endless pills for their stomachs or heart, and pain-killers for arthritis, etc., until they are nearly drugged out of their minds.

In hospital, under strictly controlled conditions, they often recover most or all of their senses. Where there has been mental or physical abuse the relief from this, together with a drop in the amount of drugs taken, will probably be sufficient to turn a confused old person into a coherent being again, but within a few weeks of release they may well be back in hospital once more. Dr Cameron, carrying out examinations on the corpses of abused old people, has found that not infrequently they had been hospitalized a couple of months or so previous to the final accident, perhaps with a stroke and heavy bruising after having 'fallen down the stairs'. He and other concerned doctors feel strongly that where suspicions are aroused it is most important that investigations should be carried out, so that if necessary home conditions may be alleviated. If this is not done further abuse will almost certainly take place.

An elderly in-patient may confide in a sympathetic nurse or a doctor if either can spare the time to listen until the point is finally reached. They are unlikely, however, to admit straight out what has happened, partly out of pride, partly because they probably dread being put into a home even more than they dread returning to their family. The only way round this problem is for all doctors to search for any suspicious signs and then to ensure that somebody has a long, easy talk with the patient in an attempt to discover the truth. Straightforward attacks with instruments or outright brutality with fists or feet are rare, so it is the smaller signs that must be looked for.

How does a family get itself into this position in the first place? Various doctors have given me their own versions of what they themselves have found to be typical patterns, but these do not entirely coincide. Dr Michael Green, medical editor of *Modern Geriatrics* and consultant geriatrician at the Royal Free Hospital, London, has mostly found three types of family situations:

(1) where the family was initially loving and quite happy to make a home for a bereaved parent, but where increasing disability has soured the relationship;

(2) where the old person was taken in reluctantly because a stroke or inability to look after themselves meant the parent could no longer live alone; and

(3) where the family is already in stress, and violence is likely to break out whether or not the old person is there.

Other doctors have found attacks occurring where an unmarried daughter or son has had to take the whole burden of an incapacitated aged parent upon themselves. Occasionally, where both spouses are surviving, one batters the other, mentally or physically.

The first situation seems to be quite common, and is in some ways the saddest to contemplate. It is worth looking more closely at how such a relationship can deteriorate, as with the rise in the numbers of surviving elderly people more and more of them will have to be looked after by their families, for the state alone will not be able to cope with the increase. At first the elderly grandparent is welcomed and no one mentions any reservations he or she may have. The old person probably tries to be unobtrusive and not to interfere. Everyone exudes good will. But if the grandparent is living completely within the family and sharing their lives in every way stresses and strains almost invariably begin to sour the relationship. Grandchildren may resent having their lives interfered with: they cannot watch television programmes of their own choice because granny or grandpa wants something else, or the radio or TV may have to be turned up loudly because of increasing deafness, so that even in their own bedrooms they cannot concentrate on homework. They must be careful how they speak, censoring their words and their subjects, lest an old person of another generation be shocked. In addition, unwelcome comments may be made on their friends, their hairstyles, their clothes

117

and their manners, until finally they storm out of the house in a fury. Their father may come in from work tired and wanting nothing so much as a quiet evening, but he may have to listen to endless chat about nothing in particular, designed not so much as true conversation but as the only means of making contact that the elderly parent has. The mother, who has already had the old person around 'under her feet' all day, may also be longing for some peace. Seeing all her family becoming more and more tense and family life breaking up, perhaps she tries to shoo the grandparent off to bed, but this move is likely to be resisted as the old person probably finds sleep at night difficult, though he or she may drop off at any time in the evening to the accompaniment of loud snores.

Increasing family tension is of course sensed by old people in this position, and they may react by falling into despondency and depression, or by trying to prove how youthful they still are. Angry at their weakening powers, perhaps they insist on joining in or doing tasks they can no longer perform properly. Perhaps they insist on wiping up when their arthritic hands can no longer safely hold a slippery piece of china and it breaks, or they lay the table but put out the wrong china, or they simply follow their busy daughter or daughter-in-law around from room to room, literally getting in her way until at last she breaks, gives an exasperated push meant only to clear the infuriating old thing out the way, never to knock her sprawling onto the floor. Or perhaps the daughter grabs hold of her parent by both arms and shakes her, just as many mothers do their exasperating children. But neither the very young nor the very old can take treatment of that kind without some damage being done, and though the daughter will probably be bitterly ashamed of herself afterwards, she knows with despair that the old person's condition can only deteriorate and she fears what might happen in the future.

It is easy enough to talk of day centres as a solution for this type of stress and these will be discussed later, but that there is no easy answer to the problem may be seen from the following letter sent to the *Guardian*:

After six years of granny watching I am not surprised to read of granny bashing. I often feel like it myself and indeed practise one form, namely silence. I have run out of emotional steam and can no longer find the energy or charity to keep my housebound, blind 87-year-old granny in touch with the outside community by relating to her the minutiae of my everyday confined domestic life. I rely more each day on the BBC Home Service to keep her going.

Jean Renvoize advocates day centres. First you have to persuade them to go. I managed this after gritting my teeth against her apprehension and dislike of change but gran returned shattered yesterday after seven hours at a centre where she had been unable to get in touch with any of the other old dears sitting in the warm and comfortable lounge. She could not see them and although she says she addressed 'remarks to the company at large' no answer came back from the void. She was told that her immediate neighbour was stone deaf. A well-meaning member of the staff turned on Radio One and left it on for the rest of the day.

Well, I've had a few fags and quite a bit of drink and now I wonder if just once a month I could find someone to come in for a few hours to take care and cook for her so that my husband and I could perhaps visit friends who have been pressing us for two years to make an hour's journey to see them or just have a walk in the country. God help those and particularly the single women who couldn't afford to employ such a treasure if she could be found.

Then I've thought what a good idea it would be if families or individuals in a similar predicament could buy or use a local house communally for their grannies and take it in turn to look after them in a group. The organisational problems are daunting. I often hear some well-meaning know-alls say that the old are best off in the bosom of the family where they are loved and wanted. But observation and experience tell me that the old are often alone in the family. On the other hand an old person, like a sick person, often receives more attention when she is the object of visits; certainly my husband spoke to his mother much more before G-day (when he visited her twice weekly).

Does it make sense as the Lift Up Your Heart brigade enjoins us to lay down our life in service to others? If we're all doing this doesn't it make self realisation, which I feel is a reasonable objective, rather difficult? Sure, we have to live without trampling on others, but isn't there a limit? I hope I will still think so when it is my turn to be someone else's predicament and that I will have the opportunity to find some solution other than living with the children.

Dr Cameron who, as a pathologist, deals with the extreme end of the spectrum, has found that in his experience the attacker is frequently an unmarried daughter living with her widowed mother. The daughter finds the stress of looking after a parent who is increasingly becoming confused, demanding and unreasonable almost more than she can bear, especially if she is going through hormonal changes caused by the menopause. Quite likely she is holding down a job which makes demands on her, but she returns home at night not to the warmth of family life but to the complaints of a lonely old woman. There are plenty of bachelors who also find themselves in the same position. The increasing strain on single people undertaking the burden of looking after such a parent must not be underestimated, especially by other married members of the family who could help by themselves taking turns in looking after the old person.

The majority of elderly people who find themselves having to face the last part of their lives without the companionship of a partner are female. Of people over 76 who are widowed or divorced two-thirds are women. In fact, over 85 per cent of women aged 75 and over are either single, widowed or divorced.

Of course, there are a few still-united couples who on retirement move in with their families, but usually this does not happen until one or other of the spouses dies. Whoever is left alone has then to cope not only with the loss of a lifelong companion, but also with a devastating sense of uselessness. In too many cases retirement itself has already left a couple with nothing to do except to look after each other. For the woman this is usually a continuation of her married life, for although she may well have worked outside the home previous to the retirement, much of her existence will remain unchanged as she continues to organize the home for the two of them, to shop and cook, etc. For a man who probably has had little to do with the daily running of the house the situation is very different. At an age when he is likely to be in physical and mental command of all his senses he is dismissed from his work and left stranded. Perhaps in a couple of decades today's changing life-styles will enable retired men to adapt better to living at home all day, but most of the present generation of retired men face the prospect of pottering around the house, doing a bit of shopping, a bit of gardening and little else. It is no wonder they tend to deteriorate rapidly, some turning into cantankerous, difficult old men with no object in life.

Marital problems between the couples may be no more than a continuation of their normal way of life, or they may be the result of their changed circumstances. As the retired couples grow older some husbands, for instance, find themselves having to cope with the unaccustomed work of looking after an invalid wife. Unused to such intimate personal service a few find their tempers flaring and they hit out at their wives, perhaps for the first time ever. An elderly wife is less likely to resort to physical violence, though this does happen, but she may employ mental violence. As she draws the weekly pension money it dawns on her that her husband is no longer the breadwinner: it is she who is now the primary caring member of the family, she who stretches out the pension to cope with reduced circumstances, who cooks and who runs the house. Her husband may help her with the domestic work but she is unlikely to be very grateful as she has probably so organized her work over the years that she hardly notices it any more.

If the relationship between them is not a good one the continual presence of her husband under her feet will probably irritate her. She may begin to nag him or denigrate him until he either rebels and strikes her, or degenerates still further into a fumbling, useless old relic. But when he eventually dies, leaving her widowed, she suddenly finds she has no one to work for, no one to nag, no point in life. If she moves in with her children she is likely to feel even more useless. She is no longer head of the kitchen, it is not she who organizes the house. After all her long experience of life she has ended up subordinate to a younger woman who cooks in a different way, eats modern food and does the housework differently. No wonder she finds her new life difficult, setting off waves of discontentment

121

which reverberate through the entire family.

One point that is sometimes overlooked is that by the time an old person has reached the age of 85 or so, his or her children are themselves likely to be reaching retirement age. They may well be feeling that at last they can relax and enjoy their new freedom, and they will not welcome very heartily an elderly parent who is likely to prove even more hard work to look after than the children who have grown up and left home. They consider they have earned a long holiday and they begrudge having a new burden put upon them. Others may have some of their family still living with them, perhaps married and with children of their own, so that if grandparents move in as well there will be four generations living in the same house. This can be an immensely rewarding and fascinating experience for all concerned, but if the physical conditions are not right it can also be exactly the opposite.

The picture I have presented so far seems a thoroughly gloomy one, but in most cases it need not be so. Obviously, some old people were always difficult to live with and old age merely makes them even more impossible. But for great numbers a combination of factors surrounding old age have turned them quite unnecessarily into unwanted burdens instead of beloved family members. Let us look more closely at some of these factors.

The onset of deafness, for example, can completely change a relationship. The old usually dislike admitting deteriorating faculties, and may insist that the speaker's pronunciation is at fault if they cannot hear properly. It could be that syringing the old person's ears to remove accumulated wax will cure the problem, or it may be that a deaf aid will be necessary, but something certainly must be done as impaired communication can cause more irritation than anything else. Much of the problem of knocking into things and breaking precious objects may simply be due to deteriorating vision. Eyesight ought to be checked annually and the recipient of a pair of glasses persuaded to wear them. Some old people suffer from incontinence, an extremely embarrassing disorder, which may result in their refusing to go outside the house at all for fear of letting themselves down. But if incontinence is tackled as soon as it first begins to show itself doctors can very often control it if not cure it, so that it causes the minimum of inconvenience. Problems with bowels, digestion, locomotion all tend to be brushed off as the inevitable accompaniment of old age, but such an attitude angers modern geriatricians who know that most of these difficulties can be considerably alleviated if not cured. They insist that nurses, social workers and doctors as well as the patient's relatives stop dismissing such complaints. with a shrug and a smile, followed by the comment, 'It's your age, grandma, you can't expect anything else', and instead take a more constructive approach. Too many drugs - sleeping pills to ensure oblivion and pep pills to lift depression, in addition to other drugs for a variety of ailments - can, as we have already seen, cause a state of confusion and bewilderment that is often mistaken for senility. As the days, months, years of boredom and mental isolation slowly pass, growing unhappiness increases the drift into senility.

But there are only a few aged people who become senile from purely physical causes. Most of us could reach a contented, busy old age still in our right minds - less agile, perhaps, but still competent, useful members of society. After all, judges, actors, doctors, writers and many other professional people go on until they drop. Activity keeps them alive, interested and comparatively healthy. To deprive them of their work would for many be no less than a death sentence.

What then can be done to avoid stresses occurring in a family which could lead to an unintended but possibly lethal attack? Perhaps most important of all, old people ought to be persuaded to take their health at least as seriously as when they were young, and assume that something can be done to treat any infirmities that might arise. Only the rarest of men and women are ennobled by illness, and even fewer by the persistent mild ill health which is the daily experience of millions of old people.

I suspect there are many elderly men and women reading this chapter who by now are fuming at my seeming to consider that all old people need others to look after them. May I hasten to assure them that I know from personal experience and general observation that there are plenty of eighty- and ninety-year-olds who have more energy, more interest in life and more ability to help others than thousands of people half their age. There are many others with a similar spirit of independence and determination, whose physical health forces them to seek some assistance from others but who still remain fully in control of their lives which they continue to enjoy to the full. But these fortunate ones should remember there are also vast numbers of elderly people dragging out their last few years, some wishing they were dead and that it was all over and done with. They are frightened of leaving the house because of modern traffic, because 'everything is so changed nowadays', because of uncertainty about their bladder or bowel control, or because they are frightened they will seem doddery and stupid. As they grow even older they may become more and more difficult, cantankerous and childish in their demands and behaviour. It is these people in particular who need our concern.

Old people should be encouraged to remain within the community for as long as possible, hospitalization being reserved as a last resort for those for whom there really is no alternative. Few actually want to enter an old people's home, but even if all did there are nothing like enough places for them. For those who have nowhere else to go and who can no longer live alone hospital is often the only place, but this is an absurd waste of scarce resources. In 1973 people over 65 occupied half of all medical beds and over a third of all orthopaedic beds. They also occupied nearly half of all psychiatric beds, although only a proportion were actually suffering from mental infirmity as a result of old age. Taking into consideration the many services that may have to be provided, it occasionally costs nearly as much or even more to keep an old person in the community than it would to put them into residential or hospital care, but usually this is not so. The cost of residential care for the elderly and disabled in 1975-6 was estimated at £142 million per annum, a large sum which will nevertheless have to be considerably increased as the years pass. Indeed, 35 per cent of the Health and Personal Social Service Budget is currently being absorbed by the over 65s.

DHSS figures suggest that between 650,000 and 1,300,000

old people in England suffer from some degree of mental infirmity and some 200,000-400,000 of these are suffering from dementia. Of these, most are living at home supported where possible by relatives. The problem must become greater in the next two or three decades as the numbers of the very old increase. Clearly, as much help as possible must be given both to the aged and to those who look after them.

About one third of our elderly people live alone. For obvious reasons these appear to be the least likely to suffer physical or mental abuse. Many will live out the rest of their lives without needing any help other than an occasional visit from their doctor. Others less fit who need some social service care should nevertheless be encouraged to be as independent as possible. It is better for them to walk to a luncheon club, for example, where they will meet other people, than to have meals on wheels brought to their homes. The importance of sheltered housing for old people who prefer their independence is at last being recognized, but there is little of it available. Day centres are obviously very useful, particularly where old people are living with their children, as this gives the family some freedom while at the same time allowing the old person to meet others of a similar age. Unfortunately day centres are not always as effective as they might be, as may be seen from the moving letter quoted a few pages back. About 14,000 day centre *places* are available at present, but there are many old people who are not within reasonable reach of one. The cost per place per annum is approximately £590, and the DHSS understandably suggest that only those with the greatest need be allocated places - the cheaper method of using adapted buildings to provide social activities which are partly run by voluntary helpers will have to be the way of the future. For many active elderly people the running and organizing of such centres could be a very useful and enjoyable way of using their otherwise wasted energies and expertise.

Many families would be considerably relieved if their aged parent could stay elsewhere for a few weeks every year so that family holidays could be taken without the continual presence of someone who cannot walk or join in the more adventurous or energetic pastimes of a younger generation. Occasional free weekends, a regular free day once or twice a week and an annual holiday would make all the difference between a grandparent being welcomed and loved, and a family torn apart by internal tension. For this some kind of temporary residential care will be necessary - perhaps the only way to achieve this in our present economic state will be to have voluntary helpers working under the supervision of the social services.

One observation made by many people is that if the grandparent lives completely within the family setting problems are likely to occur. If at all possible the grandfather or grandmother ought to have at least a good-sized bed-sitting room of his or her own, or better still, a self-contained flat, even if it consists of only two rooms. A pleasant sunny room, facilities for cooking and washing and, most helpful of all, a separate entrance so that both parts of the family have front doors behind which a sense of privacy and independence can be retained, will help ensure that the relationship stays a happy one. Such an arrangement allows the grandparent to offer occasional help which he or she knows will be welcomed, such as baby-sitting, cooking, financial or other assistance. Her pride in her own abilities is then retained, along with the great satisfaction of knowing she is genuinely needed.

One way or another vast sums of money are going to be expended on the aged, so would it not be best to spend some of it now on research? We need to plan for the future. Above all we need to rethink society. The imposition of an arbitrary retirement age must be reconsidered. Of course young people need the chance to rise, and old people cannot stay on for ever, but forcibly to retire at sixty or sixty-five someone who still has much to offer and who wishes to stay on in one capacity or another at his or her work is an absurd waste of human resources. Others will only be waiting for the day when they can step off the treadmill of a lifetime's employment, but these too may need some help if they are to get the most out of their retirement. What to do in old age, how to make it profitable, entertaining, enriching - there are many positive aspects that can be explored. Attitudes to when real old age begins must change - Dr Burston commented wryly that as far as he was concerned young people of sixty-five needed paediatricians, not geriatricians. A sense of uselessness, boredom, too much time in which to consider the possibility of approaching annihilation and despair that life will never again be enjoyable - all these contribute to the deterioration of the elderly. If we can change this and make life more fulfilling, more positive for the old so that they remain competent, companionable beings, we will certainly reduce considerably the number of elderly parents who are knocked down or verbally battered by their own exhausted children.

It will never be possible to stop all violence - human beings are too unstable and subject to fluctuating emotions - but at least we can do everything in our power to reduce its incidence.

Baby Battering

'No, at that stage he wasn't hitting me. That came later when he kept losing commissions because of his drinking and he didn't know what to do for money. When I hurt Janice it was just the opposite. He didn't feel any need to hit me then, he was having a lovely time. Out half the night with his mate, night clubs and that, fast cars, never mind me stuck at home with two kids. It was my place to be at home, he said. He'd been brought up without a father by relations who let him come and go as he pleased - they didn't care - and he felt he'd done his bit, he'd married me, gave me enough housekeeping and that was it. He couldn't see what was happening to me because in all his life he'd never had to care about anybody, nobody at all.

'The flat was too small but we couldn't get another because no one wanted to know, not with two babies. Jimmy was eighteen months, Janice was three months. We had to share the kitchen, bathroom and toilet. It wasn't a house you could feel proud of, I mean the entrance was disgusting. There were a lot of kids there and it was noisy and dirty and damp. I did my best, I was always cleaning my part but sometimes it made you feel really sick just going through the front door.

'I was caged in with two children, and I knew I was in trouble. But I thought if they take the children away I'll just die, I'll kill myself. It was bad enough that little Jimmy was jealous, he hated this thing that had arrived in Mummy's arms, you know? He used to twist the baby's feet and hands, and throw things into the pram. I was always trying to keep Janice out of harm's way, and all the time I was worried because there was something wrong with her inside, not very serious, she'd been born that way, but it meant she cried a lot.

'There was one day when she wouldn't stop crying. She'd cried in the night, and my husband didn't come home till four in the morning so he was no help. I was exhausted, honestly I was. I was only eighteen. I'd first got pregnant at sixteen. Imagine it, two kids by eighteen! I was mad, wasn't I? I hadn't had any fun at all, I was washing dirty nappies out while girl friends were living it up at the disco. Not that my husband let marriage stop him having fun. No, I don't think he was having women, he wasn't really that type; anyway, who'd fancy him, the way he was by the time he crawled home drunk!

'Well, Janice kept on and on crying and I thought I'm going mad, I'll have to do something. I got them both dressed to go to the doctor's and I'd just put Janice into her clean clothes, a pretty little jacket I'd only bought the day before, and she was sick all over it. I don't know, everything went black, I just picked her up and shook her then flung her down on the cot. Well, that's what I meant to do but somehow I didn't throw her straight and I caught her head on the windowsill. I hurt her leg too, I must have been holding it too tight, because afterwards they said it was broken. Yes, her skull was fractured. I never meant to do it, I just sort of blew up. I couldn't take any more.'

In fact medical evidence showed that the leg had been fractured at least a fortnight earlier, but Sally had wiped out all memory of earlier attacks. The only way she could cope with what she had done was by coalescing the results of her growing desperation into one terrible moment. Janice survived, just. Typically Sally delayed taking her to hospital for forty-eight hours, certain her baby would be stolen from her, and by the time she took her in it was almost too late.

Every day stories similar to Sally's are sobbed out to sympathetic doctors, health visitors, social workers. The unsympathetic workers are told lies, or are met with a sullen 'don't know, can't understand it', 'she only fell onto the carpet', 'down the stairs', 'the toddler pushed him, it doesn't make sense'.

We know a lot more now about why and how these attacks happen than we used to, and as a result people's attitudes are changing. They are beginning to say to themselves, 'In her place, what would I have done?' Since I wrote *Children in Danger* (1974) I have often found myself being asked at gatherings or parties about child abuse, and nearly everyone makes the same two comments. The first is, 'How could you bear to write about such a subject?' followed a few minutes later by an admission that they, too, had had times when they felt distraught, could almost have bashed their own children. Noticeably, this last year or so, several total strangers have admitted to me that they have once or twice hit their children considerably harder than they had intended. It is no longer quite such a taboo subject, no one any longer has to pretend to be 100 per cent 'normal'.

Normality itself is under question. What is normal? Haven't we in the past frequently meant 'ideal' when we used the word 'normal'? I think it is normal to be angry with your children sometimes, normal to feel moments of aggression that afterwards shame you when you recollect them. It is normal for people who have lost their temper to want to hit something, and it is normal for children occasionally to make their parents lose their temper. Upbringing, civilization, tenderness, love, any number of reasons stay our hand, but it is hypocritical to pretend that it is abnormal to want to hit children. Granted, the taboo against actually hitting tiny babies is far stronger than against older children because of their obvious vulnerability, so we may not even recognize the aggression that rises in us for what it is, but to those parents like Sally who break, we must try to extend our understanding, not as superior beings offering disinterested help but as fellow humans who share similar urges.

In this chapter I shall concentrate on facts. There has been much research in the last few years on child abuse, some of which is directly contradictory. Too much is still unknown; often impressive-sounding tables and percentages are based on numbers so small as to be, statistically speaking, almost worthless, but if funds do not permit 2,000 people to be investigated then the researchers must make do with 200 or even 20, and while the results may not be universally valid they will be a useful, if small, addition to the ever-growing body of knowledge.

Even the definition of what a battered child is is still under dispute. Rochdale Borough Council, for instance, for the purposes of their register of children at risk, asks for details of 'All physically injured children under sixteen years of age where the nature of the injury is not consistent with the account of how it occurred, or other factors indicate that there is reasonable suspicion that the injury occurred through acts of commission or omission by the child's parents or other person(s) having the care of the child.' For their own register the NSPCC in Leeds and Manchester asked to be notified of 'all children under four years of age, where the nature of the injury is not consistent with the account of how it occurred, or other factors indicate that it was probably caused non-accidentally.' These definitions ignore certain factors which disassociate 'baby battering' from ordinary child abuse, such as that battering parents usually, though not invariably, appear genuinely concerned about the welfare of their children, often being desperately anxious that they shall not be parted from them. This may or may not apply equally to parents who neglect or otherwise abuse their children, and there are those who argue that it is pointless to attempt to separate out any particular class of abusing parent.

In America even Professor Henry Kempe, who in 1961 deliberately originated the emotive phrase 'battered child' in order to shake public opinion, seems now to feel less strongly that battering and ordinary abuse are two quite separate

131

things. The general impression used to be that the majority of battering parents were comparatively normal but because of various psychological hang-ups (mostly due to lack of consistent and warm 'mothering' as a child) they were liable to lose control and hit out when stress became too severe. Neglect and general abuse were seen as different syndromes. For the purpose of compiling registers of children at risk it makes sense to include *all* children who have suffered physical abuse at the hands of a caretaker, regardless of the psychology and background of the attacker. But after reviewing the current research it seems to me there is still a valid distinction to be made between the two types of abuse, although the difference between them may occasionally be so blurred as to be almost indistinguishable. Some researchers find that almost all the battered children they see come from socially deprived homes with inadequate neglectful parents, and consider social causes to be the primary factor, affecting generation after generation of children doomed never to rise in the social scale. Others, such as Ray Castle, head of the NSPCC's National Advisory Centre on the Battered Child, find that neglect and lack of concern appear in only the minority of cases being investigated, regardless of the family's social class.

What matters is that we find out *why* some parents attack their own children to the point where real damage is done, whereas other parents in exactly the same situation manage to control themselves. Some of these battering parents are shattered at what they have done and long desperately for help, though not necessarily to have their lives taken over by officialdom. An interesting letter from an Australian paediatric social worker illustrates this last point.

> A very distressed mother I had been looking after for some time told me all she wanted was to feel normal. She criticized me severely for 'helping' her in such a way that she felt comfortably abnormal, complained I'd taught her to live with her abnormality which at the same time allowed me to protect her child from her. I had categorized her as a battering parent and she could not escape from it.

Many of these parents are capable of helping themselves and of breaking the terrible cycle of emotional damage passed from parent to child. To assist them to do this we need to gather every scrap of knowledge we can find. It is useless to say, as a reader recently wrote to a paper, 'to hell with the emotional problems of socially maladjusted parents, send such people to prison for criminal assault and take their children away from them permanently.' It would not even be practical - there aren't enough prisons, there aren't enough foster homes. Some 20 per cent of battered children do have to be separated from parents who will never be able to care for them properly, but most of the rest can be more or less successfully rehabilitated. The home may not be perfect, but what home ever was?

No one knows how many babies are battered or killed every year. Various estimates are made, but they are still guesswork, depending on where and how the sampling was taken. The NSPCC's Special Units in Leeds and Manchester have been so successfully publicized and used that local battering has unquestionably declined, to the point where they are able to extrapolate from their own figures that in Britain 3,360 children under 4 will suffer non-accidental injury every year, of whom 27 will die, and 1,300 be seriously injured. They add '[such an estimate] assumes that the level of professional skill nationally approximates to that in those areas where Special Units are operating'. It would be nice if it did, but it doesn't yet, as the NSPCC perfectly well knows. Dr M. H. Hall of Preston Infirmary (1975) has suggested an estimate of 4,400 cases a year with 757 annual deaths, but when these figures are revised to allow for certain problems of method they adjust to 2,500 definite cases, of which 430 would be fatal. Other estimates (Mounsey, Lancashire, 1975) suggest 1,600 cases a year with 250 fatalities. A study in north-east Wiltshire (Oliver *et al.*, 1974) suggests 3,500 annual cases with 350 deaths. Extrapolation of American studies would give us equally variant figures. If reporting of suspected cases were mandatory in Britain as it is in the USA, Kempe's 1973 American estimates would suggest we might expect 18,000 reported cases of whom over 2,000 would be seriously injured and another 2,000 severely deprived. On the other hand estimates worked out from David Gil's figures (1970) suggest a mere 1,600 reported cases, only half of which would be serious. Gil, a leading American researcher in this field, writes 'physical abuse cannot be considered a major killer and maimer of children in the United States' and considers it far more important to concentrate on tackling poverty, malnutrition, inadequate health care, education, etc.

The NSPCC, in their paper *A Report on Registers Maintained in Leeds and Manchester* (1975) write that other researchers' figures suggest 'between 3,500 and 4,500 children would be suspected by professional workers as having been non-accidentally injured each year, and that between 250 and 450 of these injuries would be fatal.' But, after discussing their own experiences and their previously mentioned lower estimate of 27 deaths a year, they write: '[Our] evidence would appear to suggest that the deaths of children under four . . . may be less frequent than has been estimated elsewhere.' On the other hand a questionnaire sent out to all local authorities by the DHSS reveals the following figures (1976):

97 English authorities, accounting for about 90 per cent of the child population, recorded some 5,700 cases (40 of them fatal) of known or suspected non-accidental injury coming to their notice *during the last three-quarters of 1974,* although not all give data for the whole 9 months.

These figures are therefore seriously incomplete, with reporting variable and in some cases non-existent.

A study of 134 battered children led by Selwyn Smith at Birmingham University produced many interesting results which will be referred to again. Out of these 134 children, 20 had serious injuries resulting in permanent damage, while 21 died (Smith and Hanson, 1974b). If 21 out of 134 die in one area alone it does seem that we may for some time to come expect a high fatality figure. The Select Committee on Violence in the Family, having considered the various figures made available to them, have come to the conclusion that over 300 children are killed every year in England and Wales alone, and 3,000 seriously injured. Four hundred receive injuries which result in chronic brain damage, while a further 40,000 children suffer mild or moderate damage (*Violence to*

Children, First Report from the Select Committee on Violence in the Family, June 1977).

The number of children who die as a result of non-accidental injury may never be known with any real accuracy: a child actually dying of pneumonia after a lethal attack is classified as having died of pneumonia, not physical assault; death from poisoning by aspirin is most likely to be classified as accidental, though who can tell how the bottle came to be lying around open in the first place? The circumstances in which a toddler falls from a window may leave deep suspicions in the investigating police officer's mind, but from lack of proof the child's death will again be classified as accidental. Whatever the true incidence may be, there is no doubt that as our knowledge increases these fatalities will be considerably reduced - we need only look at the encouraging results of the work of the NSPCC's Special Units - and one hopes that soon it will become very rare indeed for families at risk to go undetected to the point where a child is killed.

Research into the psychology of battering parents is far less contradictory. Time and time again the same factors turn up. Typically, battering parents have immature personalities, needing constant support and evidence of being loved, which unfortunately (since they tend to choose spouses with equally damaged natures) they rarely receive. Like children they want to gratify their impulses instantly; the restraint that comes with maturity has not yet been fully developed. Mostly they love their children, but this love seems to be less dogged than that of non-abusing parents. There are times when every parent has feelings towards his child which are anything but loving, but underneath the anger and aggression there flows a consciousness of what some will call love, others duty or conscience. Above all, the child continues to be seen as a child, albeit a temporarily infuriating one. To a battering parent this correct perception can disappear, the crying child perhaps being seen quite literally as the distraught parent's own mother screeching abuse, or as her husband shouting in anger.

'It was my mother's voice again, yelling at me I was no good, I couldn't do nothing right, exactly her voice just as

135

though she was there. It wasn't a baby I hit, it was my mum, I hit her right in the mouth with my fist, just like I always wanted to when I was a kid and I couldn't. I don't expect you to believe that but it's the truth. It wasn't my baby I hit at all.'

Not infrequently amnesia follows an attack, with the abusing parents as bewildered by the injuries as anyone else. Sometimes this may be due to a genuine confusion of identity at the moment of attack, but no doubt often it is the result of an inability to accept the horrifying fact that they have severely injured their own children.

But not all battering parents have even a basic love for their children. A few parents have such badly damaged personalities that immediate, permanent separation is the only possible course. At a Royal Society of Health Congress Dr John Howells, Director of the Institute of Family Psychiatry, quoted a letter from one such deeply disturbed mother to her mother-in-law who was looking after her little daughter:

If you were living nearer I would come down and throw a heavy lashing on Susan's hide . . . I will be coming up just like a devil after her, only I won't have his horns. . . . When you speak to her and she stretches out her mouth, give her a little bit of food for the week, just for her not to die, and do not give her any cover at night, and do not light the heater for her to get warmth. Just drag her out of bed in the early morning.

As Dr Howells so rightly stressed, it is time social workers dropped their insistence that the mother is the best person to rear her child - in many cases this simply is not so. Of course there can be few social workers by now who do not theoretically appreciate this fact, but most have been trained to keep the family together at all costs, and it is far more difficult than the layman realizes for them deliberately to break up a family, especially one in which they have invested much time and effort over a long period. In particular if a parent asks for a child to be taken away then his wishes should be respected, and he should not be merely told, 'Oh don't worry, everyone feels like that at times. It'll pass, it always does.' I have several times had this kind of remark repeated to me by parents who had known what danger their children were in, and who were quite unable to convince their health visitor or social worker that they meant precisely what they said when they expressed desperate fears.

Other parents, equally incapable of looking after their children, retain childhood fantasies of a united happy family and insist on keeping their children with them in the face of impossible odds. John Auckland, who had already served an eighteen-month sentence for killing one baby, requested, when his wife walked out and left him, that his fifteen-month-old daughter - at that time in foster care - should be returned to him. His wish was granted. This work-shy man, known to drink to the point of violence, now had three young children to look after, without any fully effective help. That a man with his record should have been allowed to remain in that situation shows a breathtaking incompetence on the part of the local social services and doctors, all of whom were in contact with the family. When he battered a second daughter to death public outrage was so great that an official enquiry was held.

Mr Auckland is now back in jail for another five years. *Why* did he want those children in his care, when he knew how violent he could become with drink? Was it love? loneliness? a hopeless desire for an ideal family life, a joy he had never known? In prison, if he is not protected by solitary confinement, his fellow-prisoners will no doubt be inflicting their own traditional punishment on him. But when he comes out he will still be a human being, with a human being's needs. What will happen then to his need for love, for companionship? Will he begin the same story all over again? How can we go on letting these things happen, and then pretend we are serving justice when we lock up such a damaged, damaging man for a few years behind bars?

Researchers have found evidence of abuse as far back as five generations in one family. When they were children the future battering parents learned to trust no one, that words mean nothing. They were able to develop no consistent idea of their own identity, and had little inner certainty to fall back on in times of stress. The damage they suffered in childhood may have been mainly physical or it may have been purely emotional: either way recovery is unlikely to be complete.

Psychological tests on 20 battering parents by the Battered Child Research Department showed they were consistently more reserved and detached than a group of parents chosen as controls, that they were more aggressive, more introverted, less realistic and practical. Also the fathers showed less enthusiasm and spontaneity, generally adopting a passive attitude. Over half the mothers and a few of the fathers had been given treatment by their GPs for psychiatric problems before they were referred to the Department. A few had been sent to psychiatric out-patient clinics for anxiety states or depression, and one father and four mothers had made unsuccessful attempts at suicide. Withdrawn and with little verbal facility, the fathers were unable to give much support to their wives, so that the many problems inevitable in any marriage, as well as ones more specific to people with impaired personalities, remained unaired. Many reports speak of one parent admitting to a suspicion that the other parent was damaging their child, the usual explanation being that he or she was unable to bring himself to talk about it, or even openly to face up to it in his own mind. Frank contact with another person involves a giving of the self, which these parents find almost impossibly difficult to achieve.

At Birmingham University Selwyn Smith found that nearly 62 per cent of the battering mothers he worked with had personality disorders of mild or moderate severity. Even more striking, one third of the fathers had severe personality or psychopathic disorders. Kempe found only 2 or 3 per cent of his fathers to be psychopathic, so it seems likely that Smith's team were investigating a more severely disturbed group than Kempe's, particularly in view of the high death rate of the children in their sample. Smith writes (Smith and Hanson, 1975):

Baby batterers [were] characterised by all kinds of hostility . . . against both others and themselves. This description resembles that of the depressive psychopath. Indeed, in the backgrounds of our sample there was considerable evidence of psychiatric disturbance; childhood neurotic symptoms, childhood unhappiness, a family history of psychiatric illness, physical handicaps, head injuries and lack of school success. Despite such adversities, very few baby batterers had received any formal psychiatric treatment.

What treatment were they likely to have been given other than tranquillizers, which can themselves be dangerous. Dr C. Ounsted of Park Hospital, Oxford, feels that 'many parents are disinhibited by tranquillizers given for their psychological problems without any attempt to solve their underlying causes'. John Auckland, for example, was under treatment for depression at the time of his second fatal attack - tranquillizers plus excessive alcohol are hardly conducive to self-control, even in the fairly well-balanced.

Steele and Pollock (in Helfer and Kempe, 1968) found that all the parents under study were repeating their own style of upbringing, a finding common to other researchers. As children they could never satisfy their parents, whose demands were excessive and unrealistic, so that they were perpetually crushed by a sense of their inadequacy.

> No matter what the patient as a child tried to do, it was not enough, it was not right, it was at the wrong time, it would disgrace the parents in the eyes of the world. . . . Inevitably, the growing child felt . . . he was unloved, that his own needs, desires and capabilities were disregarded, unheard, unfulfilled, and even wrong.

The child, frustrated in his natural desire for love and encouragement, feels aggression towards the parent, but guilt and shame at feeling angry at his parents lead to the aggression being turned in towards himself. This guilt, together with the suppressed aggression, 'accounts in the adult for the frequent periods of depression and contributes to the pervasive sense of inferiority and low self-esteem'. Thus abusing parents suffer from childhood a smouldering sense of unhappy aggression, of guilt combined with a sense of uselessness, and a conviction that they will fail when demands are made on them.

Unfortunately few periods of our lives are more demanding than those years when we have the care of small children.

Children make incessant demands; as babies they are totally selfish, and must be so. Satisfaction of his immediate needs is all that matters to a small baby: his will to live is immense and necessary. Small wonder that an insecure mother, frightened at the responsibility thrust upon her, looks at this red-faced squalling infant from whom in pregnancy she had fantasized nothing but coos and loving smiles, and feels shocked, ashamed, even horrified.

It doesn't matter that last week the baby slept well and smiled and she loved it. This week it bawls night and day and scowls unpleasantly at her. A potential battering mother says to herself, 'I'm his mother, but I don't know what he wants, he's telling me I'm no good. I'm a lousy mother, I knew I would be. It's all his fault, if only he loved me I'd feel different. He's a hateful little bastard.' If enough other things are wrong in her life the scene is set for tragedy. The moods of unstable parents can switch so rapidly - a baby being jiggled on a father's knee may beam with pleasure and the man is delighted. He jigs harder and faster, much too fast for the infant's age, the baby becomes frightened and screams and the father's temper flares disastrously. He flings the baby from him as a child might fling away a stuffed toy which suddenly displeases him. It has happened without reflection, apparently the result of a moment's flash of anger. But the moment has been prepared for all that father's life.

Whether or not we agree that aggression is an inevitable part of the human psyche we can see how remorselessly it is developed in many children from the first moments of life. By the time such a child is three or four he has learned that the world is totally unpredictable, that punishment is given for no apparent cause, that to make open demands for love is to invite a rebuff, or worse; that authority is condemning and harsh and unjust; that try as you may you can never be sure of pleasing. You deduce that you are not lovable, that you are an inadequate, useless sort of person, unlikely to succeed in a harsh world apparently full of confident, happy people.

Deeply suppressed anger at his fate, a desire to punish as he has been punished, will lurk beneath the appeasing exterior of the developing child. Grown up, these wounded children await the birth of their frequently unplanned first child with a mixture of feelings: underlying the hope that they will at last have the loving family they have always longed for and the intense desire to prove better parents than their own ever were, is the fear they will fail. When the child is born they cannot help to a certain degree reiterating the patterns impressed on them from their early childhood. They expect too much too soon from their babies, both in physical and emotional development, and when severe disappointment mingles with conflicting desires and memories, there is likely to be an explosion. Unfortunately, having learned in the past not to ask for help, they do not ask for it now. Battering parents are notoriously slow in approaching their doctors or social services for aid. Alone, isolated (they usually have difficulty in making friends), they hide their problems even from those attempting to help them, partly out of need to impress authority with their competence, partly out of a sense of hopelessness. Knowing little of other children, they imagine their child's performance to be abnormally slow. Tragically, by their own harsh, unloving behaviour, they often bring about the very retardation that has previously only been imagined.

To sum up, most battering parents are inadequate, self-defeating, introverted, immature people who need love but find difficulty in giving it; who want gratification for their impulses *now*, not next week; who often love their children and show great concern for them but whose love is inconsistent and incapable of standing up to the stresses life can inflict; who in a few extreme cases hate their children or are totally incapable of ever rearing a child satisfactorily and from whom the children must be taken. Frequently clinically neurotic or depressed, they usually have a poor sense of identity and very little self-esteem, and live isolated lives (particularly the mothers). Although they yearn to behave differently they cannot help inflicting on their children their own style of upbringing. Finally, frustrated in their lifelong desire to be loved and cherished, they nurse bitter anger along with their guilt, hidden from authority whom they still (how well the lesson has been learned) attempt to appease.

We now have some idea of the kind of personality many

battering parents have. What about the children? Is there a particular kind of child who is more likely to be battered than his siblings? Recent research has made considerable advance in this field and it is quite clear that the child itself is the trigger in many instances. From the moment of conception many battered babies are unwanted, over one third of them, according to American and British investigations, being illegitimate. Smith's study group found that the rate of pre-marital pregnancy and illegitimacy among their twenty- to twenty-four-year-old battering mothers was between two and three times higher than that in the general population, a striking difference. Battering parents legitimized their children far less frequently than the controls: whereas over twice as many battered children (71 per cent) were conceived out of wedlock as were control children (33 per cent), six times as many ended up illegitimate (36 per cent as compared with 6 per cent of the controls).

Illegitimacy has always been an important cause of infanticide, as far back as history has been recorded, and today's changed attitudes and improved social welfare do not seem to have made that much difference. P. J. Resnick (1969) found that problems arising from the birth of an illegitimate child were the most common cause of child murder. Another American study found that illegitimacy was present in 60 per cent of the fatal battering cases studied (Weston, Appendix B, Table 1, p. 228 in Helfer and Kempe, 1968). Battering mothers commonly find pregnancy more distressing and a greater cause of anxiety than do their non-battering sisters. You would expect, then, women whose attitude towards pregnancy is ambivalent to say the least to take steps to control their fertility, but far from it. As a group they take less interest in contraception than other women do, and social workers often find it very difficult to persuade them to adopt effective contraception, even when they express extreme distaste at the idea of another pregnancy.

In addition to not wanting the child in the first place some of these mothers have also had to face the fact that all is not well with their unborn children, or that for one reason or another their pregnancy will not be able to run its full term. What effect an unhappy, unplanned pregnancy has on the physical health of the growing foetus has yet to be proved, but it is unlikely to be beneficial. Arnold Sameroff and his colleagues at Rochester University, USA, have already found a relationship between psychiatric problems suffered by a mother during her pregnancy and complications during delivery. Over a quarter of the battered children appearing on the NSPCC London and Manchester register were below the normal birth weight of 2,500 grams, four times the national figure, while 13.6 per cent of these were below 2,000 grams, which is seven times the national figure. Some of these were premature babies, others were born at full term.

These figures are typical of international research, and some researchers find them highly significant. Others point out that when all the disadvantages these mothers commonly suffer from are taken into consideration (low social class, with poor housing, medical care and money worries, plus youth and possibly the anxieties of pre-marital conception) a high frequency of low birth weights is to be expected. It is perfectly true that most parents of underweight or premature babies do not batter their children, so that in itself low birth weight may not be of great significance, but when it is associated with other problems the child should be considered at risk.

Battering parents not only have an abnormally high number of underweight babies, but they are likely to find childbirth exceptionally difficult. Out of the 27 children studied by the Battered Child Research Team only 14 had been delivered normally. Four were induced and 7 had abnormal deliveries (breech births, forceps and caesarian sections). Many of the mothers had been extremely anxious during pregnancy and half of them recalled the birth itself as a very painful, frightening experience. Three of these children were of low birth weight, and 8 had neo-natal problems, 7 of whom had to be separated from their mother for periods of from one day to a month. Many other studies show the same sort of pattern: conception out of wedlock; anxious, distressed pregnancies followed by a high proportion of abnormal births; and babies with something medically wrong necessitating a temporary separation from the mother. Thus, in many cases even before the baby has left hospital its chances of a happy infancy have already been frighteningly decreased.

Much work, which I shall look at more closely in Chapter 7, has been done on early mother-child relationships, such as that by Drs Marshall Klaus and John Kennell (Cleveland, Ohio) who have been investigating the differences between children separated immediately from their parents after birth and normal controls. Briefly, they found that mothers who were given their naked babies to hold and explore immediately after birth for a period of an hour and who were also allowed to hold them for considerable periods during the following few days, formed closer relationships with their children than those mothers subjected to the normal separation inherent in most hospital systems, concerned as they are with hygiene and order. After a month the first group of mothers were observed to spend three times as long cuddling and fondling their babies as the controls, and they held them closer when feeding, looking at them face to face, while the second group of mothers held their babies at a greater distance, rarely looking at them face to face. Even after a year differences in smiling and contact behaviour were still noticeable, and, most important to a study of battered babies, the first group were more than three times as likely to comfort their babies when they were crying. The face-to-face contact between the first group continued, while this was much less noticeable in the separated mothers.

We all know how much more personally involved we feel when we look someone straight in the eye, and this must be particularly important in the contact between mothers and babies who cannot yet use words to express themselves. When, therefore, premature and low-birth-weight babies are separated from their mothers, sometimes for many weeks, we must expect that the growth of close communication will be impaired. Many mothers of such babies complain they cannot feel their children as being their own, that they seem to belong to the hospital or the nursing sister. It takes great persistence and will-power on the part of the mothers to overcome this vital break in nature's pattern, and unfortunately these are two attributes in which battering mothers are noticeably deficient. Easily thrown, they are quick to sense their babies' rejection, and without the right kind of professional help (rarely at present available in premature units) it is only too likely that a successful imprinting or bonding will never be achieved. It is not enough to jolly the mother along; an expert knowledge of how this bonding takes place and of how to overcome early separation problems is necessary. It can be done, but more research is still needed. The goodwill of the nurses is of the greatest importance: it is much easier for a busy staff to run a premature unit without the continuous presence of germ-carrying, nervous, depressed mothers who cannot help but be upset by the sight of strange-looking infants shut away inside glass cages more reminiscent of a science fiction film than a normal nursery.

A further problem to battering parents is the effect their babies' crying has on them. Time after time mothers report they are being driven frantic by their babies' yells and screams, but the usual social worker or health visitor's response is only too often, 'Oh, he'll grow out of it' or 'All babies cry, they need to develop their lungs', or some other such well-intentioned remark. If in despair the mother goes to her doctor, she will probably be given a sedative for him. I was appalled at the number of battering mothers who told me their children had been given bedtime spoonfuls of sleeping drugs for years on end, frequently escalating to double or even triple doses as they became habituated to them. It is still an uncommon doctor who accepts that a mother coming frequently to him about this problem is in great need of individual help, and that an automatic handout of drugs is no answer.

A certain amount of research has been done on the crying itself. We know already that babies with particular diseases have distinctive cries that can be recognized. Spectrographs - wave patterns drawn on a rolling paper drum - reveal Mongolism, brain damage and other problems. As we have seen, many battered children are born with some congenital illness, and it is quite possible that the actual timbre of their cries upsets the mothers. Some types of brain damage, for example, cause babies to have a particularly high-pitched cry of abnormal pattern, and it is very likely that at some instinctive level the mother knows that all is not well, so that extra stress is added to that already inflicted by the continuous crying of the child. This research is being continued and it could well be that in the future spectrographs will be made automatically of every newborn baby's cry, revealing not only those with some physical malfunctioning but those whose cries contain an element known to be especially irritating or exasperating to some parents. It seems that it is not only physical ailments that can be picked up by this method - Dr Barry Lester (1976) has found that neglected children have a different pattern of crying from normal children. The neglected children's cries were quieter, higher-pitched and more monotonous than those of the control group.

Whether or not some battered babies actually cry more than other babies is at present a matter of conjecture. Certainly the mothers think they do. Persistent crying, particularly at night, is one of the first things they usually complain about. Dr Martin Richards, who has been studying small children with sleeping problems, has found that their mothers had been in labour longer than normal, and though the babies had been slower to begin breathing and crying immediately after birth, once started they cried more, wanted feeding more and slept less. One or two researchers have suggested that abused babies cry less than normal ones, but perhaps by the time a baby has been battered a few times and comes under a researcher's eye it has learned it is wiser to keep quiet. Smith found his sample to be lethargic rather than hyperactive, but he also found that their mothers had a lower tolerance of their crying than normal mothers. Klaus and Kennel reported that the mothers who picked up their babies more and made more fuss of them (remember these were the mothers who had not suffered early separation) had fewer crying problems at the end of the first year, while the mothers who let the babies cry on 'for their own good' ended up with babies who continued to cry. Battering parents, mostly brought up strictly themselves, usually fall naturally into the last group, even without the reinforcement of early separation from their babies. If, as is likely, they live in restricted housing which does not allow them to move out of earshot (apart from walking out altogether on the child, which few mothers can bring themselves to do) they have no choice but to endure the noise until they can stand it no longer.

To sum up, the situations where children are potentially at risk, even without any direct consideration of the psychology of the parents, are where the child is illegitimate or where a marriage has been made because of an unplanned pregnancy; where the baby is premature or of low birth weight; where the pregnancy has been difficult and/or the birth abnormal; where the child has to be separated from its mother after birth, with the associated lack of bonding between them; where a parent is made distraught by its child's crying and where illness or wakefulness continuously disturbs the parent's sleep. At least a quarter of all battered babies have suffered a combination of these circumstances, and probably all at least one of them. Health visitors paying their initial visits to such families ought to take particular care to observe the family relationships and to sense the atmosphere. They may not have much time; half the children who are battered by their own parents are under a year old, and many are injured within a few weeks of their birth.

For obvious reasons there is less research into the personalities of the infants themselves than there is into those of their parents. Nevertheless some factual details about them have emerged, not all of which are universally agreed. The sex of the child appears to make little difference: a few studies have shown a very slight preponderance of boy children being battered but the difference is so small as to be of no significance. Handicapped children are more at risk than normal children, though different studies show varying percentages. Smith and Hanson write (1974b)

7.46 per cent (of 134 children) had serious congenital defects as compared with 1.75 per cent of the general population. There were two cases each of spina bifida, hydrocephalus, and encephalocele and one each of Hirschsprung's disease, coeliac disease, congenital spherocytosis, and congenital dislocation of the hip. A further eight children had minor congenital abnormalities.

Out of the Battered Child Research Department's group of 25 children none had major congenital anomalies, but six had minor physical defects. A further child suffered from convulsions. Other studies vary from one or two which report no congenital defects of a seriousness sufficient to cause

147

mothering problems to those which agree with Smith's results.

Obviously, handicapped children throw great strain on mothers; since it is common for mothers of such children to feel - however irrationally - in some way responsible for their children's defects, potential battering mothers who already have more than their share of guilt may not be able to bear this extra burden. They may also feel shame that they have produced a flawed child, and that they were not 'good enough' to manage a perfect child. Clearly they will need all the help they can get if they are to rear the child successfully.

The younger the child, the more likely it is to be attacked. The Leeds and Manchester NSPCC report showed the median age of battered children on their register was eighteen months (they had asked to be informed of abused children up to four years of age only). The younger infant was also likely to suffer more serious injury: the median for seriously hurt babies was only fourteen months, while that for moderately injured children was twenty months. Other studies show very similar results. Of course, older children are also battered - Maria Colwell, for example, was seven - but since the abuse of older children is often complicated by factors other than those applying to younger children, the usual line drawn at four years of age does seem to be valid, for research purposes at least.

Many people find it very difficult to imagine how a mother or father can attack such tiny children, but it must be remembered that such parents often do not see their babies as they actually are. They are cocooned from the real world by their chaotic emotions and even their own baby is sometimes outside their immediately-felt experience. It is their *own* internal crying that pierces their centre, not the crying of the child. When, in a rage, they pick up the baby, they are picking up not a defenceless infant but an accusing, malevolent being, the epitome of all that has made them miserable in their life. When, later, a full consciousness of the child's reality returns to them, they are usually appalled at what they have done.

> 'I can't understand how I did it! I love her! I look after her and watch over her, and I won't let anyone else touch her. But then sometimes, when she goes on so, it's as though she's

not a baby any more, but something evil, something deliberately taunting me. Then I could do anything to her, I know I could. The first time I hit her it was only a small blow and I cried all the rest of the day. I swore to myself I'd never lift a finger to her again. But it was only a few days after when she drove me mad with crying and I hit her harder that time. It sort of escalated, I hit a bit harder each time. But every time afterwards I could have killed myself I was so ashamed of what I'd done. I couldn't tell anyone, I couldn't tell my husband, he'd have got so mad. No one could have understood, it's not the kind of thing you can make someone understand, that you could almost kill your own baby, especially not when it's a pretty little thing like her.'

This mother fractured her child's skull but luckily no permanent physical damage was done. The baby was eventually returned to her; with continuous supervision by a friendly health visitor the outcome promises to be successful. But not every case can have a happy ending: tiny babies are frighteningly vulnerable, and even a bad shaking can permanently damage them.

Researchers have repeatedly found that the parent's perception of the child is often very different from actuality, even outside times of acute stress. Gregg and Elmer (1969), comparing two groups of children, one battered, one normal, found there was no significant difference between their mood and activity levels, but that the battered children were, if anything, easier to look after. This was in direct contrast to their mothers' perception of them. Smith and Hanson found the same with their groups: 30 per cent of battering mothers compared with 9 per cent of control mothers thought their children difficult; 27 per cent of battering mothers compared with 8 per cent of controls found the other children in their families difficult; 29 per cent of mothers of battered children as against 8 per cent of control mothers found crying, whining or clinging behaviour to be a severe problem. Yet the researchers found that in fact the battered children were less wakeful at night, less excitable and less tired during the day than the controls. There was no difference between bedtimes and rising or between their appetites, and in general they were no harder to manage than the controls. We have seen that battering parents are likely to be strict and to disapprove of picking babies up and comforting them in case they become 'spoiled'. Since it seems clear from modern research that cuddling and comforting reduces rather than increases crying in the long term it may well be that in their homes these parents induce, or at least do nothing to prevent, the very behaviour that irritates them. In hospital a child will not be left to cry continuously so that nurses or researchers are likely to see quite different behaviour from that which the mother unnecessarily forces herself to endure.

> 'He was an incredibly difficult baby from the beginning. He just cried and cried all the time and we practically had to force feed him. You could do nothing with him, you really couldn't and it made me feel so helpless. I did everything by the book for him and stuck to a routine so if he woke early, I didn't feed him. When he wouldn't take his food I used to take the teat off his bottle and pour the milk down him and occasionally I hit him with the bottle. My husband would say, "you are silly, because you're only making more mess for yourself", but at least it relieved my feelings.' (Quoted in NSPCC Battered Child Research Team, 1975)

The same team report that those mothers who saw their children as quite different to what they were in actuality also had unreasonably high expectations of them, attributing almost adult feelings to them:

> In one case in which the mother states she thought it was time for her child to mix with other children as he needed preparing for school, the worker had to remind herself that the child in question was less than a year old!

Since these children in hospital are usually no more difficult or irritable than other children in similar circumstances, it seems likely that interaction between children and parents is causing the main difficulty, rather than an inborn 'cussedness' on the part of the children. Of course, a major difficulty in considering what effect the children may have on the parent is that mostly the child is only investigated after it has either been actually battered or at least is considered dangerously 'at risk'. By then it will have been emotionally damaged to some extent, and will already have learned not to expect much comforting reaction from its mother.

Tests specially designed to show how children feel towards various members of their family have demonstrated that the control group of normal children (picked to be as close in class, age, etc. as possible to the battered children) had twice the involvement with the mother figure as had the battered children. Games, using cardboard cut-outs representing mother, father, siblings and so on, were used so that direct questioning could be avoided. Often the battered children would opt out of choosing a 'mother' card when a situation arose where a mother figure should have been chosen. Conversely, they showed greater involvement with their fathers than did the control children. Thus battering mothers, who typically long for the love and warmth they were denied in their own childhood, appear to produce, by their own impaired mothering, babies who are cool towards them and whose response to them as mothers is not normal. At the same time many reports have shown that they see their children as clinging and over-dependent. Clearly the picture is an involved one, fraught with tension for all concerned and can, alas, only result in a new generation of emotionally damaged children. Genetically these children in their turn are likely to reproduce some of their own personality traits in their own offspring, and this factor, together with the social problems their upbringing is likely to have inflicted on them, will almost certainly ensure the continuance of the unhappy cycle of child-parent difficulties.

The NSPCC found in their nursery that at first many of these children had no idea how to play on their own and made no attempt to explore or try things out for themselves. Many violently resisted any attempts to structure the day, by such means as refusing to stay on their beds at rest time and disrupting meals. All were disturbed in some way and were below average in their own development. Some were withdrawn and possessive, while others were highly active and sometimes destructive, grabbing things for themselves and refusing to share. With time this behaviour became modified, though the aggressive children needed a great deal of individual attention which could not always be given them.

Often children who have been battered are attractive to look at, their wistful pallor arousing protectiveness in those appointed to look after them. Researchers have commented on their 'frozen watchfulness' or 'expression of wariness' (NSPCC Battered Child Research Unit, 1975). But others are less attractive; they are physically unappealing, aggressive and constantly seeking attention, or drearily apathetic, unresponsive and depressed. Interestingly enough, few of any type show obvious fear towards their parents and often seem delighted to see them when they are visited in hospitals or nurseries, though this may be more a childish pleasure in seeing a familiar face than pure delight at the prospect of the parent's company.

Some researchers have found evidence that battered children learn early to respond to their parents' needs by comforting them or by being very careful to observe and respond to their parents' moods. These results have mostly come from American researches, such as Davoren (in Helfer and Kempe, 1968) and Martin (in Kempe and Helfer, 1972). On the other hand, Smith and Hanson found that the group they were working with were no more likely to be socially precocious in this way than were the control children, and in general the NSPCC studies agree with this. Obviously as a child grows older he will learn to avoid to some extent the worst of his parent's wrath, but whether or not it is general for very young battered children of under two or three years to give their parents the comfort and support that they themselves ought to be receiving has not yet been proved.

Certainly they are not precocious in their intellectual development. Most researchers have found that language development, for instance, is seriously retarded. Abused children mostly start speaking late, tend to use baby talk and speak with poor enunciation well after their speech ought to be clear and well-articulated. This is no doubt partly due to insufficient stimulation by the parents - they are often kept too long in their cots or watched over too anxiously so that they do not have sufficient opportunity to explore their surroundings like normal children. Many potential battering mothers are terrified their children may come to harm and are over-protective, a fact that can seem self-contradictory to a layman. Restricted by exaggerated care, with none of the self-confidence consistent mothering ought to have given him, the child's development is slow. This in itself is likely to irritate an ambitious parent who has no idea that he or she is the main cause. Once a parent has come to the attention of the authorities for battering, of course, the situation is even worse. 'I daren't lay a finger on him now', a mother told me, 'so he's got completely out of hand. And I daren't let him play outside in case he falls over and gets a bruise. I'm scared of the stairs, he's got no sense and he could easily fall down them, then who'd get the blame! So if I can't be with him I put his harness on and strap him in his cot. He's too big for it, I know he is, but what can I do? They're watching me the whole time, and if anything goes wrong they'll snatch him away from me. And I couldn't bear that.'

Added to this retardation caused mainly by the parent is the sad fact that a child's head is a common target for attack. Babies are usually well-shielded by nappies and woollies, and the head may be the only uncovered portion of the body. Smith and Hanson found that 15 per cent of the children they were studying suffered from permanent neurological damage, resulting in spasticity, paraplegia and blindness, amongst other problems. Children who had suffered only slight head injuries still showed some defects of response. Even the 38 per cent who had suffered no known head injuries or neurological damage had an overall ability significantly lower than that of the controls; this could have been due to previous head injuries about which nothing was known or, possibly, to their genetic endowment.

The NSPCC's study came up with more hopeful results, indicating that - where there is no permanent neurological damage - with the right treatment the children's IQ can be brought up to the normal range. At reception the IQ of the centre's 25 children ranged from 50 to 125 with a mean of 80, well below the statistical norm. The younger the child the more poorly it scored. Two years after this testing only 14 of these children were available for further assessment, but to the pleasure of the staff there was a great improvement, the mean now being 100.4, the IQs ranging from 81 to 121. Of particular interest was the fact that the more disturbed of the children had been kept in the special therapeutic nursery while the less disturbed had been put into local authority nurseries - the numbers were 7 in each case. Nevertheless the therapeutic nursery children now had a mean IQ of 106 while those in local authority nurseries had a mean IQ of 93.7, proving how effective specialized care can be.

It seems probable from these and other researches that most battered children are born with IQs normal to their social status, but that environmental damage (including abusive parents) retards them to a considerable extent, thereby adding to the disappointment of those parents. Many studies have shown how a good 'enriched' background can improve the IQ of retarded children in general, so that the outlook for battered children lucky enough to have the right kind of help is very hopeful, at least as far as their scholastic achievement is concerned. Unfortunately the same cannot yet be said for their emotional development, and clearly much work needs to be done on this, for once a child is removed from his supportive nursery and flung into the comparatively ruthless competition of ordinary school life he may well fall behind again unless his parents have undergone considerable personality changes.

I referred in the previous paragraph to environmental damage. Research at the John F. Kennedy Child Development Center and the University of Colorado finds that

> abuse of a child usually occurs in association with some other malevolent environmental condition. Experience suggests that it is not infrequent to find one of the following conditions in the abusive home: 1. Nutritional neglect to the point of malnutrition 2. Maternal or parental deprivation and/or neglect, both physical and emotional 3. Sexual abuse 4. Severe psychiatric disturbance in one or both parents 5. Social and/or economic disadvantage.

Ray Castle, head of the NSPCC Battered Child Research Department, finds that real neglect and child abuse do not often go hand in hand, but Smith and Hanson found that a significant proportion of their cases were physically neglected and had previously been in hospital because of 'failure to thrive'.

'Failure to thrive' - a condition frequently found in battered babies - is a medical term meaning that an infant does not come up to the standard of mental or physical development expected of a child of that age. It has been established that poor feeding and deprivation of good mothering can impair a child's growth both mentally and physically, and since many battered children also have low birth weights it can be seen that their lives are badly disadvantaged from the very beginning. Of Smith's sample of battered children 16 per cent compared with only 2 per cent of control children had been physically neglected, while 17 per cent as against 2 per cent had previously been admitted to hospital with failure to thrive. Half the failure-to-thrive children had been neglected. Even so, we must remember that these figures, important as they are, mean that the great majority of battered children had been at least adequately looked after, and some - if their parents followed the pattern of other studies - no doubt had excessive, even obsessive, care taken of them.

We have, then, a clearer picture than we used to of the battered child. It is not more likely to be of one sex than the other; the younger the child the more danger it is in; handicapped children, 'failure-to-thrive' babies and excessive criers are particularly at risk; the IQ of battered children is basically no different to that of their own social group in general but they are usually retarded because of environmental conditions including poor mothering; for the same reason they are likely to be dependent and clinging with no idea how to amuse themselves, thereby causing increasing stress to their parents; they tend to be either reserved and apathetic or aggressive and difficult; and, finally, the parents themselves often do not see the child as it really is, being exasperated by certain behaviour patterns which appear quite innocuous to outside observers.

Before we take a final look at what is known about battering parents it would be illuminating to see what kind of injuries they inflict on their children. In *Children in Danger* I wrote of the vast numbers of parents whose mild abuse of their children never comes to public notice. What do we mean by mild abuse? To one parent it will be a sound hiding with a leather strap, while to another it will be any kind of physical punishment, even the lightest slap. To yet another, regular beatings will be thought positively good for any child - what this type of parent would consider mild abuse will constitute a severe attack to another. I don't intend to write again of the process by which strains and stresses are built up, or how mothers often take their children with a variety of ingenious excuses to GPs, clinics and hospital emergency departments with the hope that their increasingly desperate cries for help will be picked up before severe damage is done. This section will describe only the injuries serious enough to have come to the notice of the authorities, but while reading it, it should be borne in mind that these cases are the middle and far end of the spectrum: at the other end are millions of parents who recognize much of what I have been writing about but who have been able to keep themselves under control, and whose lives have fortunately not exposed them to the worst stresses. They need not think they are alone in their guilty memories of times when they felt like lashing out. As I wrote earlier, I have hardly ever met a parent who did not admit that on at least one occasion he or she has felt him or herself close to breaking point. Most of us are, in fact, well able to cope with these testing moments, but let us keep them in mind when we read about what less fortunate parents can do to their children. Of course, there are those parents who inflict injuries of a kind as remote from our understanding as the kidnapper who murders for spite, but these are psychopaths beyond the reach of ordinary aid. The mother who in sudden desperation flings her child down is not so far from us. Whether or not the incident ends fatally often depends on pure chance - one child will suffer no damage at all, another will fracture its skull. But if such incidents continue eventually a fatal injury could well occur. The aim of every worker in the field must therefore be to step in before luck runs out.

Early injuries are often fairly straightforward, such as facial bruises, burns or abrasions, or there may be injuries to the mouth caused by a bottle being thrust angrily into it, for example, or bodily bruising caused by severe shaking or manhandling. Ocular damage, such as retinal detachment or internal bleeding, often results from these shakings; in the past this was not recognized as a symptom, but now the possibility of battering should always be considered where such a disorder is present. Damage to the head area is the most common injury: whether this is because the head is the most unprotected part of the body, or whether it is chosen because the injury might be seen by a doctor or a nurse who will intervene, a possibility which many battering parents hope for but cannot bring themselves to deliberately seek, remains an open question.

Selwyn Smith's group of 134 battered children (Smith and Hanson, 1974b) had been chosen from hospital admissions. Their injuries tended to be more severe than many of those at the NSPCC centres where children are mostly brought for protection and therapy at an earlier stage than those of Smith's group. If we take a close look at both groups we shall have a fair idea of the spread of injuries to battered babies in general, always bearing in mind those unknown thousands who are never seen by anyone at all. Smith and Hanson write (1974b)

110 [of the 134 children] had bruises, most often on the head (75 cases) and thighs (45). 23 had burns or scalds; in 9 the buttocks and in 6 the lower limbs were affected, and injuries were most commonly caused by hot liquids or a metal stove. Cigarette burns occurred in 2 cases. Children with burns or scalds were older (mean age 24.8 months) than the remainder of the sample.

They go on to report that 42 children had suffered a total of 136 recent or old fractures, the most common site being the skull (37 cases). Over a third of the children had intracranial bleeding, but 15 of these had no skull fractures and 7 did not even show any bruising to the head; these were children who had been shaken violently, suffering whiplash injury which resulted in damage to the eyes in 8 of these cases. In all, 21 children died of their injuries, 20 had serious injuries resulting in permanent damage, 62 had serious injuries but no apparent permanent damage and 31 had superficial injuries.

The NSPCC's Leeds and Manchester Report (NSPCC, 1975) shows that 23 per cent of the children presented to them who were under one year old had received skull fractures, but only 8 per cent of older children had; similarly 30 per cent of those under a year old had fractured long bones and ribs as against only 8 per cent of the older ones. But soft tissue injuries (burns, lacerations and bruising) were more common among the 12-47-month-old children - 45 per cent as against 37 per cent of those under a year old. This decrease in the seriousness of the injury as the babies grow older could be because they become less troublesome as they mature, or it could be due to the fact that the same amount of force will cause a far more severe injury to the more vulnerable younger child. Only 1 of the 124 children in this group died, while 48 suffered serious injuries and 75 moderate injuries.

Most battered children suffer a number of attacks before they are diagnosed. This is a highly distressing thought, and it seems incredible that this situation still continues today after so much publicity. Even diagnosis does not necessarily bring relief. Skinner and Castle (1969) found that 60 per cent of the children in their study were re-battered after being returned to their homes. This figure does seem to be decreasing, particularly in areas where the authorities are active in taking preventative measures. The Leeds and Manchester Report suggests that not only does re-battering after diagnosis diminish, but more and more children are being brought to the special units with a first injury. However, in the majority of areas such specialized care is not yet available. Of those 25 children looked after by the Battered Child Research Department 8 had known histories of previous injury. Five of these 8 had been injured more than once and one had suffered seven previous incidents of abuse. Remember, these were injuries picked up by the authorities - there were almost certainly other attacks which did not come to official notice. Smith and Hanson found that most of their children under two years of age had been previously battered, and their findings confirm many reports showing that battered children usually have a multiplicity of injuries in various stages of healing.

Unfortunately these earlier injuries are rarely picked up even by hospital emergency departments when a child is presented with a fresh injury: doctors are still inclined not to be suspicious of patients, and are likely to take a distressed parent's story at its face value. X-rays of battered children often reveal healing and healed fractures which are invisible on the surface. In my opinion such investigation ought to be automatic when any small child is injured except in the most obviously innocent cases.

Smith found definite evidence that one third of the dead children in his sample had been battered previously. Most fatal injuries had resulted from the effects of a single act, and the death was not due to illness caused by an accumulation of attacks. This bears out the theory that death is usually a matter of chance - many researchers now believe that the violence does not usually increase in severity. However, I personally think it likely that in most cases there will be a preliminary period of minor shakings and flingings into mattresses before the parent escalates into more dangerous attacks. After that the severity of the injury will probably depend very much on chance - whether for instance the attack takes place near the stairs or a dangerous sharp-cornered table or on the comparative safety of the parents' double bed.

It has often been thought that one particular child only is scapegoated, but most research has shown this rarely to be true, from Kempe's early work to Smith and Hanson's recent study. The latter found that of those who died, one third had a sibling who was known to have also been maltreated, and in 9 per cent of these cases the sibling had died, some under suspicious circumstances. In all, 10 of the 134 battered children had a deceased sibling and in two cases more than one sibling had died. None of the controls had a deceased sibling.

Occasionally a child is scapegoated, but often in these cases it appears on investigation that other children in the family have had their share of 'accidents' in the past, and it may be that some parents are more irritated by young children than older ones. Other mothers inexplicably attack a small and placid baby which irritates them while they are changing or feeding it, when their real aggression is felt towards an older toddler. I have had several mothers tell me this has happened to them, and it seemed to me that one of the reasons was that they were very aware of their angry feelings towards the difficult older child and took care to control themselves, but their defences were down with the 'easy' baby, so that when the older infant unexpectedly annoyed the mother her bottled-up aggression burst out onto the baby before she could stop herself.

At Park Hospital, Oxford, researchers have been investigating possible reasons why one child rather than another should receive the bulk of the aggressive acts (Lynch, Steinberg and Ounstead, 1975). Their results are particularly interesting as they confirm many of the research results mentioned earlier. By examining whole families they discovered that 60 per cent of the mothers of the abused children had had abnormal pregnancies in one way or another, as against 20 per cent of the pregnancies of the siblings. There was also a much higher abnormal delivery rate as against that of the siblings. Forty per cent of the battered children had been separated from their mothers and put into special care units as against 15 per cent of their siblings (a lower rate than the normal average). Illness appears exceptionally often in the abused children in the first year (15 out of 25 children), while the siblings were healthier than normal. This exceptional health of the siblings could have been an important factor in preventing attacks from their parents. During the battered children's first year of life at least 3 mothers tried to kill themselves and 12 out of 25 had some illness. During the siblings' first year, however, the mothers were usually very fit (only 2 out of 25 having any illness). Thus, in 21 cases out of 25 battered children either the mother or the child was ill during its first year, and in 6 instances both were ill together. Only 5 of the siblings were at all ill during their first year and never at the same time as their mothers.

The truth is we now have enough data for our caring agencies to pick out many families where a potentially dangerous situation exists, even without complicated psychological evaluation of the parents, and it is time something was done about it. Every family in the land is supposed to be visited by a health visitor when a child is born: any family where one or more of these factors are known to be present ought to be revisited and befriended. A strained mother may communicate a little of her stress over a friendly cup of tea offered during a second visit, but one short, briskly efficient call is unlikely to be of the slightest use in families of the kind we have been talking about.

The last section of this chapter will deal with general facts about battering parents. As more research is undertaken a clearer picture emerges of the typical battering parent, but it must always be remembered there will be many who hardly fit this picture at all, just as few of us conform absolutely to whatever computerized sketch the national department of statistics will have drawn of the average man or woman.

One of the questions frequently asked is, from what social strata do battering parents come? Most research shows it to occur mainly among the lower income groups, though the NSPCC (Leeds and Manchester Report) write, 'Some doctors or social workers may feel that a child of middle class parents may be adequately protected, and the mother's problems "suitably" treated by referral to private psychiatric treatment, rather than involvement with the statutory authorities.' This seems to me to be the main clue as to why various researches both in England and America contradict each other. Battering parents have a particular need to placate authority, and in any case middle- and upper-class families certainly would not relish being visited by local authority workers or NSPCC inspectors. When necessary they can, and do, employ private help - nannies, boarding schools, psychiatrists, holidays away, etc. They are not shut up in one or two rooms, and their financial problems are on a different scale to the deserted woman living on Social Security because her husband is in jail or has left her. From all the evidence I can gather it seems unquestionable that battering occurs in all classes, but more severe physical battering of the kind that comes to public notice happens among the under-privileged mostly because they have no outlets, suffer greatest pressure, and when they do see their GP they are likely to be given a couple of minutes of his time instead of the more leisurely discussion a middle-class woman will expect of her own physician. Emotional battering is another matter, and many workers I have spoken to feel that this is the main weapon of the economically privileged.

American workers have stressed the great strain that

sub-standard housing throws on many families. But Smith points out that while it is true 45 per cent of his battering families (as against 15 per cent controls) had homes lacking in one or more essential amenities such as baths, *96 per cent* of a local sample of 'inadequate' families - who had not battered their children - lived in similar accommodation. It seems clear that housing problems of one kind or another are suffered by a majority of battering parents, but these may be no worse than the problems endured by many others in similar social groups.

One of the reasons for their having to put up with poor accommodation is that the income of battering fathers is in general lower than that of the population at large, but when their age and the kind of work they do is taken into account there is no significant difference. Even so, this means they are mostly among the badly-off section of society. It can easily be imagined how difficult it must be in today's financial climate for anyone to cope successfully with growing children in inadequate, cramped accommodation when money is short, particularly if the parents are young and inexperienced.

It has often been noted that battering parents generally marry young and have children at an earlier age than most people. Many, like Sally at the beginning of this chapter, have hardly learned to cope with late adolescence when they are plunged into parenthood. Selwyn Smith's group of mothers had a mean age of 19.7 at the birth of their first child, as against the then national average of 23.3. If the low social class of most of these mothers is allowed for, this last figure still only falls to 22.6 years. The Leeds and Manchester Report shows that the average age of the mothers in their sample (with at least one child under four) was 23 years 8 months, while the national median age of mothers with a child under five is 28 years. The average age of the fathers or male caretakers in the sample was 27 years 9 months - the figure for the national median is not available. These figures are borne out by most other researchers in the field.

Although money is a problem for so many battering mothers, few of them have full-time employment. It is true that the latest census figures show that wives of unskilled workers, into which group a great number of these mothers fall, are the second least likely group to go out to work. Even so, these mothers mostly find their children less satisfying and more irritating than do other mothers, often stating a wish they could 'get out of the house and away from the kids'. So why don't they?

A psychiatrist suggested to me that it was because they are too involved with their children, and they do not have the confidence to let them go. 'They have to control every movement of their kids, and they daren't loosen up for a moment. Partly it's that they need to feel essential to someone, and partly it's a distrust of the outside world. They don't believe anyone else can look after their kids as well as they do.' Under the circumstances this may sound paradoxical, but it is certainly true of many such mothers. Perhaps because the ability to 'mother' does not come easily to them they sometimes overdo it, and are unable to relax in the way a confident mother is able to. The same psychiatrist thought that excessive protection of a child was the other face of battering, and there is no doubt it can easily lead to emotional damage. Dr Mia Pringle's recent suggestion that mothers at home should be paid a salary by the state and by their husbands - not only to stop mothers from leaving young children for financial reasons but also to improve their self-image - may have a value for some, but for most very young families a well-organized break of even a couple of hours a day would bring great benefit to everyone.

The battering parent's apparent concern for his child may to a certain extent be illusory, expressing more the desire of the mother or father to be seen to be a good parent than a genuine concern for the child itself.

In over half the cases [of hospitalized children] workers remarked on the parents' apparent lack of affection for the child, lack of concern for the child's suffering if there were injuries, and inability to sympathise with what the child must be feeling on finding himself in strange, new surroundings. Ironically, some parents were noted to be more interested in and empathetic towards other children in the ward than their own. In two cases, the mothers were described as strikingly emotionally detached, negative and hostile towards the children, almost as though they were blaming them for being injured and causing so much fuss. Some mothers expressed that they were missing their babies and felt empty or without a purpose in life, but they were preoccupied with their own needs rather than the babies'. (NSPCC Battered Child Research Unit, 1975)

Several research results show that up to half of all mothers of pre-school-age children suffer from depression, and battering mothers are no exception. The tendency to isolation that is a natural part of their make-up no doubt increases this depression. They rarely make local friends, and cut themselves off from neighbours with whom they might otherwise discuss their problems. When they need help they cannot bring themselves to ask for it, at least not openly; even when they have injured their children they typically take some hours, even days, to bring themselves to seek medical help. This delay is not because the injuries take place when you might expect them to, in the dead of night when parents are sleepy and exasperated at being woken up yet again. In fact only a small minority are battered then: of the Birmingham University group of 134 children, only 5 were battered late at night - the rest were attacked more or less equally during the day and the evening.

Researchers have repeatedly found that it is during acts of caretaking - feeding, changing, etc. - that most attacks occur. A mishap such as the baby soiling newly-changed nappies, or vomiting part of the previous meal over a clean dress, can cause a sudden outburst of uncontrollable rage. Since it is mostly mothers who have to bear the burden of looking after the child, probably more mothers than fathers do the attacking. Early research showed varying figures as to which sex is most likely to batter, but it does seem that whoever has the main role of caretaking is the most likely to do the actual damage. In many cases it is impossible to decide who battered, and where fathers are at home due to unemployment or shift work they are equally likely to attack. Final figures on this are extremely difficult to come by as usually both parents deny that either injured the child, and the workers have to make a guess. Usually there seems to be a certain amount of collusion between the parents - obviously it is almost impossible to live in cramped conditions in a small house or flat without having a very good idea of what is going on among the rest of the family. Often the non-attacking parent goads the other on, perhaps by denigrating his or her 'mothering' abilities, or by favouring one child at the expense of the other parent, or by accepting abusive behaviour as normal instead of something to be disapproved of.

The Newsons and others have pointed out the considerable class differences in the ways people discipline and punish their children. Many of the facts about the upbringing of battered children can look quite startling until allowance is made for these class differences, and then they mostly disappear. The same disciplinary pattern, though, is followed by battering parents in higher income groups, and one may fairly conclude that on the whole battering parents are either strict disciplinarians, always demanding an unrealistic standard of behaviour from their children, or they are inconsistent, sometimes smiling at a type of behaviour which another day will drive them wild. Battering parents often experiment with a variety of punishments, as though 'desperately trying to find some way of managing their children', and the subject of disciplining children is of great interest to them. Smith and Hanson found that half their sample of battering parents, as opposed to one eighth of the controls, smacked their children frequently, and a far greater number of battering parents withheld their love as a punishment.

The fathers of battered children frequently upset their wives by a basically inconsistent attitude to the behaviour of their children. Sometimes a husband will accuse the mother of being too stern, and he will cuddle the children and make a fuss of them to prove his own kindness, but another time, tired after a hard day's work or irritable from too much drink the night before, he will shout that she can't control her own kids and storm angrily out of the house, possibly giving her a nasty swipe on the way. Rarely do the husbands in battering families give their wives the support they so badly need.

Both fathers and mothers are unrealistic in the way they express their feelings for their children. They either say that a child is a nuisance and they wish it weren't there, or, more frequently, they swear it is the very centre of their lives and

165

they couldn't imagine being without it. They are rarely able to take the middle path of most parents, admitting occasional strains - even unhappiness - but remarking that on balance the relationship is unquestionably well worth while, enjoyable rather than the reverse. Battering parents' egocentricity prevents them from examining their lives and their relationships disinterestedly; as has been noted earlier, it is difficult for them to see the reality of another person, even that of their own children, so that although after an attack they may plead movingly to keep their child, the situation is rarely as simple as it seems. In their idealized picture of themselves - a vision as yet unattained - they are the centre of a happy family group, a group completed by the presence of a flourishing, delightful child. The demolition of this dream-picture would be unbearable; if a social worker or a doctor were to take away their baby this pitifully precarious self-image of themselves as ideal parents would be instantly destroyed. But at the same time a truly genuine love for the actual child which is in danger of being removed is not always very convincingly displayed: while the argument is going on the child in question may be sitting uncomforted and unnoticed on the floor.

Such a description may make us feel bitter towards such parents, but how many of us can claim that our love for our children and our spouses is 100 per cent altruistic? We love for a variety of reasons, and the totally selfless mother-love extolled by a few starry-eyed innocents very rarely, if ever, exists. There are parents who give up their entire lives to looking after a handicapped or otherwise needy child, but such devotion demands patience, will-power and a rare self-abnegation. Battering parents are deficient in these qualities, and when one looks at the way most of them have been brought up their self-distrust and immaturity become understandable.

As we have already seen, it is not easy to persuade these parents to tell the full truth about their early lives. At first they will often describe how kind their own parents were, how happy their family was, and so on. A typical research is one carried out in Wiltshire, where J. E. Oliver and his colleagues (1974) found a great disparity between the favourable reports of their early life given by many of their subjects and the truth as revealed by records and other information. The NSPCC

Battered Child Research Team (1975) found the same pattern:

Information regarding the background of the parents in our study was gleaned from informal discussions with them during the course of treatment. Many of the parents were initially reluctant to divulge this information, particularly if it was of an adverse nature. It was often through contradiction, retraction of chance negative remarks and descriptions of their emotional states during childhood, that we were able to get behind the facade of 'normality' and 'happiness' presented by them. In certain instances this occurred quite late in treatment. One mother, for example, who initially spoke in glowing terms about her own mother, later described an incident when she disagreed with her. She said that she was dragged across the room, the buttons torn off her jumper and was then given a good thrashing. In this 'normal' household the word 'no' was forbidden. At the age of fourteen years, this mother developed migraines.

This disparity may be partly due to the inconsistencies of their parents' style of upbringing, discussed earlier. A majority of Smith's group, for example, remembered their parents as having been warm and affectionate - there was no significant difference between them on this point and the controls. And yet *at the same time* one third of the mothers called their childhood unhappy, while half of all of them had suffered two or more neurotic symptoms, such as nail-biting, bed-wetting and nightmares. Also significant numbers of both mothers and fathers reported that as children they had been physically maltreated, and that their own parents had been unreasonable, harsh and rejecting.

No doubt such parents remember what it suits them to remember. Wishing to impress workers with their 'normality', they speak of the good times in their childhood. Asked more specific questions such as how their parents disciplined them, a different picture will emerge, though both can be true remembrances. The inconsistencies they themselves have suffered in the past almost invariably will be passed on in the way they treat their own children. However warm and indulgent such a parent may be on one occasion, the next day

167

or even the next minute his or her mood can change. To the child the beloved parent inexplicably becomes the Other Parent, a terrifying nightmare figure of wrath and vengeance.

Inevitably a child subjected to this kind of treatment will grow up lacking the sense of having been nurtured and loved; he will never know the basic security only consistent 'mothering' can give, 'mothering' as described so accurately by Steele and Pollock (in Helfer and Kempe, 1968) as 'a deep sense of being cared for and cared about from the beginning of one's life'. This inconsistency in parental loving extends in many cases beyond day to day care. Over half the Battered Child Research Department's sample of mothers came from broken homes. In their childhood these mothers had had a number of changes of the main caring figure, perhaps being put into care or sent away to private or local authority boarding schools.

As children this poor or broken relationship is often repeated in their relationships with their siblings; in later life it affects their ability to make friends. Half of Smith's group of parents admitted that they had no friends, a finding typical of all the reports I have ever seen on this aspect of battering parents. This difficulty in making friends is increased by their nomadic habits. Over half the families in one study, for example, had moved within the last year, and were anxious to move again as soon as possible. The inadequacy of rented housing is often given as the reason for the moves, or the families may be moving away from persistent social workers whom they fear might remove their children. I have not discovered any figures proving whether or not they move more frequently than others similar in age, class and spending power (bearing in mind they often marry young so have greater responsibilities earlier, which means they have less money to spend than others of their own age), but certainly they move more frequently than the national average.

In addition to having few, if any, friends, battering parents are also usually remote both physically and emotionally from their relatives and rarely gain any support from them. Neither do these isolated families ask for help from the social services - shut up alone in their own little hell they cannot or will not fight their way out. Mothers especially suffer from this isolation; the fathers at least meet people during working hours, and often go out on their own in the evenings, leaving the mother behind baby-sitting. Again, this may be a working-class pattern, but for potential battering mothers it can be the final straw. Although in general battering families are no larger than average, the children often come in quick succession, so that at the time of battering a mother may well be pregnant with a second or third child, or within six months or a year of parturition. These are very vulnerable times in any woman's life, and all the factors of her past history plus her present isolation and the lack of support from her husband now build up in a potential batterer to dangerous proportions. It will not take much provocation from a jealous toddler or a fractious baby to push her past breaking point.

Whether or not the lack of intellectual stimulus (a frequent complaint of intelligent mothers) is another precipitant, is open to debate. Selwyn Smith and his colleagues produced startling figures (Smith, Hanson and Noble, 1973), showing that nearly half the battering mothers in his sample had IQs on the borderline of subnormality or below. Their mean IQ was only 80 (controls were 95, 5 per cent below the norm), while fathers did better at 92 (controls 102). As a result of these tests, they suggest that 'techniques of teaching child rearing skills based realistically on their low intelligence should perhaps be explored further as a possible means of correcting such ineffectual parental care.' But Steel and Pollock had already written (in Helfer and Kempe, 1968)

> There is no evidence of a significant relationship between intelligence as measured by intelligence tests and abuse. The IQs obtained by the patients seen for testing range between 73 and 130, with most of the patients falling into the average range (90-110).

Equally the Battered Child Research Department, both in its early pilot study and in a later study frequently referred to in this book, found no evidence that in general the IQ of its subjects differed from that of the population at large, except that battering parents did better in concrete problem-solving tests than in verbal ones, whereas the reverse was true of the control parents. As Clare Hyman, a research psychologist, has written, 'This is a pattern which has been found with other delinquents and probably reflects their tendency to act on impulse, rather than think through the consequence of their acts.'

Bearing in mind the impressive gains in IQ of the NSPCC sample of battered children after they had been given specialized care, and supposing that if in their own childhood the battering parents had also received early care, one may guess that they too might have improved their scores. In all, it seems likely that battering parents come from a mixed range of intelligence, similar to that of the public in general.

Research into the brain patterns of 35 battering parents (Smith, Honigsberger and Smith, 1973) showed that 23 per cent had abnormal electroencephalograms. In the general population between 5 to 10 per cent exhibit EEG abnormalities, while among those known to have committed acts of violence, including murder, 20 per cent or more have abnormal EEGs. Since these parents were persistent batterers and had often attacked more than one child, Smith *et al.* drew the conclusion that

> It can be wrong . . . to rely too heavily on seemingly facile explanations of why parents batter their children . . . to assume that battering parents have experienced inadequate mothering in their own childhood. . . . To assume that all such parents or even the great majority can be adequately treated by a 'transfusion of mothering', as has been suggested, may not be altogether justified and in the light of our own findings may even be dangerous to the children concerned.

Most of these parents with abnormal EEGs could be classed, Smith suggests, as aggressive psychopaths: all were of low intelligence.

Smith's findings tie in with other research, for it has been generally accepted for some time now that 20 per cent or more of battering parents can never be safely reunited with their children. It may well prove to be that these parents nearly always have abnormal EEGs as in Smith's sample. If this is found to be so, then EEG findings of all battering parents could be of enormous help in the always fraught decision as to which families should not be kept together, and further research ought to be undertaken urgently.

As one might expect, many batterers, particularly the group we have just been talking about, have already come into contact with the law. Obviously the psychopathic fathers are more likely to be guilty of crimes of violence, but most of the offences committed are petty, such as small thefts, and 'loitering with intent'. Different researches show that between nearly a third and a half of the fathers have already been convicted of criminal offences, but a much smaller proportion of women have (this of course is true in general, although the rate of conviction of women offenders is creeping up). Most of these crimes are class-related. It would be very interesting to find out if this tendency to breaking the law is repeated in middle-class battering families. Driving away with someone else's car is not, in moral terms, very different from fiddling the company's accounts, or fraudulently signing cheques. However, such research would be very difficult to carry out, owing mainly to the reluctance of doctors to believe their middle-class patients could possibly have caused the child injuries they are called upon to attend, with the result that few such families would be known to researchers.

To sum up, battering parents are from all classes, but the majority of severe physical battering takes place in lower socio-economic groups; they marry or cohabit young, have their first children earlier than average, and as a result are harder-up than most young people of their age. Few of the mothers do full-time work, and the perpetual presence of small children irritates them considerably, but they won't let the children go, alternating between smothering them with affection and pushing them away. Their affection for the children is ambivalent, and at times they seem totally to forget their existence, being overwhelmed by their own inner needs. They experiment with different punishments, but are so frequently inconsistent that their disciplining is undermined: a minority are over-strict and harsh. Reluctant to tell the whole truth about their own childhood, they can easily mislead helpers, partly out of a need to show themselves normal, partly because of the inconsistencies in their upbringing: which version of their childhood they currently remember depends

171

on mood or how much they trust the interviewer. Half of them come from broken homes, and, as adults, few have good relationships with their parents or siblings. Without support from husband or friends, spurning social aid, the mothers unsuccessfully try to cope alone. Mostly the parents' intelligence is in the normal range, though not all researchers agree with this finding. A significant proportion are aggressive psychopaths. Finally, a high proportion of the fathers have committed some minor crime, while a few have been convicted of violent crimes preceding the known attacks on their children.

An important aspect of the parents' lives is, of course, marriage. The problems they face are typical of most families in trouble and these have already been explained in Chapter 2. If only potential batterers would choose supportive, helpful, generous, enthusiastic spouses they would have few problems, but (apart from the sad fact that such a paragon would not be interested in them) they unerringly select partners like themselves, duplicating their own ineffectiveness and insecurity. This selection process of like to like seems instinctive, and it is doubtful if any kind of educative process could affect the marital choice of the vast majority of humankind. Battering parents are no exception.

Incest

There is one aspect of child abuse that has been consistently ignored. Articles on battered babies and battered wives are now commonplace in newspapers and women's magazines, but editors still feel they are taking a bold step if they print a piece on the sexual abuse of children by close relatives. Difficult subjects such as homosexuality or problems such as frigidity or impotence may now be openly discussed, but incest still causes powerful distaste or even horror.

How this horror arose is unclear. It can hardly have been instinctive: the very strength of the taboos surrounding incest suggest the existence of powerful impulses which need to be strictly controlled. Today we know that from a genetic point of view incest is unwise. International research has shown that mortality and physical and mental handicaps are significantly higher in children born of incestuous unions. Dr C. Carter of the Institute of Child Health, for instance, wrote in the *Lancet* that in a group of cases he studied parents sharing a recessive gene ran four times as great a risk of producing defective

173

children if they were first-degree relatives than if they were first cousins. (For the purposes of this book I am in general adopting Funk and Wagnall's dictionary definition of incest as 'Sexual intercourse between persons too closely related for legal marriage'.) He studied thirteen children, of whom seven were the result of matings between brothers and sisters, and six of matings between fathers and daughters. Three of these children died in infancy, one is severely subnormal and four are educationally subnormal. The remaining five children are normal. If recessive genes are not present and both parents are fully healthy then the offspring is likely to be equally healthy. The problem is, of course, that the parents may be unaware they are carrying the recessive gene and its presence will not become known until mating takes place between the two carriers.

The law, as always, reflects the strength of public feelings. Incest can carry a life sentence if the child concerned is under thirteen, though such a heavy sentence is not given in practice. Last year the National Council for Civil Liberties published a report suggesting that incest should be taken off the statute book. Some of their reasons appear to be sound, such as the suggestion that 'in many instances the victim does not appear to suffer from any obvious psychological disturbance until after the case has come to court', but few of those who come into regular contact with sexually abused children would agree with the NCCL's conclusions. They will point out that psychological damage may not become apparent for many years, but as far as is known few victims escape from it altogether and therefore children must continue to be protected by law. A further suggestion of the NCCL is that children would be encouraged to talk about what has been done to them if they knew their offending relatives would not be punished. This seems a most unlikely argument. Few young children would know whether or not the law is involved, and in any case other far stronger pressures combine to make them keep their mouths shut.

This traditional silence has ensured that very little has ever been known about the subject. Rumours about certain famous people would occasionally circulate: one still sees speculations about the relationship of Byron and Wordsworth to their sisters, for example. It is only very recently that the truth has been told about the incestuous assaults made upon Virginia Woolf by her grown-up half-brother George Duckworth which began when she was a small child, and which almost certainly were a major cause of her later frigidity and possibly of her recurrent mental breakdowns also.

But what of ordinary people? How frequent is its occurrence? Again, as with wife battering, we don't really know. One can only say incest is probably rare, but not all that rare. Less than 300 cases a year are reported to the police in this country. The latest Home Office figures (1974) show that 96 men were sent to prison and 21 were given suspended sentences. Only six women were found guilty of incest. Fred Hedley, head of the NSPCC's legal department, reckons that when he was still doing casework he personally came across an average of a couple of dozen cases a year. In America Prof. D. Walters investigated a group of students and found that out of the 412 young men and women, 17 per cent as children had had some kind of physical contact with adults, while 21 per cent said they had received 'verbal signals of approaches of some sort from adults' (Walters, 1975). Not all of these approaches were of an incestuous nature.

Firm figures about incest simply do not exist and I doubt if they ever will. One researcher writes that her medical colleagues' reactions 'ranged from incredulity to frank hostility' when she asked if they knew of any evidence of incest among their patients, while another researcher wrote that when he decided to investigate incest his colleagues gave him suspicious looks as though his motives for choosing such a field of research were being queried.

There is an extraordinary conspiracy of silence surrounding incest; generally speaking it is only when social workers get to know a family very well that the subject comes out into the open, and even then it usually slips out by mistake and attempts to cover up the admission are made. Alternatively it may only be revealed years later when the victim, now an adult, sees a psychiatrist because of a breakdown in his or her ability to cope with life. N. Lukianowicz, making a study of incest in Northern Ireland which he reported in the *British Journal of Psychiatry* in 1972, found that among unselected female psychiatric patients 4 per cent had been victims of paternal incest. Among 700 psychiatric patients of both sexes 4 per cent had experienced other forms of incest.

The psychological damage done to the victim varies considerably, depending to a great extent on what relationship the couple bear to each other. The most commonly recognized form of incest is that between father and daughter. Prof. Walters reported that out of the 200 cases of sexually abused children with whom he was working the great majority involved under-age girls and their fathers, stepfathers or mothers' boyfriends. In only three of these 200 cases was an adult female accused of abusing a young boy. Of the 412 normal students mentioned earlier whom Walters investigated, the male adult who had made advances to the female students when they were children had been well known and mostly related to them by blood or marriage, uncles and brothers-in-law being frequently reported. Homosexual approaches to the males, on the other hand, were mostly not incestuous and were made by unrelated adults who were fairly well known to them, such as camp counsellors, men involved with local church functions, shopkeepers and teachers. Most of the students did not seem to have suffered any lasting damage, but it must be remembered that the majority of these cases were very mild. At the time most of the children had felt the approaches were 'distasteful, puzzling or abnormal events in child development'. Usually the child was asked to look at or touch the man's penis, or they themselves were fondled or caressed. Half the females reported that when physical contact took place the men had touched their genitals.

In Lukianowicz's study of 29 psychiatric patients who had had incestuous experiences with relatives other than their fathers, 15 had been involved in a relationship with their brothers or sisters, there had been incest between a grandfather and five of his granddaughters, between uncle and niece in 4 cases, mother and son in 3 cases, and aunt and nephew in 2. A study made in Connecticut in 1973-4 showed that 80 per cent of all cases of child molestation involved parent or parent/substitute and child. Vincent DeFrancis, director of the Children's Division of the American Humane Association, conducted a comprehensive three-year study of child molestation in New York City, at the end of which he estimated there were approximately 3,000 cases annually in New York City. Suzanne Sgroi (1975) writes of this study that 'it must be assumed [these] reported incidents represent a small fraction of the cases' and judges that DeFrancis's estimate is on the conservative side. DeFrancis found that in 72 per cent of the cases he studied the parents were involved, either by direct incest or rape (25 per cent) or 'by acts of omission or commission'. The most frequently-named abuser was the father, male relative or mother's boyfriend, all of whom had easy access to the home. The victims' ages ranged from one or two months old to seventeen or eighteen years.

Lukianowicz found that the incestuous fathers of the women patients he investigated had first approached their daughters when they were aged between five and fourteen. This young age may surprise some, but all those I spoke to agreed that these relationships frequently begin very early. Dr A. Bentovin of Great Ormond Street Hospital for Children pointed out to me that most people consider children between the ages of seven to thirteen to be in a sexually latent period, but in fact these are the early stages of puberty, and an eight- or nine-year-old child can be very sexually attractive, sometimes deliberately so.

Once incest begins it usually continues until the child grows up and leaves home. It is rare for the offending relative, who normally lives in the same house as the child, to be able to resist the temptation once it has been given way to. In cases of paternal incest the situation is particularly dangerous where there is more than one daughter in the family, as most researchers have found that almost invariably the father transfers his attention from the older daughter to the younger ones when the eldest child leaves home. Sometimes he will even begin to molest the younger daughters while still continuing his relationship with the eldest. This is the point at which incest sometimes comes to light when an elder daughter decides her sisters shall not share her fate. Her requests for help are not always taken seriously, however, for a number of reasons. Few people like to contemplate sexual deviation of this kind, and social workers and other helping agencies are no exception. Sometimes they will be disinclined to believe the girl, whose story is in any case likely to be confused, partly because of embarrassment, partly because of fear of the possible consequences that may fall on her father. They may assume her story has been invented from a malicious desire to implicate a disliked father, or they may half believe her but misconstrue her concern for her sister as jealousy. An adolescent who is bitterly ashamed of the story she has to tell is very easily put off. If this is allowed to happen her sisters will almost certainly become victims of their father's attentions, their resistance having been weakened by the knowledge of their older sister's earlier acceptance.

It is thought that most father-daughter incest begins gently, amounting at first to little more than a petting then progressing with some tenderness on the father's part, but this is not invariably so. There are reported cases of the rape of babies and very small children, and in cases such as these massive surgery may be required. A further complication is that even tiny children can be infected with venereal disease, but this may not be picked up by a family doctor to whom its possibility never occurs. Suzanne Sgroi reports the case of two siblings, a two-and-a-half-year-old boy and a four-year-old girl, both of whom were infected with gonorrhoea. They often shared their infected parents' bed, and their doctor who in this case recognized the disease the children were suffering from, persuaded himself that it was their frequent close contact with their parents which had caused the infection. Several months later a nursery school teacher became suspicious when the girl repeatedly refused to play on the rocking horse because she said 'it hurts'. On examination the school paediatrician discovered sperm in the child's vagina, and the whole truth came out. The Police Protective Service's investigation found that the father had a long history of molesting children, but nothing had ever been successfully proved against him. The mother admitted to the investigators that she had known all along what was happening, and that both the children had been assaulted by her husband on numerous occasions, but she had not stopped him.

Even if incest is suspected and a child is examined, a doctor may be extremely reluctant to consider the possibility of oral or anal penetration, and if this has been the only sexual method

used it would be possible for a father to be cleared of all
suspicion. Equally, doctors balk at the idea that a child might
have VD, so they will probably not look for signs of it. Even if
they should recognize the disease they tend to persuade
themselves that the child must have caught it by contact with
clothing or towels or bedlinen belonging to the infected
parents, although they know perfectly well that the possibility
of such transmission has long been discarded as far as adults
are concerned.

Suzanne Sgroi writes that all doctors must be aware of these
emotional difficulties when dealing with this type of incest,
and that they must train themselves to overcome them. It is
essential that a child who has suffered such an assault be
carefully and tenderly examined, not only to find out if an
assault has taken place, but also to reassure the child itself that
it has not been permanently harmed, a worry which many
children hug to themselves right into their adulthood. She
stresses that investigation of *how* the incident happened must
not take place at the same time or the child will inevitably be
deeply upset. If the child is not properly examined medically
such give-away signs as sperm in the mouth may be missed and
the child restored to a father who is so clearly totally unfitted
to be a parent.

It seems almost impossible that a mother could collude with
her husband in allowing him to assault his children, but the
mother about whom we have just read is by no means unique.
Most researchers have come to the conclusion that in nearly all
incest cases the mother knows or guesses what is going on,
although she will probably pretend to be ignorant of it. Many
of these 'affairs' continue for eight or nine years or even longer:
it is unlikely that during such a period a woman could live in
the same house and never have any suspicions of any kind. Dr
E. Christopher of Haringey Social Services Department, who
has specialized in sex education, is convinced from her wide
experience that most mothers collude, if only by ignoring the
evidence. She suggests that a primary reason for their not
interfering is that the women are frightened of being left alone
with their children and no breadwinner, and that at least it
keeps the husband's infidelity within the family. An additional
reason for the mothers' silence is that some of them dislike sex

and are glad to be able to avoid it without driving the husband into a strange woman's arms. This unprotective and self-centred attitude towards the daughter is borne out by Walters's observation that if, after the situation has been exposed, the mother is given the choice as to whether the daughter or the father should leave home, the mother almost always decides to keep the father, and it is the girl who is sent away.

When the incest becomes public knowledge, the mother usually denies all knowledge of what has been going on. As Prof. Walters writes, she plays the role of 'the aggrieved unsuspecting victim' and she will continue to play this role even after she is faced with evidence that the daughter had tried to or even succeeded in bringing her attention to what was going on. In Walters's opinion most marriages in which incest occurs are already dead, and have been so for many years. Often the parents have not had sex together for a year or more. Not all people working in the field would agree fully with this opinion, but certainly one may assume that such a marriage is in an unhealthy state, and that communication between the parents is poor. Open discovery may well finally wreck the marriage, but if the daughter leaves or is taken away the couple will probably continue to live together in spite of all that has happened, though they may be forced to leave the district because of local publicity.

What leads to incest? It is difficult for any of us to imagine how an adult can take such a step. Certainly small children can be attractive, and young girls often flirt outrageously with their fathers when they want something, to the immense satisfaction of both. But there is a wide gulf between the mildly sexy cuddling and bantering that goes on between most fathers and adolescent daughters and the overt sexual contact that occurs in an incestuous relationship.

In some cases, it is merely one aspect of a man's generally aggressive attitude towards his family. One American study of 20 incestuous relationships showed that in 65 per cent of the families involved many members of the family had suffered violent abusive behaviour from the father. Another study by M. Virkkunen (1974), investigating alcoholism and incest, showed that 87 per cent of alcoholics convicted of incest had also shown aggressive behaviour, but only 21 per cent of non-alcoholics convicted of incest had done so.

Paul Gebhard and his colleagues reported in their study *Sex Offenders* (1965) that two-thirds of the men they were investigating who had assaulted girls under the age of twelve were drunk when the offence was committed, and they concluded that alcohol was an important aid in breaking the strong taboo against forcing very young girls into sexual acts. This conclusion was reinforced when offences of a purely incestuous nature were studied. But where assaults were made on older children it seemed the taboo was more easily broken without the need for alcohol. Three-quarters of the men who incestuously assaulted girls of between twelve and fifteen were sober; indeed, far from being the result of a drunken impulse, 84 per cent of these incestuous acts were apparently premeditated.

Lukianowicz found that of the 26 fathers in his sample who had committed incest with their daughters none were diagnosed as psychotic, but 14 were considered to be inadequate psychopaths and 5 were aggressive psychopaths. Four were found to be alcoholics. The fathers, who had frequently come from broken homes, were habitually unemployed, and the families lived either in overcrowded conditions in industrial towns or were completely isolated from others in rural areas. Although most of the men had left home after little schooling and had usually worked - when they worked - as labourers, they were all of average intelligence. Many seemed to be highly-sexed, having intercourse not only with the victim whose plight had first caused the family to be examined, but also with her siblings, the mother and sometimes with a mistress as well. Other researchers have found similar backgrounds in many of the cases they have investigated.

Social factors undoubtedly play a part in promoting incest, though - as with all cases of abuse - it would be a mistake to suppose it takes place only among the underprivileged simply because one hears so little about middle-class incest. All researchers agree that incest is to be found in all income groups, but it is the economically deprived about whom we are most likely to hear. Masters and Johnson (1976) write that although we know more about the incidence of incest occurring among the underprivileged, we know more about the consequences of incest in middle-class families. This, they suggest, could be because the latter are more likely to be traumatized by incest than the disadvantaged, for whom incest can be a more commonplace fact of life, or it could be that wealthier and better-educated people are more likely to have better access to counselling. This may well be the American experience where people with problems are more likely to visit psychiatrists who later will be able to report their findings. I have seen very little written about middle-class incest in this country and presume, as in baby battering and wife battering, that know-how and money enables the more privileged to keep themselves out of the research statistics.

It has been suggested to me that incest in middle-class families is more likely to imply that something is badly wrong with the marriage, whereas in slum conditions it may mean nothing of the kind. Certainly many findings show that incest is more likely to occur where poverty brings loss of privacy together with other handicaps, or where rural isolation means there is virtually no outside contact from one month to the next. Two social workers who had spent some time working in the Glasgow slums told me that in some areas a certain amount of incest was more or less taken for granted. They had known families sleep as many as six in a bed, with the mother at one end to avoid conceiving while the father and the children slept at the other. The frustrated father would persuade one of the children to fondle him and from that stage on anything could develop. These young girls rarely became pregnant by their fathers because by the time they were thirteen or fourteen they were so sexually experienced they mostly went off and found their own boyfriends. Other social workers who were listening to this discussion assured me they had seen the same kind of thing happening in other provincial slums with which they were familiar, and that many of the delinquent girls whom they dealt with had had this kind of background. In really severe slum conditions, they suggested, incest is acknowledged by most of the inhabitants as a way of life ('Dad breaks the girls in', as one of them put it) and no one takes much notice of it.

In some low-IQ problem families incest is not considered to be particularly wrong. In one such family described to me the family had been under the social service for many years as they were considered incapable of looking after themselves without outside help. The father of the family was no longer living in the house, but his half dozen or so children remained living with their mother. All of them were more or less subnormal but none grossly so. One day a young baby - a girl - was brought into the local hospital with severe injuries. When the police called on its father (he was the eldest son of the family, a youth of about twenty) he claimed that his fox terrier had jumped up and bitten the baby. It was obvious that the injuries - slashes in the upper thigh and around the pubic area - had in fact been made by a knife and the young father, who already had a record of violence, was arrested. The police discovered that the baby's mother was the father's young sister, aged fifteen, 'a simple soul, capable of doing a bit of washing up and general kitchen work, but not much else'. The couple, who had lived together in the family house as man and wife, had welcomed the birth of the child, and all had been well until the young mother started going out with her cousin. Her brother/husband became violently jealous, with the final result that he brutally attacked the baby. The brother has ended up in the locked ward of a mental hospital, diagnosed as a psychopath. His sister will almost certainly go on to have many further pregnacies during the course of her life, no doubt passing on to her babies her own incapacities.

But it would be far too simplistic to conclude that poverty and all the adversities that tend to go with it are the main cause of incest. Everyone agrees there is never a single source. Inherent aggression on the part of the offending male relative, alcohol, overcrowding or isolation, all increase the possibility of incest, but it takes much more than these to make a family break the powerful taboo which surrounds incest.

H. Maisch concludes in his book *Incest* (1973) that marriages where incest has occurred are already deeply disturbed and the incest itself, far from being the cause of the family disorder, is only a symptom. Prof. Walters would certainly agree with this. Indeed, he goes so far as to write that the child is probably incidental to the abuse, and that 'the primary cause usually rests on the relationship between the adult male and the adult female'. Dr Bentovin, however, feels this is far too simple a viewpoint, and considers the interaction between father and daughter is of tremendous importance. As children enter early adolescence they have strong anxieties about being too close to their parents and they need to push themselves away, but once they have succeeded in this they become frightened and feel a need to regress to babyhood and be cuddled and loved. At this stage the child can be very demanding, perhaps even wanting to share a bed, and the parents who have been feeling cut off may be over-welcoming to their child. This pattern, says Dr Bentovin, is perfectly normal and can be very intense while it lasts. If, however, at the same time the parents' marriage is under strain, with the husband perhaps disappointed in his career and conscious that he is reaching middle age, while the mother is no longer as young and attractive as she was, perhaps even having to leave the home to go to hospital for a hysterectomy or some such complaint, at this point the father-daughter relationship can become over-intense. In a few instances this intensity results in mild sexual play that eventually may develop further than anyone ever originally intended. Once this barrier has been crossed it becomes extremely difficult to re-establish it, and the relationship will probably continue until the girl leaves home.

All of these things, then, help to cause incest, but we still do not know with any exactitude why one father should abuse his daughter when the great majority, under similar circumstances, do not. Little research has been done into this aspect of incest and it may be that in the future we shall understand this problem better, though it is obviously a difficult field to study.

What damage is done to the victims of incest? Many girls unquestionably enjoy such a relationship with their father once they have accepted it, even if at the same time they feel guilty about it. It gives them a sense of power, and some even indulge in petty blackmail, demanding gifts as the price for their silence. If their parents' relationship is poor they may get great satisfaction out of playing the role of 'little mother', so that as father and daughter act out their private fantasies the real mother is pushed even further into the background. Inevitably the girl will have mixed feelings about her mother. She will feel both anger that her mother is not protecting her from her father, for she will know the relationship is wrong even if she is actually enjoying it, and guilt that she is depriving her mother of her rightful place. These feelings will probably be deeply buried but they are likely to cause problems in later life when the daughter herself becomes a mother.

An interesting case illustrating this type of delayed effect was told to me by a psychiatrist who has treated many young mothers whose own childhood traumas were causing them difficulties in handling their babies. One woman had come to see the psychiatrist because she felt herself in great danger of battering her baby daughter. The mother was a middle-class intelligent woman with a busy career and, until the birth of her first child, a successful marriage. When the baby was born the mother found to her surprise and regret that she felt strangely antipathetic to it. She began to have bad dreams and one of them, a dream in which her husband was seduced by a young girl, she told to a hospital nurse. The nurse immediately commented that obviously she was dreaming about her husband and her new baby daughter. The young mother was very shocked and rejected this interpretation, but when she returned home with the baby she found herself flooded with memories of her childhood and adolescence. As a child she had had a very close incestuous relationship with her father, which had not ended in full intercourse but had nevertheless been strongly physical. The affair had continued until she had reached adolescence without, as far as the girl knew, her mother knowing anything about it.

As her memories returned her feelings for her father revived, and she became unable to continue sexual relations with her husband. This was naturally very difficult for him, particularly as their relationship had been a good one before the child's birth. She continued to look after her baby's physical needs with meticulous care, as so many battering mothers do, but its crying irritated her to the point where she longed to bash it and could hardly stop herself from doing so. She threw the baby to the floor several times and allowed herself to smack it with some force, but fortunately before any injury occurred she was able to bring herself to see her doctor. Eventually she was sent to the psychiatrist, who considered that the guilt she had suffered from all these years was causing her present distress. As a child she had continuously expected and sometimes longed to be punished by her mother for her behaviour, and now in her mind she was mixing up her child and herself. She saw her daughter as her old child-self, and her present self as her own betrayed mother, and in this role she had an overpowering need to inflict at last the punishment which was so long overdue. In addition she suffered a buried fear that her young daughter might grow up to usurp her place with her husband, just as she herself had done with her own father so many years before.

That story has a hopeful ending - treatment is restoring the relationship between the woman and her husband, and although she is still occasionally uneasy with her baby in general she feels far more relaxed with her, while the child herself seems to be a thriving and happy infant. Not all such cases end with such a hopeful prognosis, though.

Clearly, in the majority of families where incest occurs, the home is in any case not an easy one in which to grow up. Lukianowicz reports that of the 26 mothers of incestuously assaulted girls, 8 were promiscuous and showed psychopathic traits, 3 were excessively anxious, and 2 were frigid. Most were depressed, worn down by large families and husbands who were often out of work or whom they described as aggressive, demanding bullies. Most of the mothers had colluded with their husbands or pretended to themselves it was not happening.

Inevitably most of the daughters of such parents suffered. Eleven became promiscuous and took drugs or became otherwise delinquent, while five found themselves becoming frigid after they had married. Seven girls developed various symptoms such as acute anxiety neurosis or severe depression, resulting in attempted suicide in three cases. Only six girls had no apparent ill-effects from the relationship with their fathers.

However gently an incestuous father treats his daughter and however much she may come to enjoy the relationship, it is a wretched way for a girl to learn about sex. Sex becomes a thing to be ashamed of, to be hidden at all costs. (Maisch reported that three-quarters of the girls in his study had been sworn to secrecy by their fathers; half had been intimidated and some were threatened they would be sent away to a home if they spoke out, while a third was bribed.)

Guilt and shame are often suffered by young adults when the implications of 'games' played in childhood and perhaps even enjoyed suddenly become clear. Newly-formed relationships can be troubled by the overhanging shadow of an incestuous past, and sexual problems are likely to arise, particularly in the early states of marriage. A girl may long to achieve happy sexual relations with someone she really loves but may be unable to do so, and it is at this point she is likely to ask for therapy. There is more American evidence available because, as I have remarked before, it is more common for Americans to seek therapy of this kind, but probably the practice is increasing in England with the opening up of discussion of sexual problems.

Masters and Johnson report that such girls tend to go to one of two extremes. They either become promiscuous, sleeping with anyone who is around, or they are frightened of sex and avoid male companionship. As therapists, their experience has been that most of their patients feel 'very little sensation in the pelvic region . . . and almost all are nonorgasmic'. They do point out, however, that their work has inevitably been among those incest victims who have been sufficiently traumatized to need treatment: it is impossible to know just how many people have had incestuous relationships without suffering any perceptible damage. These last may be in a tiny minority or they may be a majority: it would be extremely difficult to conduct an effective survey to elucidate this point.

One problem peculiar to father-daughter incest is that usually the father becomes excessively jealous of his daughter as she grows up. Boyfriends may be banned or rejected on a variety of grounds and the girl, who is likely to be feeling very uncertain of herself because of her guilt and shame, may find it impossible to take a normal place in society among her own age group. Some fathers behave in this way even if no incestuous relationship took place with the daughters at all. They may have entirely controlled any physical expression of their desires - indeed, they quite probably were unconscious of them - but their partiality for a particular daughter may have resulted in her being thoroughly spoiled and 'babied' so that when she grows up she is quite unable to form an independent mature relationship with a young normal male, and she looks for an older man who can replace her father in petting and spoiling her.

Most of the available research deals with father-daughter incest which is probably the most common form of incest. Brother-sister incest seems to cause far less damage, perhaps because for most it is little more than early sexual experimentation not involving any emotional pressure. Out of 30 partnerships between brother and sister, Lukianowicz found that 27 were completely free from personality disorders, neurosis or psychosis. Other researchers report a similar freedom from damaging effects. Usually damage only occurs when the relationship becomes so obsessive that one or both partners cannot form normal relationships with their own peer group. Most researchers consider that if psychological problems occur among siblings who have indulged in an incestuous relationship there are usually other causes as well. An exception is where the sister is considerably older than the brother. This form of incest has much in common with mother-son incest, and is as potentially damaging.

Masters and Johnson consider mother-son incest to be the most traumatic of all such relationships. Over-protective and over-demanding, the mother isolates her son so that he becomes insecure and self-conscious, unable to discuss sex openly with his own peer group. Usually the father will have left home when the son was still very young, the boy normally being an only child or much younger than his siblings. Masters and Johnson found actual intercourse between mother and son to be so rare they could not comment on it, the pattern of seduction usually taking one or two forms. In one common pattern the mother continues washing the child in his bath long after he is capable of bathing himself, during which she stimulates him sexually. When he reaches puberty she continues to masturbate him until he ejaculates, but physical contact between the two is nearly always limited to this act. The second pattern is for the mother, having been widowed or left without a husband for one reason or another, to take her son into her bed. Probably no overt sexual contact will take place between them, but they are likely to abandon the habit of wearing night-clothes and they will certainly be sexually aware of each other, so that as the boy grows up and begins to have sex dreams they will relate almost entirely to the woman lying beside him.

Young men who have experienced either type of relationship frequently find themselves suffering problems of impotence when they become attracted to women of their own age group. This is probably due to the fact that in their relationship with their mothers actual coitus was totally forbidden, so that over the years the sons will have been conditioned to find the very idea of coitus taboo. The young adult may want to form a new sexual relationship but he is so frightened he may not be able to achieve or maintain an erection that he abandons experiment and remains faithful to the only relationship in which he can be reasonably secure, even though his emotional attachment to his mother may not be very strong.

Of the three mothers in Lukianowicz's sample who had seduced their sons, all were psychiatrically abnormal: one was schizophrenic, one was markedly neurotic and the last suffered from depression. Of the sons, one was schizophrenic, one mentally subnormal, while the third left his home within two years of the commencement of the relationship.

The effects, then, on the personalities of children who have had incestuous relationships in their childhood are very variable. Father-daughter, mother-son incest is generally accepted as being the most dangerous. How destructive other types of incest are varies according to the surrounding circumstances, how the incest occurs, what it means to the child, and how others react to it. Prof. Walters feels strongly that a great deal depends on how adults treat the victim if the incest is discovered. He reports a case where a child in hospital overheard a detective commenting that the little girl's father 'should be shot for what he did to her'. Obviously, this had a traumatic effect on the child. Equally, close relatives may be frightened that the affair will become public knowledge, and they sometimes attempt to frighten an already traumatized child into keeping silent about it. Walters suggests that no unsupervised visitors should be allowed to visit abused children in hospital, to avoid pressures of this kind being put upon them at a time when they are in an exceptionally vulnerable frame of mind. Many families will find it almost impossible to continue living in an area if such a scandal was broken, and obviously attempts will be made to keep the whole story quiet. This silence must not be bought at the price of the victim's peace of mind, for it is essential that she or he, together with the rest of the family, receive effective therapeutic treatment.

Some people consider that if incest has occurred within a family, it is best if that family is broken up. Others disagree, and feel that many families can be successfully treated, though it will probably be necessary to send the child concerned away from its parents for a while, perhaps to a relative or a temporary fosterparent. All therapists agree that police intervention should be avoided if at all possible. Police involvement means that the victim will be repeatedly questioned, and that almost inevitably neighbours will hear about the case, as well as the man's employers. The police have no choice but to prosecute if they are certain incest has been committed and if they have any sort of case, even though they may privately consider it would be better for all concerned if the whole thing were kept out of the courts. Finally, if the father is imprisoned his treatment at the hands of other prisoners is likely to be highly unpleasant but of no therapeutic value. When he comes out, unless the family situation is dramatically changed, he will probably revert to his old relationships, so that nothing will have been solved or achieved.

If the helping agencies are able to treat the family without police involvement they must ask themselves *why* the offender committed the incest. Was it primarily for sexual reasons, or was it because of deficiences in the marriage? Were there social problems, such as poverty, alcoholism, unemployment? Obviously an extremely sensitive approach is needed if therapy of any kind is to succeed. Practical help may be of more use than an analytic approach to the original causes of the offender's deviation. If the offender is the breadwinner of the family and he is out of work or has an unsatisfactory job it will help in his rehabilitation if more rewarding or interesting work is found for him. Sydney Brandon has suggested in *Violence in the Family* (M. Borland (ed.), 1976) that in cases where offending males have a particularly high sexual drive anti-androgen drugs will help reduce this drive to more manageable proportions.

The entire family, not only the offender and the victim, will need to be helped, individually and as a unit. Prof. Walters points out that treatment is complicated by the fact that in cases of father-daughter incest, at least three people 'moving at three different speeds' have to be treated simultaneously, and quite frequently none of the three are motivated for treatment. They may even be highly resistant to it. If it finally becomes evident that no progress is being made, then all researchers are agreed that the only possible course is to break up the family, either by permanently removing the victim, together with any other children who are likely to be in danger, or by persuading the offender to leave. In most cases, as we have seen earlier, it is usually the daughter who leaves the family, while the husband and wife remain holding together whatever is left of their marriage.

If the mother herself has made the first approach to the authorities half the battle is won. But even so such women often refuse to let social workers or other helpers visit their husbands because they are terrified of their husbands' reactions. In such cases the helpers may even be uncertain as to whether the mother is telling the truth, especially if the child concerned is too frightened or shy to talk openly. It is essential, therefore, that the mother's confidence be fully won so that she will eventually allow the husband to be approached.

It is no easy task for a mother who suspects that something is wrong to decide how to set about getting help. The best advice may be for her to phone her local social services so that she can find out their attitude in advance. Even professionals have their hang-ups about sex, and a few may find incest almost impossible to face. If, as is most likely, the social workers seem sympathetic then all is well, but if the mother is not reassured by their manner she could go instead to a local child guidance clinic. The advantage of this latter approach is that both she and the therapist can use any problems the child might be having as the excuse for the wife going to the clinic in the first

191

place, thereby avoiding early conflict with the husband.

Of course, if the mother has confidence in her family doctor an approach to him could be the best method of all, but this does involve the risk that he might call in the police, whereas a social worker would be most unlikely to do so. She will face the same problem if she contacts the NSPCC, as the workers are under rigid instructions to inform the police in all cases of incest and it would be very difficult for any individual worker not to do so, whatever his or her personal inclinations. A health visitor also would be a helpful ally, but unless the child is very young indeed the mother is unlikely to have any contact with one. Marriage guidance counsellors or Citizens Advice Bureaux might be able to help, but they do not have special training in this subject.

But, however difficult she finds the initial approach, it is essential that a mother who suspects some form of incest is occurring within her family contacts someone to whom she can talk, someone whose reaction will be sympathetic and not punitive. This is especially important in cases of brother-sister incest, where far more damage may be done by heavy-handed interference than anything the children are likely to do to themselves. Nevertheless, if the situation cannot be safely contained within the family setting - particularly where an adult-child relationship is concerned - the family will have to be split up for the sake of the children, regardless of what damage it may do to the family as a cohesive unit.

The Search for Answers

Several years ago Sir Keith Joseph, the then Secretary of State for Social Services, sparked off a political row by his compassionate interest in what he called the 'cycle of deprivation'. In any given group of families there will be a small nucleus who, generation after generation, claim a disproportionate amount of the social services' time. To some, Sir Keith Joseph's desire to aid these families was no more than a right-wing ploy to ensure that such families stayed exactly where they were - at the bottom of the social heap. To these militant left-wingers, 'scrap-heap' families only exist because in a capitalistic society there will always be a deprived bottom stratum. Had Sir Keith been a Labour instead of a Conservative Member no doubt only the extreme left-wingers would have attacked his theories, for everyone else knows that no society, capitalistic or otherwise, has ever existed in which all men are truly equal. As long as we are allowed to mate freely without government interference our genetic inheritances will vary to an unfair extent which must be anathema to all just-minded souls.

With the political eclipse of the Tories the phrase 'cycle of deprivation' died out, but Dr David Owen, the new Minister of State for Health, was no less enthusiastic than his predecessor in tackling the state of the country's health. Streams of memoranda and copies of speeches still continue to flow from the Department of Health and Social Security, and if words could do it, there wouldn't be an unhappy family left in Britain. But alas, children continue to be deprived, wives to be beaten, and whole families to sink under the burden of low IQ, emotional immaturity, and a total lack of know-how. The social services wade in where they can, but to some it seems a hopeless task. Financial resources are being cut instead of expanded as everyone had hoped a few years ago, *and* by a Labour government. As we all know only too well, the money is simply not there to spend.

Meanwhile, many thousands continue to live in abject misery. Their problems are so complex that there can be no single answer. Money and other benefits of being a member of the better-paid classes obviously alleviate many of these problems, but not all. The lawyer's wife who lives in dread of the sound of her husband's key in their expensive neo-Georgian door feels the same terror as her counterpart waiting in a two-room slum flat. Their children, lying awake in their beds hoping that tonight won't be a bad night, suffer the same fear whether they sleep in a pretty nursery or share three to a bed. Only, the house of the lawyer being bigger and grander, the neighbours are less likely to hear the thumps and the screams and the NSPCC won't be called in.

Where does one problem begin and another end? We have already seen how violence can involve every member of a family. In one study of battering parents a quarter of the mothers had also been beaten by their husbands. Twenty-seven per cent of the fathers had already been convicted of violence of one sort or another. In another a quarter of the men charged with child murder had also assaulted their wives. Sometimes, when only the wife had been battered, she in turn attacked her child. Yet another study showed that half of a group of men who had attacked their wives had criminal records, while 90 per cent of all of them were themselves brought up in violence.

Most of these probably came from the kind of family Sir Keith was talking about, but money alone, or better education, or rehousing, or somehow changing society so that no one is 'lower-class' any more won't, in themselves, alter these families overnight. The lawyer's family already has all of that, and they and others like them still batter each other, still produce disturbed unhappy children who drop out, take to drugs, steal or kill themselves or someone else. These problems cannot be solved by political argument or revolution alone - they are fundamental to human nature with its diversity of talents and abilities. We are animals, albeit superior ones, living very artificial stressed lives, and to me it seems totally unrealistic in our present state of evolution to expect everyone to fit successfully into the society we have made for ourselves.

We *are* evolving, however as is shown by our increasing concern for the underprivileged and the wounded members of our society. Everywhere people are getting together, forming groups such as those which help the parents of spastic children or drug-takers, the wives of prisoners or the families of schizophrenics. Self-help groups abound, from refuges for battered wives to pre-school groups. Some are supported by official backing, but most rely on their own resourcefulness. Without more money the government itself seems unable to do much more than form committees and make speeches, and these they do in abundance.

As Tom Tomlinson says (in M. Borland (ed.), 1976),

> Central government needs to re-examine its tendency to pass politically expedient legislation requiring already overloaded agencies to do even more work at a point in time when resources are actually being cut in real terms. The anxiety created by this sort of situation reduces the agencies' ability to cope even at the original level.

There are, however, certain actions the government could take which would not need vast funding. Some people have pressed for a Minister for Children. Brian Jackson, Director of the National Educational Research and Development Trust, has repeatedly pointed out that responsibility for children's welfare is split up between five major ministries. The Department of

Health and Social Security is responsible for children's welfare, but their safety on the roads is in the hands of the Department of the Environment, while the Department of Education and Science looks after their schooling unless they get into trouble, when the Home Office steps in. Thousands of children die unnecessarily every year from a variety of causes, from preventable road accidents to inadequate labelling and closures on poisonous substances. But children have no means of putting political pressure on governments; they have no vote, no lobbying power. Just as in cases of baby battering there is occasionally a disastrous lack of co-operation between social workers, health visitors, doctors and police, so - though on a different scale - there is a lack of co-ordination between the different ministries who are responsible for various aspects of the well-being of our children. We have recently created a Minister of Consumer Affairs; would it not be rather more important to create a Minister for Children whose job would be to co-ordinate all policies relating to children? He or she would be informed automatically of any plans or schemes relating, however distantly, to children, so that he could advise and keep all the relevant ministries in touch with each other and their developments. For instance, new town planning and new road schemes all ought to have the special needs of children actively borne in mind. Children don't only go to school or to baby clinics: they use nearly all the public facilities that adults use. The brief of such a minister would be to make every other department as aware as he is, of children as creatures who share our everyday lives but with special needs of their own. The lack of proper facilities for growing children is one very important cause of strain in many abusing families.

At present it would probably not be considered possible to set up a new ministry. The DHSS is already very concerned with children: could they not make room for a new minister and the small department he would need? The governmental answer would probably be that without the executive powers of a full ministry such a minister would be unable to make anyone do anything, either at government or at local level. That other ministries would make polite noises and do nothing, while many, perhaps most, schemes put forward to local councils (for when it comes down to it this is the level at which most social changes have to be implemented) would be discarded in favour of others which seemed more pressing to local councillors at the time. If that were true there would certainly be a very real danger that people would erroneously imagine there had been a great advance - a Minister for Children, by the sound of it, must be a very important man - and reforming zeal might be allowed to fade away although little of real significance had actually been achieved.

Some progress has been made, however. Dr Owen's Children's Act became law at the end of 1975. It will help some children who, as in the tragic case of Maria Colwell, do not want to be dragged away from their foster homes and returned to their natural parents, but it is still not mandatory for all children to be legally represented in their own right when parents ask for the custody of their children. If the court decides there is a conflict of interest between child and parents they are now encouraged to arrange separate representation for the child, but this throws the onus on to the magistrates, who are very busy people with extremely varied points of view and training for the task they have undertaken. Parents applying for revocation of the Care Order which has resulted in their child being removed from them may still have that child returned to them without any further investigation into their suitability if the magistrate concerned feels they are able to look after their child. The magistrate does not have to insist on seeing the original complaints which resulted in the child being removed, nor on seeing the child's social worker (though he may do so if he wishes). Often a child is returned to a totally unsatisfactory home without his social worker being aware of it, or, equally, a social worker may herself ask for the revocation when an unbiased person could see clearly that the parents are quite likely to re-abuse the child. A further snag is that even if the magistrate decides that the parents are totally unsuitable and he places a Care Order on the child intending to have it removed to safety, after a few weeks the local authorities may well return the child to his own parents to care for it on their behalf. Admittedly the child will be subject to their supervision, but the frequent ineffectiveness of this supervision has been proved in too many cases to enumerate.

This is a very complicated subject and there is no space in

this book to go into it thoroughly, but basically until children's Guardians in some form or another are appointed directly to look after the interests of every child who has come to the notice of the caring services there will continue to be unnecessary tragedies. There is much support for this view. In October 1975 the Magistrates' Association passed a resolution proposed by Mrs Phyllis Marks, Chairman of Willesden Juvenile Court, urging the establishment of the office of children's Guardians. At the moment, unless evidence of cruelty can be presented convincingly to a court (clear evidence of cruelty is very difficult and often impossible to obtain) the court's power to protect the child is too weak. We must have a number of children's Guardians, regionally based, who can collate all information from every source about children in danger, who have the power to apply for a Care Order removing a child from his home, without first having to collect evidence strong enough to convict the parents legally, and to see that the Care Order is carried out. *The safety of the child, not the punishment of the parents, would be the brief of such a Guardian.* Exactly what training and background such a Guardian would need is a matter for debate, but many feel strongly that Directors of Social Services (a frequently-made suggestion) would not be suitable. Someone who is unbiased and was not trained in the social services ethos that families should be kept together, if remotely possible, is needed if children's interests are to be properly protected. Some people will protest that parents' rights have already been eroded unnecessarily, and that all that is necessary is better facilities for disadvantaged families to enable them to provide proper care for their children. Obviously this also must be done, but meanwhile, let us put the safety of the children first. Blood may be thicker than water, but it spills as easily.

New laws may be passed and urgent memoranda posted to everyone professionally involved pressing for their co-operation, but we can never ensure, especially at grass-roots level, a common unity of viewpoint. As we have seen, social workers dislike separating families, but the police feel that protection of the citizen (including those too small even to pronounce the word) is their paramount duty; doctors are usually more concerned with repairing an injury than with its cause or its possible recurrence, while health visitors, who are better equipped than social workers to cope with some aspects of the battering situations, complain that they have too little authority. Unlike a social worker, for instance, they cannot directly apply for a Care Order even when, as trained nurses, they know that a child is not thriving properly and suspect unsatisfactory mothering.

The NSPCC's Battered Child Research team frequently found this difficulty of conflicting viewpoint. In order to safeguard their own friendly relations with the families they were looking after they had arranged with the local authorities that it would be they and not the NSPCC workers who should take all necessary steps required for the successful application of Care Orders. In theory this was accepted, but in practice the local authority social workers, understandably enough, disliked carrying out the unpleasant side of casework without the rewards of the therapeutic work. They found themselves in the position of having to break up a family when often they did not think it necessary, while the NSPCC workers, who were looked upon by the parents as trusted friends who would protect them from the law, were in fact the very ones pressing for the separation. In one case, for example, the NSPCC wanted a child removed from a mother who had admitted causing the child very severe multiple injuries which, if she survived, would result in permanent handicap; the local authorities nevertheless queried whether there was enough evidence to obtain a Place of Safety Order and were reluctant to take action.

Lawyers appointed (usually at the instigation of the NSPCC workers) to look after the parents' interests in court were equally confused by the NSPCC's dual role. As none of them had previously had much experience or interest in this particular field they mostly became emotionally involved with the parents' desire to keep their children at home. When damning evidence, previously unknown to them, was produced in court they became even further confused, no longer knowing what would be best for their clients. The NSPCC came to the firm conclusion that any lawyer dealing with such cases must be fully experienced in this emotionally disturbing field, otherwise parents, feeling themselves betrayed on all sides, may then become quite inaccessible to treatment.

When more research has been carried out it may well be that the present attitude of the social services to separating families will change. Certainly the NSPCC's team (who were already more prepared than the local authorities to remove children) concluded that 'with hindsight, we now feel we were occasionally over-optimistic and that some situations could have been better resolved by the child's being permanently removed and offered a good alternative home'. This is something most of us are reluctant to face up to - temporary separation seems severe enough, but permanently to remove a child from its home is such a drastic step that except in the most desperate cases it is understandable if workers try to dodge the issue. Clearer and more broadly-based evidence needs to be gathered of what exactly happens to children left in unsatisfactory homes and to those removed to foster homes or institutional care. There can be no easy answer, but until we have more clues all decisions must be haphazard and dependent more on the emotional response of the worker than on statistical probability.

The necessity for close co-operation between all the agencies concerned with baby battering was one of the main themes of *Children in Danger*. That this co-operation is still unsatisfactory is shown repeatedly in press stories of children who in spite of the attention of a variety of professionals still end up dead. While one must bear in mind that success stories never come to public notice, there is no question that (in spite of the establishment of Area Review Committees and Case Conference Committees as requested by the DHSS) there is still a lack of the kind of co-operation one would like to see. Much has been written on this subject and at least one can now say that the good will is there. No longer is the very fact of baby battering denied, and the diehard 'string 'em up' attitude is rarely heard except in occasional letters to the press. But co-operation needs to be properly organized (by children's Guardians, case co-ordinators on the American model or by some other means): case conferences and general get-togethers are not in themselves sufficient, however well-intentioned. Baby battering arouses anxiety and emotional response in everyone who deals with it. The social services, who have suffered much lately from media accusations of a combination of inefficiency and badly misjudged actions, are particularly vulnerable to criticism. As R. Galdston said of the American scene in 1970,

> The management of child abuse generates a particular and special form of anxiety in those who are charged with responsibility. Agencies have developed techniques . . . to facilitate the sharing of responsibility with others. When such sharing is of information, the result can be useful to the patient. When the sharing is mainly of anxiety, then the results are usually harmful to the patient.

Co-operation between client and worker is of course even more desirable but this also is fraught with difficulties. As discussed in Chapter 7 the parents retain a childish need to impress authority. At the same time they strongly dislike being returned to their old status of obedient child faced by dominating parent figure. They show this ambivalence by making appointments but rarely turning up for them, or they lie so convincingly about their children's injuries that they do themselves out of the very treatment they know quite well they need. As one mother said to me,

> 'If only they'd made me go away for treatment I'd have been grateful, it would have made all the difference, but I created such a fuss about being parted from my kids they gave in. They shouldn't have, it was up to them to be strong-minded; they could see what I really needed better than I could.'

As we saw in the chapters on marital violence, fathers are notoriously difficult to reach. Most of them are out during working hours, and while many social workers are willing to call at night to see them the mothers are likely to object to this. They feel the social worker belongs to them, is their own special confidant, and often become jealous - even sexually - of any relationship developing between workers and their husbands. This is exacerbated by the fact that the marriages are often unhappy. It is difficult to know what can be done about this particular problem other than appointing separate social workers to deal with the husbands, but this is an expensive method and one that few areas could afford.

Jealousy of the social worker is also very noticeable with regard to the children; everyone working in this field has found it is important not to make too much fuss of a child in front of its parents if they want to keep the parents' trust and friendship. Once the worker is regarded as being more interested in the child than in the parent there is an immediate drying-up of warmth, and the worker is relegated to the position of an interfering official, one of 'them'. This is unpleasant for the worker, especially if the child runs up to kiss her or wants to sit on her lap. The NSPCC, for example, refer to one mother who, being angry with her worker for briefly attending to the child, retaliated by reading a story to the child and totally ignoring the worker. An infantile piece of rudeness, perhaps, but one that can be hurtful to a worker trying to do her best to help a family.

A further problem all the helping agencies have in coping with battering parents is that, while it is often they who first bring their difficulties to the notice of the authorities, in the case of injury they usually deny they have actually battered their child. This makes correct diagnosis very difficult, especially for those professionals who are unwilling even to consider the possibility of battering. Equally, a parent's early 'cries for help' before real injury has taken place are usually so well wrapped up that no official action is taken. A complaint to her GP about the baby's eating habits or a fear that a toddler is not walking early enough will probably be taken at its face value, and unless the mother is able to indicate that what she really wants is to talk about her violent feelings she is unlikely to obtain the help she badly needs. With present-day publicity more and more parents are asking for help directly, but even so they often do not get proper assistance. One hears of many cases of mothers who have reported their worries about their husbands' violence, or of fathers who complain to doctors or social workers about their wives' attitudes to their children, but official action was inadequate or taken too late to prevent at least one severe battering.

Of course there is the other side of the picture, one that can cause ill-will especially among those who already feel that too much attention is paid to battering at the cost of other more widely-spread problems. I have been told by several workers in the field (hospital emergency departments included) that some over-conscientious parents are now coming to them to express their fears about their occasional violent feelings, who, the workers are convinced, would never actually lift a finger to their children. Guilt is strong in most of us, and a broken night coming soon after reading an article on baby battering is enough to make most of us wonder just how far we might go if pressed too far. But doctors and hospitals simply could not cope with a rush of uneasy but basically safe parents who want a reassuring chat. It is easy enough for me to say that if one parent out of a hundred is actually a potential batterer that is sufficient justification for any time wasted, but a busy doctor must see it otherwise. Perhaps a kind of Samaritans service run by volunteers could be set up. Certainly on a radio phone-in programme recently I was amazed and appalled at the queue of callers all wanting to discuss their fears, most of which seemed only too frighteningly valid. To talk to someone is a major need of many stressed parents, not only of potential batterers, and an anonymous chat to an understanding person could be a very useful outlet leading, where necessary, to a referral to professional help. It might turn out that few genuinely potential batterers were among the callers, as notoriously they find any kind of communication very difficult, but at least it would clear many others out of the way, leaving the professional field open for those who need it most.

We can see, then, that if battering parents are to be effectively helped wholehearted co-operation between every-one concerned is the first necessity. But again, this is easier said than done. In addition to the problems of differing points of view there is the question of status. The medical profession in particular has a firmly defined hierarchical structure; senior consultants do not take too kindly to submitting to the wisdom of middle- or lower-rank social workers. Some older professionals will dislike the enthusiasm of young colleagues, feeling their new ideas are all untried theory, bearing little relation to reality. A senior policeman is likely to feel himself apart from the other members of a committee, knowing that at any point he can break up the whole working situation by insisting on a prosecution; an awareness of this superior power is only too obvious in the attitudes of some policemen, to the chagrin of their committee colleagues.

Most committees are deliberately formulated to contain a high number of participants of senior status so that any decisions made can then be put into action without the need to obtain permission from a higher level. This means, however, that those working on a daily basis with clients have less say, if they are present at all. As a result the discussions are likely to be rather formal, with varying effect. John Pickett in discussing case conferences (in M. Borland (ed.), 1976) writes:

> A well ordered and efficient case conferencing system is no guarantee against failures in communication; at its best it merely ensures that, at a given point in time, adequate communication is occurring. Good case management requires a high level of therapeutic skill and effective communication and co-operation throughout the life span of the case. Most cases are managed, however, against a background of inadequate record-keeping, faulty communications and seemingly endless changes in the personnel involved. For these reasons a process of constant monitoring seems essential.

Confidentiality between doctor and patient is less of a problem to co-operation than it used to be. It is now generally considered permissible for a doctor to pass on information if he is worried about the safety of a child, though the police are still unlikely to be informed because of their powers of prosecution. It is here that personal contact is particularly useful - a hint dropped to a working acquaintance is far less drastic than the sending of a formal memorandum which would have to be officially noted and filed. Doctors do not want to believe a patient could actually batter her own children, and if it should be proved they prefer to offload the whole thing on to the social services. Few doctors will attend case conferences, partly for this reason, and partly because they are very busy, though which of the other professionals concerned are not equally overworked? Smith and Hanson write (1974a):

> It almost seems as if the medical profession has abdicated its responsibility to local authorities and voluntary organizations, whose roles in some respects are complementary but in others may not always be harmonious. Both agencies rely heavily upon inexperienced and possibly inadequately trained social workers who are as yet ill-equipped to deal with these difficult cases.

An illustration of the difficulties inherent in genuine co-operation between such differently orientated groups as police, doctors and social workers is their attitudes to a suspected battering parent. For instance, doctors and social workers want to believe whatever the client tells them; the attitude of the police is exactly opposite. They are trained to find out the truth as far as they can, and whereas a doctor or social worker will avoid stringent or lengthy questioning so as not to upset a client, the police have no such inhibitions. This causes great annoyance to the other professionals who see much of their therapeutic work being undone. In reply the police will claim that their sceptical attitude means they arrive at the truth quickly and positive action can be taken promptly, perhaps with the result of a child's life being saved; this to them is of greater importance than the possible undermining of a client's growing confidence. They add that social workers, etc. are unlikely to object if the person being questioned is a burglar who has stolen their own household goods. All the same, the police are very aware of these differences of approach and many are now making great efforts to work closely and sympathetically with medical and social services colleagues in battering cases.

Nevertheless, in the end most of the day-to-day work falls on to the shoulders of social workers and health visitors. Health visitors, who are qualified nurses employed by the Area Health Authorities, see all new babies, and often work in close collaboration with GPs or hospitals. They have far too high a caseload to do more than give clients simple social advice, but their medical recognition of an ailing child is invaluable in picking out cases where the social services need to be called in.

It is then up to the social workers to keep in regular touch with a family to give it the support it needs.

Bad publicity has not helped social workers, who have become very self-conscious on the subject of baby-battering. They know battering parents are most likely to deny everything but also they know that the parents desperately want help; they know that if they don't get results in time and a tragedy happens they will take their turn at being pilloried by the media, but they also know that a delicate approach is necessary if they are not to scare off their clients. Some social workers pass through a relationship lasting for years with parents who have severely injured their children without the word 'battered' crossing anyone's lips, both workers and parents colluding in pretending the injuries were caused accidentally. This may be partly because the workers are unable to admit the actual facts even to themselves - a form of mental cowardice, if you like - but it is also partly due to a fear of alienating the client. Sometimes this collusion is even kept up when other professionals become involved, such as doctors or hospital staff. As to the police, I doubt if any social worker would voluntarily let them know about a client who has abused his child except in the most violent cases, and even then many would see no point in bringing in the law.

If a field worker is able to discuss cases regularly with an uninvolved senior the exclusiveness of the bond between worker and client can be loosened sufficiently for the field worker to stand back and take a cool look at what is happening in the family, but many workers have totally inadequate supervision. In this case the emotional involvement can become so complete that the worker can genuinely convince herself the child is accident-prone or the mother merely hasty-tempered, even if a child has been hospitalized, perhaps suffering permanent injury. This may sound incredible to a lay reader, but clients such as these make great emotional demands on their workers. If they do not give fully of themselves the parents will not accept them - they have no time for 'cold' professionals whom they feel are judging and probably condemning them. The result can be that the social worker loses her professional detachment and begins to make the same excuses that families make among themselves.

It is this sort of experience that makes some people question the value of social workers to society as a whole. Much as I would like to explore this subject, for reasons of space I can only offer one or two comments. At a British Association of Social Workers' conference Bill Jordan, a lecturer in social work at Exeter University, said, 'I personally believe that social workers are *helping* to precipitate baby battering.' Taken out of context these words sound startling, but it is obvious to many that we are asking far too much of our junior social workers, many of whom are untrained. In November 1976 David Ennals, Secretary of State for Social Services, agreed to consider setting a date by which time anyone being appointed to a social work job would have to be properly qualified. It has been revealed that three-fifths of field social workers are untrained, while nearly nine-tenths of residential social workers have no recognized qualifications. Christopher Andrews, secretary of the British Association of Social Workers, said that he hoped this date would not be more than two years away. Obviously untrained social workers already in jobs will need to go through a training course to bring them up to the necessary standard, and it is hoped to have half of all present social workers qualified by the mid-1980s, although Mr Ennals is believed to consider that economic constraints may prevent this.

At the moment most of our qualified social workers are having to spend the majority of their time organizing the rest and can rarely be spared to go out on the job themselves. Untrained workers with insufficient supervision struggle to keep families together, to help them get all the public aid they can, to bolster up their confidence and support them through endless dramas and conflicts. Sometimes the results are heartwarming, and I am full of admiration for those who persevere with such a backbreaking, stressful job.

But there is another side to this type of supportive care which is beginning to attract attention. Some families have received continuous support for several generations and cannot conceive a life without it. One worker told me of the remark of a client of hers. Two generations of the family had been looked after by a succession of agencies, and now the eldest daughter (a girl of fifteen who all her life had been in and out of trouble) found herself pregnant. 'Ah well,' she said to the current social worker, 'I'll miss you.' 'Why?' said the social worker, 'I'm not changing my job.' The girl looked at her, puzzled. 'But now I'm starting my own family', she said, 'I'll need my *own* social worker from now on, won't I?' No one in that girl's family had ever filled in any forms, kept any interviews, taken any jobs, appeared before any court, without the active support of a social worker. It was inconceivable to her that she should be expected to manage on her own. It is true that some families are of such low intelligence it would be impossible for them to cope alone; even so, an emphasis on training them to be as independent as possible rather than on gentle supportive friendship might in the long run make for a more healthy society.

In the autumn of 1976 the British Association of Social Workers brought out a code of practice with regard to child abuse for social workers to follow. It stresses the need for co-ordination with other agencies, the proper reporting of every incident, etc., and emphasizes the need for more resources to be made available. 'The code clearly states that a great deal more investment is required if an adequate service is to be provided,' says Chris Andrews, General Secretary of BASW. He wants to see more workers trained so that less responsibility is laid on juniors, more foster homes for permanent and temporary placements made available, more children's homes, along with better housing and other kinds of support for the families. There can be no doubt that more money is desperately needed in every branch of the social services, local authorities, hospitals - the list is endless - not just for battered babies but for everyone else too. Unfortunately it does not look as though it is forthcoming, at least not for some considerable time. So until circumstances change we must make do with what we have, and try not to expect too much of a service that is grossly undermanned and overworked.

We have seen what the government and other official bodies are doing to help battering families. There has been progress, but most of it has been aimed at directly helping individual families known to have battered. Broader approaches, some not even concerned with battering at all but with inter-family relationships or early mother-child interaction, may in the long run be of more use. Unfortunately prophylactic medicine is still in its infancy, and for some time is likely to remain a failure-to-thrive infant. Immense rewards would be given to a team of researchers who produced vaccines to cure common cancers such as breast, womb, prostate or stomach; but researchers who discover environmental causes of cancer such as pollution, food additives, diet, stress, etc., because they cannot dramatically change cancer figures overnight, earn little more than a paragraph or two in the papers. No one actually doubts it is better to prevent an illness in the first place than to cure it after it has occurred, but the relevant statistics are inevitably negative ones and impossible to prove. Who can tell how much changes in social attitudes, economics, even climate might also have affected whichever illness or problem has been alleviated? Whereas if ninety-nine out of a hundred people recover from a disease which previously carried a four out of five chance of being fatal, there can be no doubt a miraculous break-through has been discovered.

It is obvious that improving family relationships will lower the incidence of inter-family violence, and most probably lead to an eventual lessening of violence in society as a whole, but it would be impossible to pin down such a success to any one particular cause. If only we could inoculate babies against unhappiness as easily as we now inoculate them against polio! Yet the body of knowledge is growing so fast that if we were really determined we could go a good way along this path. We shall never be able fully to protect anyone against the random tragedies of life - death of a loved one, physical handicap, accidents - but already we could do so much more to improve people's mental health than we do at present.

I mentioned briefly in Chapter 4 the work done by Drs Marshall Klaus and John Kennell at Case Western Reserve University in Cleveland on the reactions between mothers and babies immediately after birth. This is an excellent example of the kind of study being carried out by many researchers which could have important repercussions on our future society if its implications were fully understood and assimilated. Hospitals, naturally enough, are at present mainly concerned with the physical health of the mothers and babies in their maternity wards. The need for hygiene and the necessity of monitoring babies for any early symptoms of malfunctioning mean that normally babies are removed from their mothers within a minute or two of birth. In America, apart from feeding times they are usually kept apart in nurseries; in Britain more and more hospitals leave the babies in cots at the mothers' bedsides during part of the day, but even then the mothers are not normally encouraged to take them up except during feeding or visiting hours.

Hospitalization of expectant mothers for the birth is rapidly becoming as universal in Britain as it already is in the USA, against the desires of many people. Undoubtedly many mothers and children are alive and well today who might otherwise not be because of the instant availability of expert care and complicated machinery. A mother can bleed to death from a massive haemorrhage or a child die or be permanently brain-damaged for lack of an oxygen tent. No one, however healthy, can be certain such an emergency will not happen to her.

Against this unquestioned benefit must be set a number of losses, however. Toddlers temporarily lose their mothers and their jealousy of the new baby may be heightened. The father is still frequently denied access to the mother during the birth, who - as she is in hospital - may consider herself a 'patient' as though she were sick. But more important than any of these is the interruption of the establishment of an immediate bond between mother and child. For several years Klaus and Kennell's work (briefly discussed earlier) has centred around this bonding, and from it has come a series of interesting results. To take an example of one of their studies, a group of 28 first-time mothers and their normal full-term babies - all carefully matched for age, marriage, socio-economic status, and the weight and sex of the infants - was split into two. The first group of 14 were given their nude babies to hold and explore for an hour within the first two hours after delivery and they also had them for an extra five hours each day in addition to feeding time for the next three days. The other 14 mothers went through the routine common to most American hospitals - they were briefly shown their babies at birth, saw them for a moment a few hours later, then were given them for feeding purposes for twenty to thirty minutes every four hours. Apart from that the babies were kept in the nursery. There was thus quite a difference between the two groups, but not as great as would be expected in a home delivery: all the babies were still separated from their mothers for a while immediately after birth, and more drugs and anaesthesia were given than would be the case in most home births.

Even so, the differences in mother-child relationships between the two groups were clear-cut. After a month the first group of mothers who had returned for medical checks to the hospital stood closer to their babies during examination, soothed the babies more, were more reluctant to leave them in someone else's care, and when nursing them engaged in greater eye-to-eye contact and fondled them more than the second group. A year later there were still significant differences. They spent more time helping the doctor examine their babies and soothed them more when they cried. At two years the mothers were talking to their babies differently, but this study has to be re-checked as only five mothers from each group were tested, which is too small a sample to be valid. Further studies have had similar results, and there seems little doubt that those few extra hours of contact in the first days of life can make a noticeable difference to the relations between mother and child for at least twelve months and probably much longer.

An earlier filmed study by the same team of newly-born babies and their mothers, confirmed by later studies, showed that, at the first contact between them, all the mothers first touched their nude infants' extremities with their fingertips, then within four to eight minutes began gently to massage or lay the palms of their hands on the babies' trunks. Every mother made this changeover from fingertip exploring to firmer holding with the palms. Often the mother grew progressively more excited, then the excitement would quieten and sometimes she even fell asleep. During this study the mothers were alone in a room, and time-lapse films were made through a two-way mirror. Klaus and his colleagues in their article 'Does human maternal behaviour after delivery show a characteristic pattern?' (1975b) note that in another research project (Rubin, 1963) mothers given their babies wrapped up in blankets instead of nude took several days to pass from fingertip touching to palm contact. Mothers of premature babies were even slower to make this change.

The excitement of the mother during this 'recognition' period is felt by others too, particularly in home births where a group of people may be present. A kind of general euphoria can take place with everybody present feeling intense joy. Clearly such reactions can have repercussions in the acceptance into the family of the child, particularly in the case of the father, who is too often ignored. Dr John Lind has found that when fathers were asked twice to undress their newborn babies and establish eye-to-eye contact with them, there was a significant difference between their caretaking behaviour and that of controls three months later.

An important finding was that the fingertip touching, etc., was seriously inhibited if, under hospital conditions, other people were present, whereas the presence of known observers in a home birth such as family, friends or a familiar midwife added to rather than subtracted from the relaxation and pleasure of the mother. American mothers in the hospital experiment were not particularly disturbed by the camera and audio-tape technique, but Guatemalan mothers were almost as disturbed by this as by the actual presence of doctors and nurses in the delivery room after the birth.

Of even greater interest was the confirmation of the profound importance of eye-to-eye contact. Some researchers doubt whether a baby can focus properly on its mother's eyes until four weeks of age, but certainly many mothers feel direct contact seems to be taking place right from the beginning. Researchers at Park Hospital, Oxford, are perfecting an eye-movement recorder which they hope will help elucidate this point, as they have found reactions similar to the American women's among their mothers.

The Americans clearly wanted to wake their sleeping babies to see their eyes, and were recorded as saying things like, 'If you open your eyes I will know you are alive.' They reported feeling much closer to their babies once they had simultaneously looked at each other. The time spent thus was quite considerable: in a 10-minute session the mothers increased the time spent looking at the babies *en face* from 10 per cent in the first 3 minutes to 23 per cent in the final 3 minutes.

It is thought that such eye-to-eye contact is an important releaser of caretaking feelings in the mother. It can take a long time for mothers to establish a close relationship with blind babies, and they find it difficult to interpret their babies' needs. One mother of a baby born without eyes reported that she could only regard her child as 'a person' when glass eye-prostheses were implanted at the age of 18 months. Klaus has pointed out that in the USA most mothers are not given their babies until several hours after birth when they are sleeping and are not easily aroused, and in any case the eyelids are usually partially closed because of the instillation of silver nitrate. In addition drugs given to help the birth can dampen responses of both mother and child for some hours afterwards. Martin Richards and his colleagues at Cambridge have found that such drug effects persist for some time, and that up to 60 weeks the affected babies have less social interchange with their mothers than babies whose mothers were not given analgesics.

But mothers who have been separated from their babies by over-efficient hospital care need not despair, for this 'maternal sensitive period', as Klaus and Kennell call it, is not a once-and-for-all affair, as is imprinting. Such bonding can be achieved at a later date, but it will take longer and be more difficult to attain. The importance of the sensitivity of this period is shown by an occurrence in an Israeli hospital reported by Klaus and Kennell, when two babies were accidentally switched and the unsuspecting mothers took the wrong infants home. Two weeks later the error was discovered, but now the mothers who had cared for these children as their own had come to love them and they wanted to keep them. It was the fathers who insisted on the change, pointing out the importance of facial and other family characteristics. Similar reactions have been reported by others in similar circumstances.

We seem to have spent a long time on research not directly related to baby battering, but when one remembers how frequently mothers of battered children were parted temporarily from their babies because of illness or prematurity, we see more clearly how the vital union between mother and baby can be inhibited. In the research just discussed it was found that mothers temporarily separated from their children were clumsy and hesitant when they began to look after them, taking much longer than normal to learn how to cope with ordinary simple caretaking tasks. Significantly R E. Helfer has found the incidence of battering of children born by Caesarean section to be ten times greater than with normal deliveries, a figure which points to similar conclusions.

What can be done to help where separation is necessary? Klaus and Kennell investigated a group of mothers whose infants were born prematurely. Half the mothers were allowed to visit their babies in the premature unit as soon as they were physically able, but the other half did not see their infants for three weeks. The early contact mothers were found on the babies' discharge to look at their babies more while feeding them, and the mothers of girl babies to hold them closer than the mothers of girls in the late-contact group. Standford Binet IQ tests at 42 months showed significantly higher scoring in the early-contact babies (mean IQ 99 against 85). They also found a correlation between the IQ at 42 months of the two groups and the amount of time the mothers had spent looking at their babies while feeding them at one month of age. A follow-up study of these children will obviously be of great interest, but its significance as far as battering is concerned is that since so many babies are attacked or killed in the first weeks of their life, successful mother-child interaction at that stage is of vital importance, regardless of whether or not the children make up any bonding or intellectual difference at a later age.

The mother's visiting in the premature unit must of course go beyond a mere peering at the child inside its cot. Dr T. B. Brazelton reports that, since premature or damaged babies have difficulty in establishing the vitally important eye-to-eye contact with their mothers, he has been examining babies' responses to auditory stimulation. He and his colleagues find that infants respond automatically to female voices, will quieten on hearing one and turn towards its source. Their faces show they are expecting some response from the owner of the voice, and when a mother (who may be disappointed in and rejecting towards her child) has this reaction pointed out to her she 'softens and gets locked onto the baby's face'. The doctors are able to show her that the baby is already responding to her and explain that by the time he is ready to go home he will have improved further. They also take this opportunity to discuss any problems with her. She is thus helped to attach herself to her baby and also to adjust to any physical defects he may have. When she takes the baby home she is given a goal to work towards with advice on how to achieve it; with such help it is often found that when the mothers return for checks they have doubled the expected rate of progress. With this type of aid such a mother's attitude can change dramatically. As Brazelton says in Klaus *et al.* (1975a): 'It is partly her own self-image which is at stake, not just her image of the baby. By giving her an active therapeutic role, you are giving her credit for having the capacity to respond to and nurture even a damaged baby.'

Such studies as these show what may be achieved in the future. There is unfortunately no space to elaborate on other examples of research into early mother-child relationships, such as Frederick Leboyer's work on peaceful childbirth; William Condon's work in Boston on language development in babies; Aiden Macfarlane at Park Hospital, Oxford, on interaction between mother and child from the moment of birth, particularly the development of communication between them; Colwyn Trevarthen at Edinburgh who has found that if a mother, instead of continuing to respond to her baby's attempts at communication (eight-to-ten-week-old babies were used in this experiment) suddenly freezes her face and presents an absolutely blank expression to him, the baby is deeply puzzled, soon becomes dejected and withdrawn, then enters a state of acute depression which persists for some minutes after the mother has returned to her normal responsive behaviour. The significance of this last discovery with regard to battering mothers, who so often have severely ambivalent feelings towards their babies, is obvious.

This once neglected field is now one of the most thriving areas of psychological research activity. How can we persuade all those concerned to take full advantage of these studies? For the true roots of violence, to my mind, do not stem from poverty but from man's complicated make-up, no longer animal, not yet saint. It is not enough to argue that if we cure poverty we cure violence: we alleviate misery but that is not at all the same thing. To be happy, humans need a complicated interwoven set of circumstances, and freedom from want is only one strand of this net. I have often heard old people talking regretfully of their pinched pasts - 'We were happy then, in spite of having nothing' was a phrase repeated again and again. My first reaction was always anger that a cheap rag doll or an orange and a bag of sweets doled out by some well-heeled middle-class matriarch at a Sunday School outing should be remembered with such gratitude and joy seventy years later, yet, looking at the bursting cupboards of today's kids, I wonder whether *any* of their toys will be remembered in that way when they are old? While we are improving the social lot of the many thousands amongst us who are still too short of comforts which the rest of us take for granted, we must not lose sight of the fact that it is something else again that makes us happy or unhappy.

Fewer people in the middle and upper economic ranges commit violent crimes, certainly, but to deduce from this that the high rate of crime in the unskilled classes is solely due to poverty is too simplistic. Yet one still hears this outdated argument. Society is constantly changing, the less bright and the emotionally crippled slipping down the social ladder and the healthy, bright ones climbing up. People at the bottom of the ladder are not just poor, they are also the residue of generations of social movement. The children of low-IQ parents tend to revert upwards to the normal mean, while the children of highly intelligent parents tend to revert back a few points. This basic pattern will continue whatever social aid we give: however much social engineering we perform we can never ever achieve a state of total equality. We can give everyone the same pay, house everyone in identical houses, make every man a socially-equal brother, but there will still be some who make a success of whatever they do and others whose ability is far lower. To pretend otherwise is criminally wilful, as harmful to true progress as is the obnoxious attitude of the high Tory or the blinkered racialist.

All of this is perfectly obvious, even trite, but it is something that people do not actually like to say. But we must say it, and then we must ask ourselves what are the main reasons for this persisting inequality and is there anything we can do about it? Innate variance in IQ is the most obvious cause of social inequality, and since genetic engineering is unacceptable to the great majority of people we must accept that some intellectual differences between people will continue to exist. But another factor, which so strongly affects what we make of our natural endowments, emotional stability, maturity - call it what you will - we can do something about. We have already examined various studies which show that abused children improve their IQs when they are properly cared for, and that the IQ of premature babies improves if their mother is helped to establish a close link with them. Self-confidence, a feeling of being wanted, warmth towards others - without these none of us can achieve our full potential. Right from the very first moments of birth, perhaps before, our future ability to achieve happiness lies in the balance. By 'happiness' in this context I do not mean the odd moment of pure joy, but a fairly consistent feeling that all is well with our particular world, that we are in charge of our destiny, that even in times of deep sadness we can sense the existence of a light beyond the blackness.

Few of us have as much as we would like of this emotional security. No longer propped up by religion, most of us manage as best we can, fortunate that our upbringing was good enough not to inflict on us gross disabilities. But significant numbers of people never have even a glimpse of what it is like to be emotionally secure. Their life is full of distress, bitterness, jealousy of others and repressed or not-so-repressed violence. If they come under the care of psychiatrists they will probably begin to understand why they are so unhappy, but this knowledge rarely seems to do them much good. Therapy sometimes helps them, as does consistent friendship and support, but the damage such unhappy people can do to society around them and their own families is only too obvious.

Whether or not society is more violent than it used to be is an impossible question to answer: we have totally different standards from our ancestors. We don't cut off heads and exhibit them as warnings on stakes any more, but we do drop bombs and fry people alive. At least previous generations had the guts to look what they had done squarely in the face. We prefer to do it by remote push-button, and if some social aberrant actually kicks an old lady in the face with his own two feet we are appalled, but I don't know whether that makes us a less or a more violent society.

Most of us nowadays have some smattering of psychology, but we still want it both ways. We accept that a violent criminal's childhood has caused him to be overtly violent, but we still want him punished. We say, 'Others have had dreadful backgrounds like his, but they don't do what he did.' True. So why is he different? What extra factor or factors caused him to break into violence while his brother is merely a defeated little man of mild temper?

Many people know many of the answers. Research never stops. But what happens to it? Other researchers and seriously interested people read the original published papers. If its appeal is wide enough it is picked up by the media, there are a few articles, maybe a few moments in a television magazine or even the accolade of a whole programme to itself. The gist of it may enter the consciousness of a fairly large number of people, and a few rare practitioners of whatever discipline is involved will relate it to their everyday work. But the ordinary person will continue his way unaffected.

For years now researchers have been discovering the importance of those first vital days between mother and baby, and still most hospitals snatch the baby away within seconds of its first breath. For fifteen years battered children have been news, yet there is still no nationwide attempt to teach all new mothers and fathers the reality of rearing children, with all its stresses and disappointments as well as its joys, still no support offered freely after birth *before* problems arise. The damage has to be done first before the authorities will move in. As we have seen, battered wives are getting better treatment at last, but apart from a new project by the NSPCC nothing much is being done to prevent the young children of such marriages from growing up into a new generation of oppressors and victims.

If only we could change our priorities and overhaul the way our system works, have closer liaison between those who find out *why* and those who *do*, we could make rapid strides forward. After all, when financial profits are involved there is no such problem. New proprietary drugs leave the scientist's laboratory and arrive on the GP's desk with indecent haste. The knowledge that a baby is happier if its mother looks into its eyes within a few minutes of birth brings immediate financial benefit to no one. But in the long run, how we should all prosper if every child born into this world had such a start in life. There are a few evangelists here and there trying to ensure that new knowledge does percolate through to the medical establishment and others, but they only convince those who are ready to listen. Most are not. These argue, with some justification, that they are busy, that resources are limited, and new theories are seldom properly validated. Move with caution, don't rush into the unknown. It is true that the Thalidomide tragedy taught us not to *run*, but as long as the physical health of mother and child is properly guarded it is difficult to see what harm is likely to come from copying much of the eminently sensible research that we have been looking at.

Another piece of research which has an important bearing on the kind of atmosphere in which many children are brought up is being carried out by Prof. George Brown and his colleagues at Bedford College, on depression in women. By depression they mean not the sort of general unhappiness and dissatisfactions which seems endemic now amongst so many mothers at home looking after children, but depression involving physical and mental symptoms severe enough to be classified as needing treatment if a psychiatrist were to examine the woman concerned.

For the purposes of the research they found it simplest to divide the women they were studying into working-class (not only semi-skilled and manual labour but also what was originally labelled an intermediate group, such as skilled manual labour, tailors, typists and builders' foremen) and middle-class (the upper end of the intermediate group, mainly defined by husband or wife having received education until sixteen, and managers, professional, and small business owners, etc.). Incredibly, their research has found that 25 per cent of working-class women in the area studied (Camberwell) were psychiatrically disturbed as compared with 5 per cent middle-class women. Yet hardly any of these had seen a psychiatrist, and less than half had even been to their GP about their symptoms. When the sample was reduced to mothers with children under six years of age the class differences became even more marked. Forty-two per cent of working-class mothers were psychiatrically disturbed while the proportion of middle-class mothers remained unchanged at 5 per cent.

One's first reaction to such extraordinary figures is that the research is biased or incomplete, but Prof. Brown's work has been conducted scrupulously and bears close examination by anyone who cares to check out his figures. I should perhaps repeat that these figures refer to clinically depressed women. Very many middle-class women suffer from some form of depression, but the majority of these are at the most borderline cases which are not considered severe enough to warrant treatment by a psychiatrist. When Prof. Brown and his colleagues went on to discover why these figures should be so disparate it became clear that severe life events such as a dangerous illness of someone close, the loss of a job, an unwanted pregnancy, failure to obtain a house, or an eviction, etc., caused working-class women greater psychiatric distress than they did middle-class women. This was particularly marked among women with children: 39 per cent of working-class mothers developed a psychiatric disorder after a severe event as against 6 per cent of middle-class mothers.

To compound this vulnerability, working-class women with young children were considerably more likely to be faced with a life crisis involving husband, children or housing than their middle-class counterpart - other severe life events occurred equally between the classes. Active motherhood was the only period when the total number of crises was significantly different between the classes, the researchers finding that in general, from childbirth until the children leave home, middle-class women were well protected. Only 18 per cent of middle-class mothers suffered a severe event as against 41 per cent of similarly-placed working-class women during the year under study. The former may have problems, but they usually have adequate housing, their husbands are rarely sent to prison or their children arrested for breaking and entering or soliciting. Added to these differences is the important fact that middle-class women have something to look forward to; they feel more in control of their lives. They make sacrifices for their children expecting them eventually to prosper, they accept a small income now hoping their husband's career will soon flourish, and know that once the children are at school they themselves can go out and recommence their careers or study for a new one. Female middle-class angst is real enough, but the opportunities are there if enough energy and determination can be summoned to take advantage of them. For working-class women the picture is different: generally speaking they have no such promising outlook. Of course there are exceptions, but among the group studied the future outlook was a dreary one. In any case, the working-class ethos has always been to look at the present rather than the future, and present problems were often quite overwhelming.

This discovery that working-class mothers are much more likely to suffer the kind of event that can cause psychiatric distress than middle-class mothers, combined with the knowledge that, when faced with such a severe event, they are also considerably more likely to become psychiatrically ill than a middle-class woman, might be thought by some to be sufficient explanation of why eight times as many working-class mothers with children under six are disturbed as middle-class ones. But Prof. Brown and his colleagues decided to take their research further and have now come up with some revealing results.

The first is that close intimacy with a husband or lover gives almost complete protection against the onset of psychiatric disorder caused by a severe event such as we have been discussing. Faced with such a happening only 4 per cent of the women with an intimate relationship became disturbed. But the lack of intimacy does not in itself cause breakdown - there was little difference in disturbance between those with and those without such a tie who had not suffered an unpleasant life event.

The researchers found a substantial difference in intimacy rating between the classes, which was sufficient in itself to account for much of working-class vulnerability. The middle-class women stayed very close to their husbands when their children were young, but by the time their children had left home only 73 per cent were still as intimate. Working-class women started well, but the birth of children caused a dramatic change. Only 37 per cent were rated as intimate when they had a child under six. Thus their intimacy with their husbands while caring for young children (the very time they were most subjected to severe life events) was considerably less than that of the middle-class woman. However, by the time their children had left home they had regained much of their intimacy with their husbands and were only slightly less intimate than middle-class women at that later stage in their lives.

Three further factors were found to be important in precipitating mental disturbance, when the subject was faced by a severe event (but not otherwise). Having suffered the loss of or separation from a mother before the age of eleven, experienced by 9 per cent of working-class women against 3 per cent of middle-class women, was one such factor. Another was having three or more children under the age of fourteen at home (this applied to 43 per cent of working-class as opposed to 14 per cent of middle-class women). Not working outside the home was the third factor, and although there was no class difference in the age at which the mothers of both classes were prepared to leave their children to go out to work, fewer middle-class women were tied by having a child under the age of six present. After their children had passed that age three-quarters of all the women worked.

Having a job was clearly helpful in preventing an unpleasant event from causing psychiatric disorder. Of the women kept at home by children who were not on intimate terms with their husbands 79 per cent became disturbed when faced with a severe difficulty as against only 14 per cent of those who were working. Prof. Brown does not feel that the companionship of others is the simple answer to why this should be so, as close relationships even with the woman's father, mother or siblings gave nothing like the same protection as intimacy with a husband. He suggests that a sense of achievement might be the crucial factor, as self-esteem and a sense of being someone in their own right are qualities lacking in many of the women he tested. As one working-class woman who had recently started work commented, 'The money wasn't much but it gave me a great boost.' Poor marital relations make a woman, who has been brought up to consider marriage as the high point of her life, feel a failure, and if bad housing conditions leading to an uncomfortable, unattractive home are added to her worries, one may understand her lack of self-esteem. Unable to work because of small children, she may feel too tired, or too tied, to go to her doctor, let alone a psychiatrist. Of the women who were not on intimate terms with their husbands, only half as many saw their doctors as those who were, which suggests that the husbands themselves might have persuaded their wives to seek treatment.

Prof. Brown concludes,

> Certain groups of women in our society have a significantly greater than average risk of suffering from depressive conditions. To the extent that the unequal distribution of such risk is the result of more widely recognized inequalities within our society, and our findings certainly point in this direction, we believe that it constitutes a major social injustice.

I have gone into this research in some detail because from it one can begin to see the roots of much of the disturbance in our society. If further studies bear out Prof. Brown's figures (an earlier 1971 study by Naomi Richman found similar figures of depression in working-class women) we will have to accept that nearly half the working-class children in Britain are brought up by mothers who for certain periods of their childhood are suffering from borderline or severe depression. Their own emerging personalities must inevitably be affected by this, and the grounds laid for yet another generation of disturbed, unhappy adults.

Finally, with regard to baby battering, Prof. Brown found some very disturbing evidence indeed. When he investigated the number of children of borderline or psychiatrically disturbed mothers who had received emergency treatment after an accident, he found it was more than twice as high as the children of normal undisturbed mothers. Of the women who became depressed during the year in which they were being studied, the rate of accidents to their children prior to this onset of depression had been the same as among normal women. How many of these 'accidents' were genuine and how many were directly caused by the distressed mother is unknown, but even if none of them were intentional the implication is of great importance in the study of baby battering.

One point that has emerged time and time again during discussions with battering mothers is their sense of isolation. This is by no means unique to them - it is the constant plaint of nearly every young mother tied to her children. In this chapter we have broadened out the study of battered children to include those emotionally damaged by their parents and by the actions of society around them. Whereas comparatively few of us physically batter our children, I wonder whether any of us can claim never to have done them some - however little - emotional damage? One might even argue that a child brought up in truly ideal conditions would still be harmed, because he would be dangerously unprepared for life as an adult in normal adult society. We all of us inflict some damage on our children partly because, still young ourselves, we are not yet mature enough to cope easily with the complications and demands of marriage and child-raising, and partly because society as a whole is still light-years away from taking seriously the delicate demands of the human psyche.

One of the most worrying aspects of our present society because of its possible long-term effects - the isolation of the young mother - is by its nature eminently suited to group aid. The Pre-school Playgroup Association, which was started by just such a nucleus of mothers, has now spread right across the country. The provision of nursery schools is still woefully inadequate, and the Playgroup Association fulfils a deep need of mothers and small children to meet and socialize. Each group has a trained playgroup leader, and the mothers are encouraged to take some training themselves. All newcomers are encouraged to participate, and although a few use the groups merely as dumping grounds the essential basis is that mothers should work in rota to assist the leader in looking after the children.

The many advantages of such a scheme to both mothers and children are obvious. This is an excellent example of what seems to me to be the right way of tackling many of society's problems, actively to draw people into a situation where they are not only being helped but are also taught to help themselves and others at the same time. An isolated mother often feels useless, narrow, out of the main flow of life, and to tell her that bringing up a child is the most important thing in the world is quite beside the point. If she is depressed and lonely she will look at her grizzling infant (she is unlikely under these circumstances to have a cheerful well-balanced child) and tell herself that if child-rearing is the most important thing, then she's making a lousy job of it. But at a playgroup she will meet other mothers and find she is not the only one to have these feelings. Gradually, as she talks to the mothers and works with the children, her attitude towards herself will change and her self-esteem grow, while the children, relieved from solitary contact with a depressive woman, will probably blossom.

Not enough of this active participation takes place. For instance, at the turn of the century the LCC Education Committee later replaced by the ILEA, arranged for volunteer workers to visit homes of children who were showing disturbed behaviour at school. This scheme has been very successful, and the ILEA's sole complaint about these voluntary workers is that there are too few of them. At the moment this help to the families is all one-way. No one I spoke to at the ILEA was aware of any of the volunteers bringing together several of their families with the aim of encouraging mutual aid and support. Now, one of their particular virtues is that as volunteers they are much freer than the professionals to try out different methods. I feel that here would be an excellent opportunity for introducing parents who after all share the same school and the same neighbourhood, and who no doubt have many problems in common. They would have much to gain from chatting with each other over a cup of coffee. Evening groups would help to draw fathers, who normally cannot be contacted during day visits, into the discussion. Where such a group is successful it could be extended to one or two others as yet uninvolved parents known to the participants to be experiencing some trouble, and mutual support given. While these families are merely the passive receivers of individual help they are unlikely to make the kind of progress that could be expected of more deeply involved families. Since self-help groups can be extraordinarily effective perhaps someone would care to try such an experiment?

There is a warning that must be made, though. One of the greatest advantages of group therapy is that a trained therapist in charge of the group can see far more people in the course of a week than if the clients were treated on a one-to-one basis. When the group leader knows exactly what he is doing the results can be outstanding, but groups run by untrained amateurs can have disastrous effects. One professional social worker told me that on several occasions he had been horrified to see people 'destroyed', as he put it, by the destructive criticism of other members of a group, while the leaders had no idea how to control or correct the process. The kind of groups I have in mind are not of this searing self-exposure type, but instead small gatherings together of people with similar problems for mutual support, during which they can discuss shared difficulties, thus overcoming social isolation at the same time as discovering they are wrong to believe that they alone have feelings of being totally inadequate or desolate. If such a group can progress to draw in others and to take active steps to promote improvement of their particular problems, just as the Playgroup Association founders did, then these advances are an additional bonus. But no one, however well-intentioned, ought to instigate the first kind of group without specialized training. It is a dangerous game, and much damage can be done.

Islington's social services department, together with local health visitors, are now promoting a number of groups not only for mothers but for anyone who feels themselves to be isolated or in need of support, such as pensioners living alone. Ordinary people help run these and are instrumental in bringing in neighbours whom they feel the group would benefit. The groups are kept very small, not usually more than four or five people in any one group, and never more than ten. They make up their own programmes, meeting in places such as community halls on housing estates where the children have room to play. The organizers feel that the housing department needs to be more closely involved than it is at present so that the local authorities and the social services may know when new young mothers or anyone else vulnerable moves in. Otherwise they feel the groups are proving very helpful to a previously neglected range of people.

The London Council of Social Services has been running a pilot study in Greater London with similar groups, whose leaders are non-professionals attracted by publicity about the project, and who have undergone a seven-day training course. The leaders found it easiest to attract young mothers to the groups, which are activity-based; older people tend to drift away after half an hour or so, perhaps disturbed by the children's noise. Again, everyone is pleased with the results and the groups will no doubt be extended.

These are both good examples of attempts to involve lonely people in their local society before a breakdown has occurred, before a child has been battered or its life soured by an unhappy upbringing. The problem is always that those who most need to be involved are those most reluctant to present themselves at any group - they rarely turn up at a community centre on their own. Even when they come it won't always be possible to achieve the additional success of teaching them to help others - there will be many who are incapable of doing much more than keeping their own heads above water - although useful social aid can often be garnered from the most unlikely places.

In this broader approach to child abuse we have looked at research into the relationships between mother and baby in their first few months of getting to know each other, at the frightening incidence of depression in working-class mothers and at a variety of groups whose aim is to involve isolated people within the community. I shall close this chapter by returning more directly to work actually centering around baby battering.

The NSPCC Battered Child Research Department found that the mothers of children in their nursery were greatly helped by contact with others in a similar situation. These women had been most reluctant to be separated from their children, and when facilities were provided for them to spend the day at the nursery this became a way of life for some. They

227

would arrive with the children, drink coffee, chat with the other mothers or the staff, go out to the shops but return for lunch, and so on. It was thought wiser to have a separate mothers' room which was apart from the children's nursery, as the mothers very easily became jealous of attention paid to the children, demanding that the workers should focus on themselves instead. This was a difficult situation for the workers, whose instincts and training were to put the children first. As the mothers grew in confidence the situation eased to a certain extent, but it is obviously something that will always prove a problem in this type of group.

A couple of the mothers eventually progressed to the stage where they were able to help others, and one has recently become an official Mothering Aide. She calls on distressed mothers, comforts them or helps in practical ways such as temporarily taking charge of their children. Because of her own frightening experiences (she fractured her baby's skull and arm) she is able to reach the mothers in a way that no one else could. As she said to me, 'Mothers accept me more readily than a social worker. I would have done when I was in that situation, if someone had come round and knocked on my door and said, "Look, I know how you feel. I've done the same myself. I know what you're going through."' Both these mothers attend the nursery regularly and help settle in new mothers by chatting and listening and talking to them about their own sufferings. Not all battering mothers will be able to reach that stage of development, but the centre feel hopeful that many will achieve it. They doubt if any battering mother could eventually become so balanced and confident that she would be able to become a fully-fledged social worker (even the most successful tend to regress occasionally and need a certain amount of support) but they say that the help of these two mothers has been invaluable.

One of the major causes of battering is that the babies are unwanted or turn out to be quite different from the unreal fantasy the mother had built up in her mind during pregnancy. An unfortunate fact is that the sort of girl who is most ill-equipped to take on motherhood is often the one who is most careless about contraception. Insecure, unhappy at home or living alone, perhaps unconsciously wanting to start a family of her own so that she can know love at last, this type of girl will often start sleeping around as early as thirteen or fourteen years of age. Sooner or later she will become pregnant, probably by any of several men. Although the idea of a baby might entrance her, the actuality is likely to be very different from her expectations. Women police and social service workers have often told me how impossible it is to get this sort of girl to go on the pill, or to persuade her to take it regularly. Even if the baby is taken into care or adopted, and the mother doesn't want it back, she is likely to become pregnant again within a few months.

The same problem has been found with battering mothers, but the NSPCC report a welcome success in this field. By the end of the first year of treatment by their research team most of the mothers had started using regular contraceptive methods, mostly the pill. Previously contraception had either not been used, or it was used intermittently or carelessly, even though the mothers frequently expressed a strong desire not to have any more children. The importance of family planning in this context can hardly be overstressed.

During the last few years there has been a general reduction in illegitimate births, partly thanks to impressive work of the Family Planning Association. Between 1972 and 1974 there were 10 per cent fewer unplanned pregnancies among single women in the 16 to 19 age group, and 15 per cent fewer among the 20 to 24 age group. While this reduction in the number of unwanted babies is certainly an advance, it will mostly be the more responsible, emotionally mature girls who will have contributed to the lowering of these figures. This supposition is strengthened by the fact that the rate among girls between 11 and 15 remains unchanged at 1 in 400. Since most schools already include sex education in their syllabus it seems likely that these girls will have to be reached in some other way. The problem seems as intractable as trying to stop young people from smoking. Warnings about danger to health or ruined lives have virtually no effect on this age group, to whom the future is so distant as to have little or no bearing on their current lives.

In *Children in Danger* I discussed the desirability of nationwide registers of children at risk. Since then the DHSS has asked all local authorities to set up such registers. Most have already done so, but as at present no one is legally obliged to furnish names for inclusion, the value of the list varies greatly from authority to authority. This is a highly controversial subject, and there are many who disapprove strongly of registers altogether. These range from those who object on political grounds to citizens' names being put on any sort of official 'black list', especially if they do not have a chance to defend themselves, to those who fear that such a register could get into the hands of the wrong people. This last is most unlikely: stringent precautions are taken to ensure that only bona fide enquirers are given information. These precautions are sometimes so effective as to hamper the usefulness of the register: there are complaints that at night or at weekends it can be virtually impossible for junior workers to obtain this permission. Instant removal of an infant from a dangerous home is occasionally vital, and the delay of a day or so could result in death. But obviously it would be intolerable if any busybody could ring up and satisfy her curiosity about a neighbour. This aspect needs to be worked out thoroughly - since each local authority is in charge of the way it handles its own register perhaps the DHSS will make investigations into which methods prove to be the most successful.

Some object that parents on the list have no means of knowing what is said about them, and no way of ensuring that their name is removed after a suitable period has elapsed. One case was recently quoted of a mother who found out that her baby's name was listed in the local register. She asked for her name to be removed on the grounds that the child never had been battered and was in no danger of being battered in the future, but she was refused. She openly admitted that she had had a nervous breakdown, had undergone treatment by a psychiatrist, had a 'volatile temperament' and during pregnancy had considered having an abortion. In addition the social workers claimed that the woman, when asking for a baby-minder to look after her child for one day a week so that she could do some research work, had said, 'If I don't get a baby-minder, who is going to stop me battering my baby?'

Now, this case is a very interesting one because it is a perfect illustration of what people are arguing about. Some feel that, if we have to have registers at all, they ought only to contain the names of children who have actually been battered. Others, myself included, feel that the real value of a register is that it should be a very wide-reaching one, so that if, for example, a child has been taken for any sort of injury to a hospital, or if either of the parents has a background such as that in the case above, or if there exists two or more of the risk factors mentioned in the previous chapter (illegitimacy, low birth weight, temporary separation at birth, etc.) the child's name should be entered. Each time a new entry is made against the same name, previous entries can be scrutinized, and action taken when it is thought desirable. There will be comparatively few cases on such a list of children genuinely in danger, but I know of no other way to ensure that these few children are picked up *before* severe damage is done. I cannot believe that many parents would object to their names being entered on such a broadly based list if its purpose and workings were properly understood and publicized.

Most psychiatrists dealing with baby battering would consider the mother just described to be at some risk of attacking her child if her domestic circumstances were to deteriorate. Nevertheless some people will still object that it is wrong for innocent people to be marked out like this. But if one balances against this objection the thought that a certain number of children will escape physical and mental pain or possibly death, then surely we can only conclude that registers are worthwhile. American and Canadian authorities have been using such registers for some time, and have found them very effective not only in helping prevent abuse but also as invaluable sources of information about battering.

The final word on registers must lie for the moment with the East Sussex social services department, who were severely criticized over their inefficiency in the tragic Maria Colwell case. In the last two or three years they have considerably improved their procedures for dealing with at-risk cases, and they consider their register has played an important part in this improvement. They report that over 900 children are now on their register and, as all professionals involved in local cases are referring them to the register, the list is steadily growing. Because children are being picked up earlier fewer are now being injured badly enough for them to need treatment by a paediatrician, and even those who do need treatment have less serious injuries than formerly. As the director of social services says,

> We are now pretty confident that there is a very much lower risk that a child will die in the same circumstances as Maria. . . . There is no room for complacency, but there are signs that the level of professional competence is rising and that communications and collaboration between services are better.

Lack of efficient and willing collaboration between all the different professionals involved has always been the weakest link in the prevention of baby battering: an efficient system of registers will only be as useful as people are prepared to make it. By merely existing, a register can help no one: people must feed information into it *and* take the information out and use it. Without consistent, intelligent use the most perfect register system in the world will be worthless. Can it be that some people don't want to share their knowledge? That they don't trust other professionals to use that knowledge properly? If so, their doubts may be understandable, but their effect on the usefulness of the register system will be about as profound as that of car workers who make an essential part going on strike - the entire works comes to a grinding halt. East Sussex had a particular reason for wanting to improve their inter-professional collaboration: if they have found registers a success, cannot other local authorities who are still dragging their feet follow their example?

Finally, what can we do straight away to improve the prognosis for the future? So far, treatment has not proved all that effective. The NSPCC's research team found that while the parents' marriages and social relationships in general improved, relationships with their children were less affected by treatment. There was some improvement, discipline being less strongly enforced, with severe punishment becoming a rarity and unreal expectations lowered, though this last may have been more a result of the children's behaviour changing as they grew older rather than an improvement in the parents' understanding of children. The workers were disappointed that there was only a slight change in the basic attitude of the parents to their children, considering that while physically the children were much safer, emotionally they were still being deprived. Researchers like Selwyn Smith and his colleagues feel that 'the combination of symptomatic relief with a programme of social relearning conducted by skilled therapists seems to us to be far more beneficial than relying solely on programmes of "mothering" and other methods that tend to reinforce their dependent behaviour.' It may well be that directly teaching battering parents how to react with their children, not just by telling them but by working with them and their children in groups over a lengthy period of time, could be more effective than concentrating on the parents' personality problems.

Currently it is common practice for social workers to avoid causing guilt in parents by ignoring any harsh treatment of children which happens to take place under their eyes. It is true that if the social worker were to intervene openly the child might suffer once the worker is safely out of the way. But is it not equally likely that the parents will interpret the worker's non-intervention as condoning their actions? You can teach dog-owners new and better methods of training their puppies, and remarkable results have been achieved. Cannot parents be trained in the same manner? Obviously not everyone will be accessible to such treatment, but great numbers of battering mothers are unhappy, neurotic women who might well respond better to such positive action (taught in groups with other mothers) than to psychiatric treatment concentrating on the causes of their own unhappiness. You cannot really teach someone to love, to be empathetic and warm, but you can teach them how a certain action will provoke a certain kind of reaction, and give them rules to remember which may help them to hang on to their tempers for the necessary fraction of time. This sounds a primitive approach, but some groups in America have found it works better than endless analysis. For a worker to look away when a parent strikes a child and pretend not to notice seems to me a dubious method of treatment, although I can understand the reasons for this approach.

233

Obviously an authoritarian reprimand is no answer, especially in front of older children who might use the reprimand later as a weapon against the parent. For this reason group therapy aiming at directly changing parents' responses to their children, conducted outside the parent's home together with other mothers and young infants so that everyone's actions can be discussed openly, would be necessary. Since the present methods are not proving very effective, others must be tried.

Fathers can and should be involved in such therapy also. As we have seen, they are too rarely seen by workers, mainly because of clashes of working hours. It may mean therapists have to work during weekends, but it is essential that both parents should work together to change their approach to their children, each supporting the other. Many men are reluctant to be dragged into this kind of involvement, but unless the worker achieves this her treatment of the family can only be partially successful at best.

Another great advance would be to kill the myth that babies mend marriages. They may tie two unhappy people together for a while, but the misery will only be compounded. Hand in hand with this myth goes another, that every woman needs a child to be properly fulfilled. Whatever the truth behind this might be, there can be no doubt that there are many women who ought never to have children, who don't want them and who only have them because they feel motherhood is expected of them. If television advertisements showing burbling little cherubs and helpful little toddlers were to be replaced by film of piles of dirty nappies and jealous toddlers squabbling endlessly over who has which toy then perhaps young women might be less tempted to rush into motherhood. Reality has to be faced. Most babies cry a good deal and all cause a great deal of hard work; most toddlers squabble and fight with each other and make endless demands of their parents. They can also be joyous and immensely rewarding, but large numbers of over-stressed parents rarely see this happy side of the coin.

Yet another piece of reality has to be faced. Government expenditure on social sevices will probably continue to be lopped rather than expanded. The kind of treatment the NSPCC units are able to offer cannot in any foreseeable future become universal. So we must snatch at every straw we can.

For example, registers cost little but provide invaluable information. Much research has already been done - we must publicize it and use-it. Children's Guardians or Advocates will cost some money, but the total will be less than the whole caravan of hospitals, police, courts and prisons once a child has been severely or mortally injured.

And finally, where an injury has taken place, we must separate children and parents long enough to find out just how likely a successful reunion is. We must learn to put the child before the parent, not the other way around. Sooner or later the child himself will become a parent, and an emotionally damaged adult cannot produce a wholly stable family. Such an attitude may be hard on the present parents, but it is their grandchildren we must think about. Someone has to stop the cycle at some point, and it may be beyond the capabilities of the parents to do it for themselves.

In a comforting passage in his book *Physical and Sexual Abuse of Children* (1975), Prof. Walters has written that he has been surprised how often abused children recover from their experiences without suffering any severe long-term damage. Unlike adults they can be resilient enough to recover from happenings which would have a severe and lasting effect on most adults. Nevertheless, 'universally one thing seems to remain with the physically abused child and that is the utilization of violence as a means of solving problems. And so we know with certainty that today's abused child is tomorrow's abusive parent.'

The message is always the same. We need to treat today's victims not only for their own sakes, but for the sake of the generations to come. It doesn't much matter whom we consider the victim to be - the offender has in his or her time been victim too. Battered baby grown up to be battering father or mother, battered wife relating again and again to the wrong man, maladjusted adult sexually assaulting a loved child: all are victims and all sooner or later will be offenders, even if their offence is one of omission rather than commission. Inadequate, immature, insecure people can cause as much emotional damage to those they live with and give birth to as any aggressive, overbearing bully. The web of violence which traps every newborn member of long-ensnared families must be destroyed so that future generations may be born free.

Bibliography

Borland, M. (ed.) (1976), *Violence in the Family*, Manchester University Press.

Brown, G. W., Bhrolchain, M. and Harris, T. (1975), 'Social class and psychiatric disturbance among women in an urban population', *Sociology*, vol. 9, no. 2, May, pp. 225-54.

Carter, C. (1967), 'Risk to offspring of incest', *Lancet*, i, 436.

Castle, R. and Kerr, A. (1972), *A Study of Suspected Child Abuse*, NSPCC.

Faulk, M. (1974), 'Men who assault their wives', *Medicine, Science and the Law*, vol. 14, no. 3, pp. 180-3.

Gayford, J. J. (1975a), 'Wife battering: a preliminary survey of 100 cases', *British Medical Journal*, no. 1, pp. 194-7.

Gayford, J. J. (1975b), 'Research on battered wives', *Royal Society of Health Journal*, vol. 95, no. 6, December, pp. 288-9.

Gebhard, P. (1965), *Sex Offenders, An Analysis of Types*, Heinemann.

Gelles, R. J. (1972), *The Violent Home*, Sage (Library of Social Research).

Gil, D. (1970), *Violence Against Children*, Harvard University Press.

Gregg, G. S. and Elmer, E. (1969), 'Infant injuries: accident or abuse?', *Pediatrics*, vol. 44, pp. 434-9.

Guttmacher, M. (1960), *The Mind of the Murderer*, Farrar, Straus & Cudahy.

Hall, M. H. (1975), 'A view from the emergency and accident department', in Franklin, A. W. (ed.), *Concerning Child Abuse*, Churchill-Livingstone.

Helfer, R. and Kempe, H. (eds) (1968), *The Battered Child*, University of Chicago Press.

House of Commons (Session 1974-5). *Minutes of Evidence of the Select Committee on Violence in Marriage*, HMSO.

House of Commons, (Session 1974-5), *Report from the Select Committee on Violence in Marriage*, vol. 1, HMSO.

House of Commons (Session 1975-6), *Minutes of Evidence of the Select Committee on Violence in Marriage*, HMSO.

House of Commons (Session 1976-7), *Violence to Children, First Report from the Select Committee on Violence in the Family*, HMSO.

Howells, J. G. (1976), 'Death and disorganization', *Royal Society of Health Journal*, June.

Kempe, H. and Helfer, R. (eds) (1972), *Helping the Battered Child and his Family*, Blackwell, and J. B. Lippincott.

Kennell, J. H. *et al.* (1974), 'Maternal behaviour one year after early and extended post-partum contact', *Developmental Medicine and Child Neurology*, vol. 16, no. 2, April, pp. 172-9.

Kennell, J. H., Trause, M. A. and Klaus, M. H. (1975), 'Evidence for a sensitive period in the human mother', *Parent-Infant Interaction*, Ciba Foundation Symposium 33, pub. ASP, Amsterdam.

Klaus, M. H., Leger, T. and Trause, M. A. (1975a), *Maternal Attachment and Mothering Disorders*, Johnson & Johnson.

Klaus, M. H., Trause, M. A. and Kennell, J. H. (1975b), 'Does human maternal behaviour after delivery show a characteristic pattern?' *Parent-Infant Interaction*, Ciba Foundation Symposium 33, pub. ASP, Amsterdam.

Lester, B. (1976), *Child Development*, vol. 47, p. 237.

Levine, M. B. (1975), 'Interparental violence and its effect on the children: a study of 50 families in general practice', *Medicine, Science and the Law*, vol. 15, no. 3, pp. 172-6.

Levinger, G. (1966), 'Sources of marital dissatisfaction among applicants for divorce', *American Journal of Orthopsychiatry*, no. 26, October, pp. 803-7.

Lewin, R. (ed.) (1975), *Child Alive*, Temple Smith.

Lorenz, Konrad (1966), *On Aggression*, Methuen (first pub. Vienna 1963).

Lukianowicz, N. (1972), I, 'Paternal incest'; II, 'Other types of incest', *British Journal of Psychiatry*, no. 120, pp. 301-13.

Lynch, M., Steinberg, D. and Ounstead, C. (1975), 'Family unit in a children's psychiatric hospital', *British Medical Journal*, 19 April.

Maisch, H. (1973), *Incest*, André Deutsch.

Masters, W. H. and Johnson, V. E. (1976), 'Incest: the ultimate sexual taboo', *Redbook Magazine*, April.

Mounsey, J. (1975), 'Offences of criminal violence, cruelty and neglect against children in Lancashire', *Concerning Child Abuse*, Churchill-Livingstone.

NSPCC (1974), *Yo-Yo Children, A Study of 23 Violent Matrimonial Cases*.

NSPCC (1975), *Registers of Suspected Non-Accidental Injury, a Report on Registers Maintained in Leeds and Manchester by NSPCC Special Units*.

NSPCC Battered Child Research Team (1975), *At Risk*, Routledge & Kegan Paul.

National Women's Aid Federation (1976), *Battered Women Need Refuges*.

Newsweek (1973), 'The deadliest city', 1 January, 20-1.

Oliver, J. E. and Taylor, A. (1971), 'Five generations of ill-treated children in one family pedigree', *British Journal of Psychiatry*, no. 119, pp. 437-80.

Oliver, J. E., Cox, J., Taylor, A. and Baldwin, J. A. (1974), *Severely Ill-treated Children in North-east Wiltshire*, Oxford Unit of Clinical Epidemiology.

Pizzey, E. (1974), *Scream Quietly or the Neighbours Will Hear*, Penguin.

Renvoize, J. (1974), *Children in Danger*, Routledge & Kegan Paul.

Resnick, P. J. (1969), 'Child murder by parents: a psychiatric review of filicide', *American Journal of Psychiatry*, vol. 126, no. 3, pp. 325-34.

Rice, E. P. *et al.* (1971), *Children of Mentally Ill Parents*, N.Y. Publications.

Scott, P. D. (1973), 'Fatal battered baby cases', *Medicine, Science and the Law*, no. 13, pp. 197-206.

Scott, P. D. (1974), 'Battered wives', *British Journal of Psychiatry*, no. 125, pp. 433-41.

Sgroi, S. (1975), 'Sexual molestation of children: the last frontier in child abuse', *Children Today*, vol. 4, May/June, pp. 18-21 and 44.

Skinner, A. and Castle, R. (1969), *78 Battered Children: A Retrospective Study*, NSPCC.

Smith, S. M. and Hanson, R. (1974a), 'Social aspects of the battered baby syndrome', *British Journal of Psychiatry*, no. 125, pp. 568-82.

Smith, S. M. and Hanson, R. (1974b), '134 battered children: a medical and psychological study', *British Medical Journal*, no. iii, pp. 666-70.

Smith, S. M. and Hanson, R. (1975), 'Interpersonal relationships and child-rearing practices in 214 parents of battered children', *British Journal of Psychiatry*, no. 127, pp. 513-25.

Smith, S. M., Hanson, R. and Noble, S. (1973), 'Parents of battered babies: a controlled study', *British Medical Journal*, no. iv, pp. 388-91.

Smith, S. M., Honigsberger, L. and Smith, C. A. (1973), 'EEG and personality factors in baby batterers', *British Medical Journal*, no. ii, pp. 20-2.

Snell, J. E., Rosenwald, R. J. and Robey, A. (1964), 'The wifebeater's wife: a study of family interaction', *Archives of General Psychiatry*, no. 11, August, pp. 107-13.

Tanay, E. (1969), 'Psychiatric study of homicide', *American Journal of Psychiatry*, vol. 125, no. 9, pp. 1252-8.

Tutt, N. (ed.) (1976), *Violence*, DHSS.

Virkkunen, M. (1974), 'Incest offences and alcoholism', *Medicine, Science and the Law*, vol. 14, p. 124.

Walters, D. (1975), *Physical and Sexual Abuse of Children*, Indiana University Press.